Denise Welch has had starring roles in hit dramas such as *Soldier, Soldier, The Vice, Down to Earth* and *Coronation Street*. She also starred as Steph Haydock in *Waterloo Road*, for which she won the Best Actress Award two years running at the *TV Quick* and *TV Choice Awards*. She was a popular contestant on *Dancing on Ice* in 2011, and won *Celebrity Big Brother* in January 2012. She is a regular presenter on *Loose Women*, where she has won the hearts of the British people for her honesty and witty humour. In 2012 she started up Welch Morgan Locations with her good friend Gaynor Morgan, and is working with her partner Lincoln Townley's company, Lincoln Townley Entertainment.

Also by Denise Welch

Pulling Myself Together

DENISE WELCH

Starting Over

PAN BOOKS

For my beloved mum Annie,
just for being my mum.
Love you for ever.

First published 2012 by Sidgwick & Jackson
First published in paperback 2013 by Pan Books

This edition published 2018 by Pan Books
an imprint of Pan Macmillan
20 New Wharf Road, London N1 9RR
Associated companies throughout the world
www.panmacmillan.com

ISBN 978-1-5098-9360-7

Visit **www.panmacmillan.com** to read more about all our books
and to buy them. You will also find features, author interviews and
news of any author events, and you can sign up for e-newsletters
so that you're always first to hear about our new releases.

Contents

Prologue

I'm in my hotel room in London and I can't stop crying. There are newspapers spread out all over the bed. My life is staring up at me in big, bold headlines: DENISE SPLITS WITH HUSBAND OF 24 YEARS; LOVE SPLIT DENISE; DENISE: 'MY MARRIAGE IS OVER.' It's a shock to read the words and see the bald fact of my separation in black and white. It fills me with a horrible, wrenching sadness. It feels so final.

Long minutes pass and I'm still sobbing hysterically. The tears won't stop. I feel as if I'm drowning in tears, as if I'm going under. Why is this happening? I shouldn't be feeling this way. Tim and I agreed to separate some time ago, and I'm glad we're moving on. We both know it's the right thing to do and the right time to do it. So why does it feel like my heart is breaking into tiny pieces?

I've hardly had a minute to myself in the last ten days.

There's been too much going on. I haven't had time to think or get my head around what's been happening. The days have flown past at a hundred miles an hour since I came out of the Big Brother house: as well as working flat out and trying to spend time with my family, I've had to deal with a massive press bombardment. Perhaps it's no wonder I'm feeling weak and emotional. I don't know. I'm too tired and confused to work it out.

Did I really go on television yesterday to tell the world that Tim and I have separated? It sounds like a crazy idea; I can hardly believe I did it. I mean, who announces the end of their marriage on live TV? I didn't plan it to happen that way, but my hand was forced. The newspapers were having a field day printing hurtful things about me and my family, so we felt we had to take control of the situation before any more damage was done. We did it to stop the rumour mill going into overdrive, to let people know what was really happening in our lives. And so it became official, live on TV at lunchtime, in front of two million viewers: Tim and I have split up.

I should be used to the idea by now, so why do I feel so miserable? A part of me can't believe it, even though we made the decision before Christmas. Tim and I have been through so much together; we have so many shared memories and experiences. We've worked together and brought up our children; we have two wonderful sons, a fantastic family and a wide circle of good friends. Tim has been there for me in my darkest moments, and I have helped him through the tough times in his life. We are incredibly close, best friends and allies, and for most of our marriage we've been very, very happy. So although I know it's for the best, and although I know that we will be happier apart, it's sad and very difficult to acknowledge that our marriage is over.

I was very emotional as I tried to explain the situation yesterday. I couldn't help it; I faltered over my words as I tried to hold back the tears. But I got through it with the help of my close friends and colleagues, supporting me and willing me on, and in the end it was a relief to get it out after weeks of bottling it up. It felt good to take control back from the media. So why can't I stop crying?

It's unbelievable what the papers and online forums have been saying about me in the past few weeks. It's been open season; I've been attacked from all angles and the criticism has been vicious. I don't understand what I've done to deserve it. You would think I had killed somebody's mother. But I haven't killed anyone; I haven't even threatened anyone.

I'm the first to admit that I have made mistakes, and maybe I don't act in a conventional way for a fifty-three-year-old woman. But I'm not a bad person, so why am I getting such a kicking? What have I done to attract all this malice and ill will? I've been denounced for getting my boobs out in a hot tub. I've been condemned for having an affair – even though, strictly speaking, I wasn't having an affair, because Tim and I were both aware of each other's situation. And now I'm being criticized for separating from my husband after nearly a quarter of a century together. Not two months but twenty-four years together! To make things worse, a couple of so-called 'friends' have been trying to cash in by selling stories about me, peddling false scandal and lies to the highest bidder.

It feels like I'm being bullied all over again and I just can't cope. After what happened in the Big Brother house, after all the viciousness and nastiness that went on in there, I don't know if I can stand any more criticism. Three weeks in that house left me feeling very fragile, and now I'm being picked on again. But I'm sick of being bullied. I've had enough of being attacked.

My manager says I've been approached about writing another book. Oh God! I don't think I can face it after what happened when my autobiography was published. After dealing with all the flak and finger-pointing back then, I swore I would never do it again. But I'm faced with a stark choice: either I talk about my life in my own words, tell my own story and take back control, or I sit down with someone who barely knows me and leave them to spin it however they want to.

I'll do it, I suddenly decide. I want people to know what has really happened over the last few years – the truth, not the media lies. I'm sure many people have been through something similar; perhaps just as many feel stuck in a life that *should* make them happy, but in their heart they know they've lost sight of who they are and what they need to be fulfilled. I hope they won't judge me too harshly.

I can't make any other decisions right now. This is a scary time for me. Although I have the total support of my wonderful family and friends, I know I'll feel less confident without the solid base of a long-term marriage shoring me up. And although I'm not single, my relationship is too new for me to be sure where it's going. I feel hopeful about the future, about my new relationship, but it could be going nowhere for all I know. It's too soon to say.

For now, I'm just going to stay locked in my hotel room, crying my eyes out until there are no tears left to cry. After that, I'll pick myself up and carry on. It's definitely time for a new beginning in my life, and there's so much to look forward to. I just pray I am strong enough to make it happen.

Right now, though, I can't see how I'm going to make it through today.

1

Horrific Headlines and Another Betrayal

It was February 2010 and we were at Carol McGiffin's fiftieth birthday party in Bangkok. Everyone was having a ball. Fifty guests had met at a jetty on the river to take a speedboat to a beautiful restaurant on stilts, which was decorated with twinkling lights and flowers. There were great pals from *Loose Women* and lots of Carol's friends whom I hadn't met before. She has a wild, wacky, crazy bunch of pals who all clearly adore her, which was lovely to see, and she was very touched that so many people had travelled all that way to celebrate with her.

Everything was so well organized it almost felt like a wedding: the champagne flowed, the chairs were covered in silk and bows, and we had a beautiful sit-down dinner. It was a very jolly evening. Carol's fiancé, Mark, made a sweet, moving speech about how much he loved Carol and then Tim sang a song. He had changed the words to 'Have I Told You Lately That I Love You?' to 'Have We Told You

Lately That We Love You?' Carol and Mark were really chuffed by it. People who don't know that Tim can sing are always surprised when he picks up his guitar. I enjoy watching the look on their faces as they realize what a fabulous voice he has.

It was a brilliant trip and Tim and I were getting on great. As the evening came to a close, we were still fairly sober and were planning to go off to bed. But before we left, I had a dance with a couple of my pals, and when I came back, Tim was talking to a plant! I quickly realized he'd been at the whisky, something I'd banned him from doing years earlier. He had stayed sober to sing for Carol and then he'd thought, I'll have a couple of quick whiskies while our lass is dancing. Now he was making no sense at all. When he drinks whisky, he turns from a ha-ha, falling-about drunk into an argumentative arsehole. And I'm speaking as someone who's done the same herself – more of which later.

I felt really angry. I wanted him to come back to the hotel with me, but he told me to go on without him. He insisted on taking a riverboat and eventually hitched a lift on an old steamer that went past. As I waited for him back at our hotel, I started worrying that he'd fallen into the river. It was an old but familiar anxiety that I remembered from the days before I'd banned whisky.

The next day, I knew Tim would be hung-over. He was supposed to be going on a motorbike trip, but I doubted whether he would even get out of bed. Right, well, you ruined the night for me, so I'm going off to meet Steve! I thought. In hindsight, I realize that it should have taken more than that to send me off to see an ex-lover who happened to now live in Thailand, but that's how I justified it to myself at the time. I didn't think my meeting with Steve Murray would be anything other than innocent: the way I imagined it, we'd have a few drinks and a chat before going our separate ways again. I had no idea how much I would come to bitterly regret seeing him that day.

Tim was totally behind me in my decision to write my autobiography, *Pulling Myself Together*, in 2010. He read it as I was writing it and was very supportive. It must have been difficult for him to read certain sections that concerned him and our marriage, but he understood how important it was for me to write about my depression, and reluctantly accepted that it meant opening up about other areas of my life.

I maintained that I needed to include an account of my affair with Steve Murray, the set carpenter I met on the drama series *Down to Earth* in 2003. I fought my corner and eventually Tim went along with it. To recap briefly, *Down to Earth* was set and filmed in Devon and starred Angela Griffin, Ian Kelsey, Ricky Tomlinson and me. In the third series, Ricky and I played a couple who owned the local pub. It was a really fun job and very well paid, but the downside was that it was a long way from home and it meant leaving my younger son Louis, who was only three. Thankfully, Tim was at home looking after him, but I knew I would desperately miss him and fourteen-year-old Matthew.

I was less worried about leaving Tim, because our marriage wasn't great at the time. We weren't getting on very well and he was drinking a lot, much more than usual, which meant we often ended up having arguments. Looking back, I realize that I could have been a lot more sympathetic, because he was obviously having a hard time and drinking to numb the pain. There were moments when we both felt very lonely in our marriage, but Tim tended to keep his anxieties to himself, in order to spare me any worry. He felt I had enough to deal with coping with my depression.

The affair with Steve began at the start of filming *Down to Earth*, just after the onset of an awful, debilitating bout of depression. I became very close to him over the next six months; I suppose I fell in love with him. Unfortunately, Tim found out about the relationship when I mistakenly left a message for Steve on Tim's answerphone, and it very nearly ended our marriage. After a lot of soul-searching, and after the *Sun* ran an exposé about the affair, I walked away from Steve and reconciled with Tim, a decision I have never regretted. Then, nine months after I ended the affair, I saw this headline on the front of the *Sunday People*: MY NIGHTS OF WILD SEX WITH CORRIE STAR. The story seemed to have come from Steve, and I felt very exposed and betrayed.

I spent that Sunday feeling extremely embarrassed and

upset, but throughout the intense press attention over the following weeks, Tim behaved magnanimously and was a rock to me. As a result, we were able to move on.

Nevertheless, I was deeply shocked that Steve seemed to have sold a story about me, because he had promised never to stoop so low. We had been good friends as well as lovers, and he wasn't a horrible person, so I couldn't understand it. When I phoned him to confront him, he claimed he had been set up, and I very much wanted to believe him. I knew the press had been pestering him for his side of the story, so it didn't seem that far-fetched. On reflection, once the dust had settled, I decided that he had probably been pressured into spilling the beans. Certainly, I couldn't imagine him ringing the celeb desk to sell his story; it was far more likely that he had been talked into giving his version of events. It was odd that the exposé was in interview form and appeared in the *Mail* as well as the *Sunday People*, alongside a photo of Steve posing under a tree, but I wanted to give him the benefit of the doubt.

That was that, or so I thought. There was no reason to see Steve again, though I looked back on our time together with fondness. Even if he had sold his story deliberately, I decided, I could sort of see why he'd done it. He had felt betrayed when I'd ended the affair; it broke his heart. He also held me responsible for the fact that he wasn't taken on for the next series of *Down to Earth*, because the producers felt there was a clash of interests. He was left single and without work, whereas I had my marriage and family and was still employed. It can't have seemed fair and I don't blame him for being resentful, even if that doesn't justify doing a kiss and tell.

Steve and I didn't see each other again for several years and I heard he had moved to Thailand. He knew Thailand well because he'd once been married to a Thai woman. While I was writing *Pulling Myself Together*, I got his contact details from a friend so that I could let him know I was writing about our relationship. We exchanged a couple of friendly texts, but nothing more, until Tim and I flew to Bangkok to celebrate Carol's fiftieth birthday.

I couldn't help thinking about Steve while we were there. He was living about an hour away from Bangkok and I wondered what it would be like to see him again. Since we were practically in the same city, I told myself, it seemed a good opportunity to meet up and make peace. I had broken his heart; he had done the dirty on me by going to the newspapers; but it had all happened a long time ago and was so much water under the bridge. I still thought of him with affection.

I was undecided about whether to see him until the day after Carol's birthday, when my anger with Tim made my mind up for me. In the end, I told Tim a white lie and went off to meet Steve. People might not understand why I did that if I was happy with Tim, but I suppose it's like looking up an old flame on Friends Reunited. I was curious, and it was lovely to see Steve again, even though I felt slightly guilty about lying to Tim. It was good to talk over the past and say a proper goodbye, as we'd parted very abruptly after the newspaper story. I had loved Steve, even if, ultimately, I had decided not to see him again.

We met in a hotel and went to his room, where we sat and chatted about our lives for hours. Steve told me how much he had loved me and how heartbroken he had been when I'd ended the relationship. He explained what had motivated him to give the newspaper interview and I made it clear how hurt I had been when the story hit the papers. It felt very much like we had met up to forgive past wrongs and clear the air, so I was prepared to let bygones be bygones.

I was pleased to hear that Steve had a girlfriend and seemed happy, and he was pleased for me that I felt I'd made the right decision in staying with Tim. All in all, we had a very nice time putting things to rights and talking about our families. There had always been a strong chemistry between us, and as we talked and laughed, it became clear that it was still there, even after several years. Attraction, emotion and nostalgia overwhelmed me. This was Steve, the man I'd once loved, and somehow it seemed natural that, caught up in the moment, things would become physical between us. It was very stupid of me, but the encounter was like a swansong, a last farewell. We both knew it was never going to go any further than one stolen evening in Bangkok.

Despite the deceit involved in meeting up with Steve, I came back from Thailand having had a brilliant holiday with

Tim. Again, people may find that hard to comprehend, but you have to understand that fidelity wasn't the top priority in our marriage. Other things were always more important, and we had a lot of fun together while we were away.

When it came to Steve, after pouring out our hearts and happily forgiving one another, I thought we had drawn a line under the past and moved on. How wrong I was.

The last thing I expected was for the publication of my book to knock the general election off the front pages – and for all the wrong reasons!

It was May 2010 and I had agreed to serialize *Pulling Myself Together* in a red-top newspaper, because it's a good way of letting people know that it's coming out. I was under no illusions about which sections they were likely to zone in on; I knew they'd focus on the fact that I had used cocaine. But I had written about it in the context of coping with my crippling depression, so I felt it would stand up to scrutiny. There was so much more to the book than my attempts to self-medicate my illness.

It didn't occur to me to ask the newspaper for control over headlines, so I was totally unprepared for the headline they chose to run on the first day of serialization, MY COCAINE SHAME, which appeared in big, bold black letters, screaming for attention and giving out completely the wrong message. I was appalled. As far as I was concerned, it was pure sensationalism, unjustifiable and unrepresentative of my story.

I woke up to this headline on the day I was due to fly to Los Angeles to film a road trip for *GMTV* with Carla Romano, who was *GMTV*'s Hollywood correspondent at the time. The trip had been planned for months and the timing was purely coincidental, but some people said I was flying the nest to escape the fallout from the serialization. On the contrary, the last thing I wanted to do was leave my family to pick up the pieces while I was thousands of miles away on the other side of the world and in a totally different time zone. I was very upset when I heard that reporters had been turning up on the doorstep at home, at my parents' and at my sister's houses.

I immediately complained to the newspaper and received what seemed to be a sincere apology. Certainly, they toned down the headlines that appeared over the following days. Of course, I didn't expect them to run with something like, I SAT WITH GRANNY AND HAD A CUP OF TEA, because that's not going to sell newspapers, but I was glad they acknowledged that they had gone too far the other way. Even without sensationalist headlines, my story seemed to hog the news. I was told that Gordon Brown was quite bewildered when he saw the papers. 'Who the hell is this Denise Welch with her coke hell?' he apparently asked his advisers. His election campaign was relegated to one thin column, while I virtually monopolized the front and inside pages! It was all very odd. The other tabloids seized on the story and I came in for quite a bit of criticism.

Far from home and missing my family even more than

usual, I was getting up at four in the morning to do publicity interviews for the book back home, then working long days filming for *GMTV*. It was exhausting, but I was there to do a job, so I tried to put my worries about my family and the press aside and concentrate on the amazing experiences I was having. I got on really well with Carla Romano and the rest of the crew, and we went to some brilliant places that I would otherwise never have visited. Among the highlights of the trip was interviewing Jackie Collins at her house in Beverly Hills, which was pure Hollywood and totally thrilling.

We talked about her latest book and I mentioned that I'd just written my autobiography. 'Could I have a copy?' Jackie asked. Wow! I arranged to have one sent to her, even though I didn't expect her to read it. I assumed she was just being polite.

The trip to LA had many high points, but it was marred by one truly awful day that I will never forget for as long as I live. Words fail me when I think back to that sunny California morning when Carla and I arrived at Hearst Castle in San Simeon to shoot a segment of the film. It was around eleven o'clock and I was just getting off the crew bus when my phone rang.

'Hi, Denise,' said a cheery female voice on the other end of the line. She introduced herself as a journalist from the *Sunday People*.

I didn't flinch, because I assumed the phone call would somehow be related to the press I was doing for the publication of my book. 'Hi,' I said, equally cheerily. I was totally loving the trip, which was getting better by the day. The night before, Carla and I had spent a brilliant evening at Robbie Williams's house.

'Where are you? You sound like you're abroad,' said the journalist.

'Yes, I'm in LA filming,' I told her.

'That sounds nice,' she said. 'Anyway, Denise, I'm sorry to be the bearer of bad news, but I'm ringing to let you know that Steve Murray has sold his story. We heard that you spent time with him in Bangkok.'

I felt the blood drain from my face. 'No, no, no,' I protested. Everything went blurry, my legs turned to jelly, and my knees buckled. I very nearly collapsed.

'I'm really sorry, but we have your texts to him,' the journalist said.

My mind went into a scramble. I tried to place the texts that she was referring to, but my thoughts were all over the place. Had I sent Steve raunchy texts? I was pretty sure I hadn't, but at that moment I just couldn't remember.

'Do you have anything to say?' the woman on the phone asked me.

'No comment,' I said automatically, and immediately hung up.

'Denise?' Carla said, her expression full of concern. 'What's wrong?' She later told me she thought someone must have died, judging by the look on my face.

I couldn't reply. I couldn't speak. After all we had talked

about, after everything we had said about the importance of family and forgiveness, it seemed inconceivable that Steve had sold another story about me. It made no sense at all; I just couldn't understand it.

It can't be true, I thought. Having put things to rights in Thailand, Steve and I had been texting each other now and again. It wasn't flirty texting, because that side of things was well and truly over. He had a girlfriend and I was married; we were friends now. The past was behind us. His last text had asked, 'What are you doing?' and I had replied, 'Oh my God! How camp is this? I'm at Jackie Collins's house, about to interview her.' His response was, 'How amazing!' It all seemed very innocent, until I realized that he would have already sold the story by then.

I had five minutes to sort my head out before filming the segment about Hearst Castle. My professional side must have kicked in because somehow I managed it. As soon as I'd finished, I phoned my manager, Neil, and told him about the call from the *Sunday People*.

'What did you say?' he asked.

'"No comment."'

'You shouldn't have said anything. You should have said, "I'm getting my lawyer on to it."'

'I didn't think,' I said miserably.

The rest of the day dragged by in a long, painful haze. We left the castle and drove for hours and hours along the Great Pacific Highway towards San Francisco. Phone reception is very patchy along the coast, so I couldn't find out the details of the story, however hard I tried. My heart pounded relentlessly as I went through all the worst-case scenarios. I was overcome by panic at the thought of what I would say to Tim. There was no way I wanted my marriage to break up. I know that people reading this might think, Well, you shouldn't have done it, then. Of course I shouldn't, but I had.

Everything felt surreal. Carla kept having to stop the car so that I could be sick out of the passenger door. It was just awful. I remember stopping off at a couple of remote hick towns, but it all seemed like a dream. I managed to speak briefly to Neil, who had scoured the papers online and found nothing. 'I think it might have gone away,' he said a couple of times. 'I think it might be OK.' I desperately wanted him to be right, but something told me it was a false hope.

We arrived at a house that I think Marlon Brando had built for Rita Hayworth, but she never saw it because they'd split up by the time it was finished. It's now a restaurant and we sat down to eat a late dinner, but my mouth was dry and I had no appetite. I tried to pretend everything was all right, but it was almost impossible to conceal my feelings and how devastated I was.

At eleven o'clock, exactly twelve hours after the call from the *Sunday People*, my phone rang again. It was Neil, who had finally got hold of the Saturday-night editions of the Sunday papers. 'I'm really sorry, it's front page,' he said. 'Shall I read it to you?'

I swallowed hard. 'Yes,' I said, steeling myself. He read

it out and it was even worse than I had imagined, utterly horrendous and full of untruths. 'I have to call Tim,' I said. The line went fuzzy. The reception was gone again.

We arrived at our hotel in San Francisco at around half past midnight, which meant it was eight thirty in the morning in the UK. Tim was on his way to go clay pigeon shooting.

'I'm so sorry,' I blurted out, tears streaming down my cheeks, 'but there's something I have to tell you, because it's going to be on the front page of the Sunday papers. I saw Steve Murray in Bangkok and he sold his story.'

There was a long pause. 'OK,' Tim said, and he put the phone down.

I barely slept that night. I lay there thinking about the headlines, knowing that by now everyone would have seen it, even people buying the *Observer* or the *Sunday Times*, who would never even dream of buying the *Sunday People*. I felt so embarrassed when I thought of my family reading it, especially my children. I knew that anybody with an ounce of sense would say, 'You went to see the guy who sold a story on you – and you're surprised that he's done it again?' It might seem strange but I was more than surprised; I was totally shocked – I had trusted him.

The article was horribly tabloided-up, with fabricated scenes and dialogue. Steve gave the impression that things had been a lot more physical between us than they had, but what could I say in my defence? It was pointless making a statement claiming that this or that sentence was fictional.

I'd met him; I'd done it; I had to take what came with it. Frustratingly, when I eventually saw the screen grabs of the texts I had sent him, they turned out to say nothing more than 'What are your plans for the next few days?' There was nothing raunchy about them, not even a hint of sex.

I started to wonder whether I had made a massive mistake by publishing my autobiography. First the horrendous 'cocaine shame' headlines; now the betrayal by Steve. It worried me that I hadn't anticipated any of it. Were there going to be further unexpected consequences? The thought made me very anxious. My first worry was about the impact on my family, but what if my work was affected as well? My account of the darkest days of my depression – and everything that went with it – dated back many years; would future employers hold it against me?

The next day, I was up at five to go to Alcatraz, where the next surreal episode of my life unfolded. I can laugh about it now, but at the time it was too bizarre being on this bleak prison island in San Francisco Bay trying to interview the warden for *GMTV*, while fielding phone calls from my friends and family about the Steve Murray story. I kept feeling dizzy, but I refused to stop working.

That evening, I flew back to the UK, where I had a meeting arranged in Manchester as soon as I got home. I arrived home with severe jet lag and literally had time to walk into the house and say hello to the children before going back out again, taking Louis with me. Fortunately, they have both learned to take press stories with a pinch of salt, and they greeted me with hugs and eager questions about my trip.

I was filming a pilot for a new daytime show in Manchester the following day and there was a lot to discuss. It was horrendous. I didn't know if I was coming or going and I couldn't focus or concentrate. Once again I managed to get through it by switching to autopilot and letting my professional side take over.

I texted Steve during a break in filming the next day. 'I cannot believe how you have devastated my life yet again,' I wrote. 'You have hurt my family and children. It was lovely to see you and I thought we had made our peace and that we were friends, but you have ruined everything. I sincerely hope you enjoy spending your blood money.'

He didn't reply for a couple of months. I was doing a massive book signing when I finally received a text. 'Please forgive me,' it said. 'They were going to do it anyway.'

At first, I was tempted to believe him. Oh, it's the same as the last time, I thought. The papers went to him and talked him into spilling the beans. But then I realized that the papers would have had no idea that I'd seen Steve in Thailand. Only he and I knew. This time, whatever he said to the contrary, he must have made that call.

I could have worked myself into a stew about it, but I decided to put it all behind me. I acknowledge that I made a huge mistake seeing Steve Murray again. It was a very stupid and naive thing to do, and I hold my hands up to that, but I think a lot of people would do the same if they found themselves in similar circumstances. Curiosity is hard to resist, even when you know how dangerous it can be.

The weeks after Steve sold his story were bumpy for Tim and me, but we got through it, as we always tended to do. I apologized and he forgave me. It wasn't that he didn't care, because he did, and he was disappointed that I'd put myself in a situation that allowed Steve to sell me out again. But, as I've said, fidelity wasn't the glue that held us together, so we were able to move on. Neither of us wanted our marriage to break down. We loved each other and our children, and our family life was more important to us than anything.

I was aware that the marriage was far from perfect, but there was also a great deal about it that was solid. It didn't follow the conventions of other people's marriages, but there was a deep mutual respect and love underpinning the relationship that felt far stronger than all its shortcomings. There may have been infidelities on both sides, but our view was that far worse things could have come between us. The important thing was that Tim wanted to make me happy and I wanted to make him happy. It wasn't always possible, but we did our best.

After more than twenty years together, the physical side of our relationship was no longer as passionate as it had once been, but it hadn't died in the way that it does for so many couples. We had been sleeping in separate beds for a few years, but that was only because I like to have my own space. It didn't mean we stopped having sex. It was just that my snoring and duvet-pulling and his sleep-talking weren't conducive to getting a good night's rest, especially as one of us is a light sleeper and the other's a heavy sleeper. And when I say Tim talked in his sleep, it wasn't just the odd random murmur. He used to tell himself entire jokes and laugh hysterically at them, in between whistling for our dog, Pip!

I know that Tim sometimes missed the physicality of being in bed with someone, whereas I like sleeping in bed on my own, but it was more practical to sleep separately, especially as I was often getting up at the crack of dawn to go off to work. I've always said that our marriage lasted because we were apart from each other a lot of the time. We aren't people who can live in each other's pockets, especially me. I need space to be myself and do my own thing. On the other hand, although I like being alone, I also rely on the knowledge that there are people looking out for me. I can be independent, but only when I know everyone's at home if I need them!

The nature of our jobs – with both of us being actors – has meant that we've had to be away from home for stretches of time. When we were first married, Tim was absent more than I was, but in recent years, I've done most of the travelling. I enjoy my work, but I always look forward to going home and being with my family. A massive downside of doing what I do is that I have to spend time away from my children, which is always difficult. We try to make the best of it, which means we're often on the phone to one another twenty times a day, but it doesn't make up for being together at home.

One of the lovely things about being married to Tim was that he would always ring me when I was on the train back and ask me what I wanted to eat when I got in. If I was feeling totally exhausted and in need of some comfort food, I'd ask him to make one of his steak and kidney pies. His cooking worked the kind of magic that you associate with your mum's cooking as a child, especially when you're feeling ill: it's deeply nurturing, as well as being delicious.

Whenever people asked me if Tim was romantic, I'd say, 'No, not in the hearts and flowers way.' But if ever I was a bit down, he would make me a pie with my initials on the crust, or a love heart, which felt deeply romantic to me.

He wasn't a perfect husband by any stretch of the imagination, and he often drove me up the wall, but he also made me feel safe and looked after. He provided a security blanket for me throughout our marriage, and he was a tower of strength during the years I suffered from serious depression. He has always been the person I've gone to when I have a problem.

It was Tim I turned to when I had my last major depressive attack in 2010. My depression is mainly endogenous, which means it isn't so much affected by external factors such as stress and exhaustion. One of the features of endogenous depression that makes it so difficult to cope with is that there are no warning signs, and this time was no exception. I was in New York to make a DVD with some of the *Loose Women* girls, just after getting back from my trip to Los Angeles, and there was absolutely nothing to indicate that I was about to be poorly.

It's true that I had been feeling quite stressed after my autobiography came out and I was given a battering by the press. The fallout lasted for weeks and was very painful for me and my family at times. Baring your soul to the nation is traumatic enough, without the added complications of horrific headlines and a kiss-and-tell betrayal. All my girl-friends who have written books agree, and they don't suffer from depression.

But although I was overtired, I wasn't feeling sad or under pressure while I was in New York. On the contrary, I was excited to be working in America for the second time in a year, with some of my best friends. I felt well and happy; I'd had nothing to drink; there was nothing to compound it.

'Night-night!' I called out cheerfully as I went to my room in our gorgeous SoHo hotel. I snuggled into bed and instantly fell asleep.

When I woke up the next morning, it was as if some-thing had gone 'bang' in my head. I felt absolutely terrible: my world went dark; my limbs were heavy; I was barely able to drag myself out of bed. By late morning, I was crouching in the corner of Toys R Us in Times Square, crying and ringing Tim. Lisa Maxwell and I had gone there to look for presents for our children. I was making myself go, in the desperate hope that a change of scene might help lift my depression. But it was even worse being out of the hotel. As usual, Tim was the only person I wanted to speak to. Just hearing his voice soothed me. All it took was for him to say, 'It will be fine,' and I'd know I would somehow manage to get through it. He was always able to reassure me and calm me down. 'I can't cope! I don't know what to do,' I sobbed.

'Darling, you'll be ok,' he kept telling me, which really helped. 'Just remember that this will lift. It's horrible for you that you're working through it, but I've seen the end results of work you've done when you've had it – and you may notice, but nobody else does.' It was everything I needed to hear – and he'd had twenty years practice at saying it!

We were meant to be doing some filming in Times Square in the afternoon, but I wasn't well enough and the other girls did it for me. I had to go back to my room, feeling desperate. It was just awful, and I suffered for days afterwards, which ruined my lovely trip.

It was a heavy blow, because by then I had established that my illness was hormonally linked and I was being treated with hormones. I had been feeling better for a couple of years, so I couldn't understand why it had struck me so hard again. I suspected that it might be something to do with the fact that I had stopped taking my low-dose antidepressants, because I thought I didn't need them. But could there be another reason?

For some years, I had been terrified of the hormonal havoc that menopause would wreak on my body and mind. Was this it? Was the black cloud that I had fought so hard to escape about to descend on me again?

2

The Sequins, the Glitter, the Pirouettes on Ice . . .

It was always obvious to me that my illness was linked to my hormones because I first became depressed five days after my first child, Matthew, was born. The onset was dramatic: one day, I was an exhilarated new mother with a touch of very normal baby blues; the following day, a terrible blackness enveloped me and I had an overwhelming compulsion to kill myself. When I wasn't sobbing uncontrollably and trying to jump out of a window, I felt totally detached from life and motherhood, as if it was all a dream. It got so bad that I used to look at Matthew and wonder why there was a baby in the living room.

There was very little awareness of post-natal depression twenty years ago, so I was fortunate that my mother was a psychiatric nurse and recognized the symptoms. It also meant that my family accepted without question that I had an illness. They never saw it as an indulgence or told me to 'snap out of it', as some people did. But it was still almost impossible to get a correct diagnosis and find the right treatment.

The first doctor I saw tried to blame my condition on things that had happened in my past. Next, I saw a very unsympathetic female GP – it wasn't uncommon for doctors back then to dismiss post-natal depression as a myth – and my friends seemed to think that a new dress might cheer me up, which was thoughtful of them, but hopeless. Then I went to see a psychiatrist who tried to link my depression with something traumatic that might have happened during my childhood. He asked pointed questions like 'Did you spend too long in the bath with your father?' I was very poorly at the time and left his office feeling extremely confused.

I have talked and written about how, over the next twenty years, I suffered from harrowing, nightmarish bouts of depression. To this day, there are photographs in the family album that I can't bear to look at, because they take me straight back to some of my darkest days and I remember how awful I felt behind the camera smile. There were times when I was plunged into deepest despair, when I lost hope of ever feeling better again. However, with Tim's incredible support and the love and understanding of my family, I battled through.

Since I was convinced that my illness was hormonally linked, I had been dreading the onset of menopause. I know that women who are afflicted by severe post-natal depression are likely to suffer with a vengeance during menopause, because it causes a similar hormonal chaos to birth. The way I imagined it happening was that I would wake up one day and my periods would have stopped; I'd be deeply depressed and automatically know that I had hit the menopause. It was a terrible thought.

After struggling for years, my depression seemed to be lifting around 2002, but then I had a breakdown in 2004 and it started getting progressively worse. While I was filming the BBC series *Waterloo Road*, the BBC drama in which I played the shambolic French teacher Steph, it began to overpower me again. Not only was I working for fourteen hours a day, but the bad spells were outweighing the good and I was depressed more than I wasn't depressed. Life became incredibly hard. Without wishing to sound dramatic, I remember thinking, I'm losing the battle here. I don't know how much longer I can go on fighting this. My illness is winning.

At this point, there was no particular link with my periods that I could see, although my cycle had been irregular for quite a while. I now think that this was possibly a symptom of the perimenopause, which is the transition phase leading up to your final period, but it didn't occur to me at the time. I just tried to stay afloat and hold on to my sanity, however precariously. I was desperate to find someone to treat me hormonally and kept looking online for any information I could find. The only lead I found was an article about a doctor in Baltimore, USA, who was apparently using hormones to combat depression in some of his patients.

Meanwhile, I was being seen by a psychiatrist who insisted that there was no connection between my hormones and my condition.

'But I didn't have a psychiatric illness; I had a baby,' I kept saying. 'I produced another human being and then I fell into severe depression. There must be some link.' He refused to accept it, so I got no help at all.

When I was asked repeatedly to recount how my depression starts, I described it as a 'whoosh'. I said, 'I feel a tingling in my palms and then, whoosh, it's on me within thirty seconds.'

'This whoosh,' the psychiatrist said hopefully. 'It sounds like it might be temporal lobe epilepsy.'

I was desperate for it to be something, because I wanted a doctor to say, 'For twenty years you've been undiagnosed, but now that we know what it is, here's the remedy.' So even though temporal lobe epilepsy is a serious condition and I knew I might risk losing my driving licence, I just wanted my illness to be something known and specific that could be treated. Especially when I found out that temporal lobe epilepsy can be controlled by medicine.

However, when I went for a special brain scan, it showed I wasn't suffering from temporal lobe epilepsy. I've subsequently met someone with the condition and discovered that the whoosh I was describing is a quite different whoosh to the one experienced by them.

I was back to square one. I didn't have temporal lobe epilepsy, and none of the medical professionals I'd seen agreed with me that my condition was hormonally linked. I began to despair of ever finding a correct diagnosis.

I vividly remember being at Beverley Callard's fiftieth birthday party in 2007 and telling my close friend Daran Little, who at that time wrote for *Coronation Street*, how awful I was feeling. 'I'm really struggling,' I said. 'I'm even thinking about going to see a doctor in Baltimore.'

Daran was very sympathetic. He told me about an actress friend of his who had also suffered from debilitating depression, to the extent that she'd had to pull out of a West End show because of it. 'She went to see a doctor in London called Professor John Studd,' he said. 'I'll find out his details for you, if you like.' At last, a ray of hope.

Professor Studd diagnosed me within minutes of seeing me. 'I think you've been progesterone intolerant for twenty years,' he told me, just before he whipped out my Mirena contraceptive coil, which works using progesterone. 'And you are so deficient in oestrogen that I don't know how you've survived,' he said.

Tears welled up in my eyes. I didn't know how I'd survived, either. 'I nearly didn't,' I said.

It was a huge relief to find a doctor who had no hesitation in agreeing that my condition was linked to a hormone imbalance. I had literally been waiting decades to hear those words. He gave me oestrogen in gel form to rub on my skin, along with a small amount of the male hormone testosterone, to revive my non-existent libido. It was as simple as that. I started to get better.

Professor Studd didn't say I was pre-menopausal, but the oestrogen gel was obviously a form of hormone replacement therapy (HRT), because it was replacing my missing oestrogen. However, it was different to the HRT I would have been given at the onset of menopause, which is usually a combined form of oestrogen and progesterone.

'You know that there's a risk of breast cancer with HRT?' people kept saying.

Again, it probably sounds dramatic to someone who doesn't understand, but breast cancer was a risk I was prepared to take in order to be free – or freer – of my depression. The fact was, I couldn't live with my depression, but hopefully I could recover from breast cancer. Yes, I was playing with high odds, but coping with serious depression was becoming harder and harder, and I was prepared to try absolutely anything to feel better. If the doctors had told me I needed to have a hysterectomy to get better, which can sometimes be the case with hormonally linked depression, I would have gone for it immediately. After all, I knew I wasn't going to have any more children, not after the miraculous accident that was Louis!

Actually, I say that, but there was one crazy moment, aged fifty, when I had thought I might be pregnant. I'd had unprotected sex and no trace of a period thereafter. I kept saying to people, 'You can't get pregnant at fifty!'

'Yes, you can,' they replied.

Then, of course, I remembered that I'd got pregnant very quickly and very easily, without trying, when I was forty-two, by having sex just one time in a month. Oh dear, I must be quite fertile, I thought, with a momentary sense of panic. It was a big eek, but quite a quick eek, fortunately.

When I was around fifty-one, I had a few hot flushes in supermarkets, but it wasn't anything very drastic compared with the sweats my friends were experiencing. Some women I knew were having night sweats that literally drenched their beds and duvets, whereas I was generally getting hot and sweaty, but only when the weather was quite warm.

Now, Carol McGiffin is the 'neshest' person I know, 'nesh' being the word Geordies use for someone who can't stand the cold. So there would be lots of 'Menopause Minnie' jokes on the set of *Loose Women*, because I'd be boiling and having to be checked for sweat marks, while Carol sat next to me wearing seventy-five cardigans!

I'm sweaty anyway – I was just ten times hotter than everybody else for a few months – so I couldn't be absolutely sure that I was approaching or going through the meno-pause, especially since taking HRT masks those kinds of changes in your body. Subsequently, although my depres-sion was a hundred times better than it had been, I lived in fear of it returning.

The New York trip for *Loose Women* revived that fear, because the illness hit me with a vengeance. I arrived back in the UK feeling very low. Both of my exciting trips to America in 2010 had been spoilt in one way or another, leaving me weary and drained, and the press were still picking on me. They loved to depict me as an out-of-control, party-going wild woman with a long-suffering husband. I knew that my family and friends didn't see me that way, but it was still difficult.

The good news was that my autobiography was a best-seller and people were constantly contacting me to say how moving or inspirational they found my account of my illness. That made me realize it was worth all the flak I received as a result of being honest. Even now, there's not a day that goes by without someone telling me how much the book has helped them. It's been described as a depression bible and I know of people who have read it three or four times. One woman even wrote to me to say how she sleeps with it by her bed. It makes me glad that I opened up about my depression, even though there were consequences.

I needed to slow things down in the summer of 2010 and was lucky enough to have two lovely holidays in Spain and Portugal. Admittedly, I felt a bit wobbly at times, but my depression didn't return in a serious way and there was no further evidence that I was going through the dreaded menopause. By the autumn, I felt refreshed and balanced again.

The new season of *Loose Women* kicked off with some great guest appearances. Jackie Collins came on the show and said, 'The last time I was with Denise, she came to my home in Beverly Hills.' How glam I felt! 'I tell you what,' she added, 'I've read her book. What a racy read that is!' I was thrilled.

I began to feel a lot better in myself. Having a relaxed few weeks in the summer had done me good; Tim and I had got through the problems of earlier in the year and were getting on well. Life was looking up. Perhaps that's why my manager suggested I take part in ITV's 2011 *Dancing on Ice*.

'You've got to be joking!' I said, immediately dismissing the idea. 'Putting a pair of skates on, at my age?'

Dancing on Ice was something I said I'd never do. Oh my God, I couldn't cope with the nerves! I used to think as I watched my friends take part over the years. I wouldn't try that. Why would anyone put themselves through it?

'Think it over,' he said. 'I think you'd be great.' It was nice that he had so much confidence in me, so I took his advice and thought it over.

My family were dead against it at first. *Dancing on Ice* is a high-pressure show and they were worried that the stress and physical exhaustion involved might bring on my depression again. The last thing they wanted was to be answering weepy phone calls at three in the morning from me crying my eyes out and wailing, 'I ca-a-n't do-oo-oo it!' (Sniff!)

'Perhaps you should turn them down, Mum,' Matthew ventured.

Tim nodded vigorously.

'No, you've got to do it!' Louis squealed.

'Don't do it, Den!' warned my good friend Coleen Nolan, who'd been a contestant the year before. 'You'd be mad even to think about it!' She told me how punishing the schedule was, how rigorous the training. But did I listen?

I've often said that I'm a gay man trapped inside a woman's body – and *Dancing on Ice* really appealed to the gay man within me. I'd been approached about *Strictly Come Dancing*, too, but nothing could be camper than *Dancing on Ice*, could it?

I kept thinking about the sequins, the glitter, the pirouettes – and how fit I might become if I trained really hard. I thought, When are Torvill and Dean ever going to offer to teach me to skate again? If I say no this time, they're not going to ask me next year.

In the end, it was a bit of a snap decision. What the hell, I'll do it! I thought. It was only later that I realized it might not be the most sensible choice I've made in my life.

I looked pretty shaky on the ice to start with. I'd skated a little as an eleven-year-old, but that's where my experience began and ended. Fortunately, in the first two weeks after I signed up, I had a course of lessons with a trainer called Donna, who was fantastic. She gets you up on the ice doing the basics. After the first lesson, Torvill and Dean came to watch me and grade my skating. They gave me a B plus, which I was very proud of. Sadly, my beginner's luck didn't last, and the next time they came, I was given a D minus. It soon became obvious that I wasn't going to be getting the call from Team GB about the next Olympic figure-skating championships!

Very gradually, I progressed. One day, Donna was unable

to give me my usual lesson. 'I'm leaving you in the capable hands of a lovely lady called Sam,' she told me. That was the day I got into doing bunny-hops, which are the first jumps you learn. To do a bunny-hop, you glide forward on your left leg, swing your right leg forward, jump and land on the toe pick of your right foot, then push onto the left foot. It's a handy little move that can be used to connect steps in a routine.

Having grasped the technique quite quickly, I became a bit cocky with my bunny-hops. When Sam left the ice to answer a call from one of her kids, I confidently bounded down the rink, feeling pretty gung-ho about my new skills. This was strictly against orders, because I wasn't meant to skate unsupervised, not even for a second. I really shouldn't have done it. Inevitably, I went one bunny-hop too far, slipped and fell over at the other end of the rink. You can imagine how Sam felt when she looked round to see me flat on my back on the ice. She nearly had a fit.

I was rushed straight to hospital in case I had a head injury. Thankfully, I didn't have concussion, even though I felt giddy and my head hurt. 'Can I go back on the ice tomorrow?' I asked the doctor, because I couldn't wait to get bunny-hopping again.

Up until then, I hadn't thought of myself as being physically fearless, because I'm the opposite of an adrenaline junkie. I don't do slides or pool fun, for instance, and I'm not one for roller coasters, either. Yet I never worried about falling over and hurting myself when I was skating, even after the bunny-hop mishap. I don't know why, because I'm not a brave person.

Both Coleen and Nadia Sawalha had told me their main fear was of falling and breaking something, but I was far more worried about becoming poorly with my illness than I was about physical injury. I was also slightly anxious about gouging out huge chunks of my partner's flesh as he spun me round by my feet, but that didn't happen, either. In the end, we had a couple of spills, but I didn't have any injuries. I had lots of bruises, obviously – you fall over; that's skating! – but we didn't have any major disasters.

They were very clever about matching me up with a partner. I desperately wanted either Dan Whiston or Matt Evers and I think I would have been disappointed if I'd been matched with anyone else. I already knew Dan, who's a Yorkshire lad, because he had skated with my friend Gaynor Faye in the first series of *Dancing on Ice*. I was also keen on Matt, as I'd met him a few times and liked him a lot. So I was thrilled when Matt skated onto the ice with a bottle of champagne for me. I thought, Yep, that's my man!

We gelled immediately and he has gone on to become one of my really good friends. I love beauty in men and women and, to me, he's a beautiful man, inside and out. We are really close, even though I haven't known him very long. I know that some people suspected there might be a *frisson* of romance between us, but there never was. Our friendship is based on laughing our heads off and having fun. Still, I can understand how situations develop between celebrities and their partners on a programme like *Dancing on Ice*. You spend more time together than you do with your own family, so if you fancy each other, something might easily happen.

Your experience of the show is very dependent on who you get as your partner, so I was fortunate, as it wouldn't have been such a pleasant experience if I hadn't formed a strong bond with Matt. We just clicked and made each other laugh. Some of the other contestants didn't have such a good rapport with their skating partners and enjoyed the process a lot less than I did. I practically wet myself laughing every time I was on the ice. It wasn't that I didn't take it seriously – I did, and I tried my absolute hardest and was sometimes nervous to the point of being sick – I just didn't take *myself* too seriously.

From the moment I was paired with Matt, I loved every single session. Don't get me wrong, there were plenty of tears. God, there were tears! It's hard not to cry when you can't get the routine and you know you only have one more session to get it right. Your tension levels rise and you think, Oh no, I'll never get this. It's very different to *Strictly*. If you're doing *Strictly* and can't get to the studio, you can practise your dance routine at home, or almost anywhere. You can go over your routine for nine hours a day if you want. But with *Dancing on Ice*, once you get your routine, you usually have only six hours on the ice before you're in the studio. Sometimes it's only four hours, but mostly you have three two-hour sessions of ice skating, which isn't very much at all.

To my surprise, I found being on the ice incredibly mentally therapeutic. While you're skating, you don't think about anything else. You can't! You have to focus completely on learning the routine and staying upright, and you forget about everything, because you're moving at such a fast pace. It's a wonderful feeling.

After a couple of weeks, I found myself craving to be on the ice. I couldn't wait to be skating again, even at six o'clock in the morning. There's no glamour about an ice rink first thing in the morning – in fact, ice rinks are often pretty grim places – but I just loved the moment when I stepped onto the ice and pushed off. I found ice skating mentally and physically stimulating. It's a fantastic sport and I'm totally in awe of professional skaters.

I'm someone who has been very vocal about hating exercise, but suddenly I had found a really enjoyable way to get fit. I began to feel physically better than I'd ever felt before, and I loved the fact that I was thinner than I'd ever been. In the past, I had lost weight because I was depressed, or by going on crazy diets, but this time I was losing weight in the right way, because I had to eat well to keep my energy levels up. Ice skating is really hard work. There was no time for snacking because I was busier than ever, so I simply ate three healthy meals a day and tried to have eight hours sleep as often as possible.

As time went on, I loved the way my body wasn't just

getting slimmer but firming up and lifting. By the time I left the competition, my legs were like steel. It felt miraculous, but of course there was no miracle about it. It was just the result of eating well – and less – and exercising. Suddenly, I was doing bikini shoots without feeling a bit embarrassed. Actually, I looked better than I had looked in a bikini in my thirties.

It was around this time that my point of view altered completely when it came to thinking about the future. Instead of feeling flat and unfulfilled, I experienced a total reversal in perspective. Instead of thinking, I'm fifty-two, so I can't expect much, I suddenly realized, Hang on, I'm *only* fifty-two! It struck me that I had so much to look forward to in the coming years, and it didn't seem unrealistic to expect big things from life. Just like that, everything changed. The world was my oyster again.

I'll always remember the moment it dawned on me that it wasn't all over for 'Nana' Denise. I was skating my way round a cordoned-off section of the ice rink at Altrincham when, instead of wobbling as I went into the pose I was practising, I started to move quite fluidly. I felt graceful and in control as I stretched one leg behind me and glided forward across the ice. My limbs were doing what my brain told them to do, and my muscles were supporting me; it was a moment of total focus and it felt completely exhilarating. Just then, I forgot that I was practically the oldest contestant ever to compete on *Dancing on Ice*. I felt fitter and physically stronger than I had for twenty-five years.

I felt empowered by the whole experience, even though I wasn't one of the best skaters. I was under no illusions about that. There were people like Laura Hamilton and Sam Attwater, who were fabulous from the beginning. Then there were people who were worse than I was, like Johnson Beharry, the ex-soldier who won the Victoria Cross for incredible bravery – what an amazing story that was. At the start, he could barely stand up on the ice, but by the time he got through to the semi-final, he was doing lifts with his partner, Jodeyne Higgins, through sheer determination. He was totally inspiring.

Learning a new routine every week was tough. I stretched myself to my limit and often woke up aching all over. But I was determined to get it right. If I was finding it hard to learn a new move, I refused to give up. There was a lot of repetition, but I didn't care, and my skating definitely improved as time went on. I was lucky to have a very good teacher and I did what I was told. Apparently, people get a little bit cocky sometimes and that can be their downfall, but I was a very obedient pupil – I'd learned my lesson after my bunny-hop disaster.

The series began in early January 2011 and I was set to make my first appearance in the qualifying rounds a week later. Brilliantly, Tim made a pie that said, 'Good luck, Den and Matt,' on the crust; it gave us some much-needed extra strength for our final rehearsals. Our first performance was a 1940s-inspired routine to the Eliza Doolittle song 'Pack Up', and Matt and I wore matching 1940s military-style outfits.

There were some seriously nerve-racking moments before I skated on to do that number! I am nervous enough when I'm doing a play, but this was totally different from going on stage. I mean, I was fifty-two and I was ice skating in front of ten million people. So much could have gone wrong.

As I've said, I was never scared of injury, and I wasn't scared of the judges' comments, either. However, like everybody else, I dreaded the thought of being voted out in the first week. No one wants to be the first to go, and that applies to all those kinds of shows, from *Dancing on Ice* to *Celebrity Big Brother*. For two months, I had been learning to skate and preparing for my first routine, so the disappointment would have been enormous. I really hoped I could skate to the best of my ability and get through the first week without letting my partner down.

Our first weekend in the studio was pretty fraught, because everything was leading up to our performance. The whole of the Saturday was taken up with studio rehearsals, which is more about planning camera angles than anything else and involves endless waiting around doing nothing. It's so much better to be busy when you're nervous. Hanging around with nothing to do is fatal, because all you can think about is how anxious you are.

On the Sunday, there was a dress rehearsal, which the judges watched to give them ideas of what they might say about the routines. Then came the live performance, followed by the results show. You don't know until about three in the afternoon what the order of skating will be. I didn't want us to be the first couple to go on, but my heart sank when I found out that we were last on. It meant that I would have to stand in the green room and watch everybody else doing their routines first. My nerves jangled furiously. I was absolutely terrified. It didn't help that I'd been in full make-up since ten o'clock that morning and had to be careful not to smear my mascara. There were so many people to get ready that they'd had to call me into make-up ridiculously early.

Once we had changed into our costumes, there was more waiting around, and you couldn't wander off alone to chew your nails in a corner because they were scared you'd disappear. It would have been disastrous for one of the contestants to be missing from a live show, so you could barely go to the toilet without a chaperone.

About two skates before you go on, they take you down to the ice. I was trembling all over as I walked towards the rink. I kept thinking, I'm actually going to be on *Dancing on Ice* in a minute! It seemed incredible. An image flashed through my mind of the time, several years earlier, when I'd sat in the lounge and my mouth had dropped open as I watched Gaynor Faye skate in the first series. How can Gaynor be doing that? I'd thought. How is it possible? It was the same when I watched Coleen Nolan and Suzanne Shaw.

Now I was walking around in my little dress, thinking, What the hell am I doing?

The music started up and Matt and I stepped onto a tiny

area of ice, about two feet square, and stood in a pool of light. 'You'll be fine,' Matt whispered. 'Left, right, left,' he reminded me. I looked up and glimpsed Phillip Schofield and Holly Willoughby ahead of us. Suddenly, I caught sight of my friends in the audience, who were waving cardboard cutouts of my head on sticks! Even from where I was standing, I could see the 'Deirdre Barlow veins' bulging in their necks, which told me how tense they were feeling about my upcoming performance. Oh no, Nana's coming on in a minute! they were thinking.

Then I spotted Tim, Matthew and Louis. Matthew worries about me more than anybody, so he was on the edge of his seat. He said later that he couldn't have been more scared if it had been his first night at Madison Square Garden with his band. 'Mum, don't ever put me through that again,' he said afterwards. 'I was so nervous for you that I honestly felt like I was going to vomit over the person in front of me.'

He, Tim and Louis hadn't seen me training, so they had no idea how much I'd improved. All they had seen was someone who could barely stand up properly on the ice two months earlier. So it was always going to be an uneasy moment for them when the announcer said, 'Ladies and gentlemen, will you welcome onto the ice Denise Welch and her skating partner, Matt Evers!'

At that moment, everything went hazy for me. I don't remember much, just smiling at the cameras with a rictus grin as the music started. Then, as I skated forward, my hair-net snagged on a sequin on my costume and yanked my head back. Oh God! I thought, but I couldn't let it hold me back. I ripped the sequin off with a quick flick of my hand and skated on.

The next couple of minutes were spent concentrating on getting through the routine, which felt like it was over in a flash. The audience applauded and Matt and I skated to a podium to talk to Phil and Holly as the judges' scores came up: ten points out of a possible thirty. Phillip asked me for a reaction and I said, 'Listen, I've been having dreams for weeks where my teeth fall out and I get *nul points*, so *any* points is good for me.'

Phillip laughed.

'I thoroughly enjoyed it. I was very nervous,' I went on breathlessly. 'I just want to say thank you to the viewer who sent in the incontinence pants because they've come in really, really handy.'

Jayne Torvill said some nice things about the performance and how much I had improved, and then it was time for the judges to give their comments. Nothing they said came as a surprise to me. Jason being nasty was just as I'd expected and it was water off a duck's back. It didn't matter to me that he said something about us looking like 'Matt skating with his mum', even though it was a bit below the belt and not very funny. I laughed the next day when I heard that Ally Ross had written about it in the Sunday papers, saying something like, 'We watched Denise Welch doing her impression of Gracie Fields on ice.' That was amusing, but Jason Gardiner was mean without being humorous. Still, I didn't care what he said. What was important was that I had done my best and stayed upright.

Anyway, the judges' scores were less important to me than they were to some of the other contestants. I always knew that whether I stayed in the show or not would be dependent on the public vote. On the other hand, I didn't want anyone to be voting for me if I was terrible – I didn't want to be the Todd Carty of the 2011 series!

I could tell that my family and friends were absolutely stunned when they saw what I could do, just as I had been when I first saw Gaynor skate years earlier. For all they knew, I was going to come on like 'Zimmerframe Zelda', taking shaky, tentative steps as I shuffled across the ice. So seeing me going under Matt's legs and doing a forward roller-up onto his shoulders took them completely by surprise. They were far more concerned about my mental well-being than they were about me being a rubbish skater, but they would have hated to see me fall over and hurt myself. I think it was a relief for all of us that I didn't land on my bum during the first week's routine.

Next, I skated off backstage and did a quick interview about how it had gone; then, an hour later, Matt and I skated back on for the results show. We glided over to wave to our supporters and then lined up to wait for the results of the public vote. I knew from having watched the show that they build up the suspense with lots of well-timed expect-ant pauses, but I wasn't prepared for the violence of my thumping heart as I waited to hear our names being announced. I thought it would smash its way out of my ribcage.

Finally, Phillip said, 'Denise and Matt!' We were through to the next round. The relief was immense.

3

You're Not Past It When You're Over Fifty

The weeks flew past and, to my amazement, I was still in the competition. I didn't expect to do so well, not in a million years. I had no idea I would enjoy it all so much, either. The whole experience was addictive. I had thought I wouldn't care what happened after the first week, once I had got over the fear of being the first to be voted out, so it was a surprise to find that I was desperate to continue skating. I longed for the mental freedom that came with rehearsing on the ice; I also got hooked on the competitive aspect of the show. I really wanted to skate well and make it through to each new round.

Another reason to stay was my friendship with Matt. I loved spending time with him and didn't want to say goodbye quite yet. I made some good friends among the other skaters and contestants, too. I can honestly say there wasn't really anybody with whom I didn't get on. There were a few people I'd known before, like Hayley Tamaddon, and Chloe Madeley became a good friend. There was an element of people wanting Chloe to fail because they thought she was hitching a ride on her mum and dad's coat-tails, but she worked her bollocks off and did brilliantly; she came third by proving that she's a lovely girl.

There were people I would never have met in the course of my normal life or had the opportunity to become friends with, like Comedy Dave Vitty, Johnson Beharry and Vanilla Ice. It was wonderful. Vanilla Ice was fantastic with Louis and they had a brilliant relationship. He missed his own kids, so when he knew Louis was coming, he'd always say, 'Hey, where's Louis? Come on, Louis,' and they would do that complicated hip-hop handshake thing. They spent hours together. Louis knew the whole of Vanilla Ice's rap, of course. I was delighted, because Louis would never have had the experience of meeting him otherwise.

I loved the dressing-up side of the show. Wearing sparkly skating costumes is a little girl's dream, and I was fifty-two! It was orgasm central for my gay friends in the audience to see me in sequins and ice skates. Plus, I was slim enough to wear the outfits without any fear of revealing a muffin top or other bulges. It felt fantastic. I loved skating with a man who has the best bum I've ever seen in my entire life, and knowing that every gay man and every straight woman watching was envious of the fact that I was dancing with Matt Evers.

The *Dancing on Ice* costume team are brilliant and incredibly creative. I was astounded by my opening-number outfit, which cost thousands of pounds because every sparkly little piece on the bodice was real gold. Actually, I couldn't understand it. Why not just go to the haberdashery department at John Lewis and get some gold beads? Who's going to know? Still, I felt amazing in my little top and skirt.

My second-week costume for our routine to the Abba song 'Gimme! Gimme! Gimme!' went several steps further. It was an all-in-one metallic gold lamé outfit with flared bits on the sleeves and trousers. At the time, I just went along with whatever they wanted to put me in, but when I look back, I wonder why I didn't question it. Carol McGiffin said later that she felt sorry for me having to stand around for ages waiting for the results wearing 'a gold condom', which pretty much summed it up. It was definitely my worst outfit.

Still, I can't complain, because it obviously rated with the public and we got the most votes that week, despite the fact that I skated terribly. At one point, I couldn't feel Matt behind me and everything went a bit wobbly. I lost the rhythm completely and almost came to a dead halt, so when the judges gave me nine out of thirty, I thought it was fair dos. It wasn't a great skate. I really beat myself up about it afterwards and my confidence levels dropped to an all-time low, but I picked myself up and went on to skate much better in our routine to 'Slow' by Rumer the following week. This was one of my best skates, I felt. I'd wanted fast, camp routines, but they gave me a slow number to get rid of what they called my 'Deniseness', which was impeding my ability to let go on the ice. I enjoyed it much more than I thought

I would, and the costume was fab, a classic little yellow skating leotard and fringed skirt.

I was horribly nervous before our Shirley Bassey routine to the song ''S Wonderful'. Although things hadn't gone too terribly the week before, I was still convinced that I was a rubbish skater and was worried that I might not get through the routine, which was very pacey. It didn't help that the dress rehearsal went badly, and by the time we went on for the live performance, I was sure I would make a mess of the whole thing. In desperation, I decided to camp it up. I was wearing bright pink and there was room for some really dramatic gestures, so I went for it.

Since I'm not going to wow them with my skating, I thought determinedly, I'll wow them with my acting and drama. The actress in me came out and everything seemed to gel. The judges gave me my best marks yet and told me that I had turned a corner. The next week, I camped it up again, to 'Roxy' from *Chicago*, which I loved, even though I was slightly worried about wearing nothing but a leotard on national television.

We were given our highest score for our slow routine to the Cyndi Lauper song 'True Colors'; the judges gave us 16.5. I was totally gobsmacked and thrilled. Christopher Dean said that he was very proud of me and he actually used the word 'serenity' when describing my performance! Again, I loved my costume, which had a fringed skirt. Part of its appeal was knowing that I would have died and gone to heaven if I'd had the chance to wear it as a ten-year-old.

Having short hair turned out to be a downside. Most of the other female contestants had longer hair than me and I'd sit in hair and make-up watching in awe as they were given these beautiful creations with hairpieces and a dazzling array of hair accessories. To make up for it, I wore a couple of wigs, which was fun. One of my favourite routines was the one we did to the Jennifer Lopez song, 'Let's Get Loud', in which I wore a shoulder-length blonde wig. I loved it, but Christopher Biggins told me he thought I looked utterly ridiculous, 'like my dad when he's dressed as a tranny'. But he always says things like that, so I brushed it off. He's just jealous! I loved the bright orange Latino costume I wore for this routine, which was really fast and furious. We didn't get a good score from the judges, but it didn't matter to me, because I had a lot of fun doing it.

Funnily enough, the lower my scores from the judges, the more people picked up the phone to vote for me. Public opinion was definitely with me and that's what got me through. It didn't seem to make much difference what I did on the ice, really; people were voting for me because I was having a go and trying my best. It was a big confidence boost for me to get so much support.

It was brilliant to know that people had rung up and said, 'We want Denise and Matt to skate again.' Of course that's going to make you happy. It's human nature. You're delighted to have another week of this experience ahead of you, because you're absolutely loving it. It's fantastic, especially when you know that you're not the best skater.

People kept asking, 'Doesn't it bother you that the judges make snidey comments and you're constantly bottom of the leader board?'

OK, it would have been lovely to get good marks, but it was also a great feeling to be voted through each week despite being bottom of the leader board. Johnson and I were always last, which meant we had to do so much better in the public vote than the people at the top of the board in order to stay in the competition. Conversely, people like Sam Attwater and Laura Hamilton were having to skate incredibly well to keep going through, because they were less well known, so the public weren't as likely to vote for them. Luckily for them, they were amazing skaters.

I was bowled over every time we made it through. When you hear, 'Denise and Matt!' when you've only scored 13.5, while other people's scores are 26.5, you can't help thinking, Wow! It's amazing to have so much public affection and backing when you're trying so hard. I felt I was striking a blow for the older birds!

Around the third week, Carol McGiffin got me on to Twitter. She made me go on it because her followers were saying, 'We'll vote for Denzi, but you have to get her on Twitter.' After that, people in ice rinks all over the country were tweeting me, which was great. I was getting tweets from people who owned ice rinks from Dumfries and Deeside, saying, 'We've had all these forty- and fifty-somethings taking up skating as their new hobby.'

Apparently, they were saying, 'If Denise Welch can do

it, so can we.' How fantastic. It was showing people that you're not past it when you're over fifty. It was showing that age really is just a number.

I was in awe of the professional skaters on the show, so it was wonderful to get to know them. As well as being close to my partner, Matt, I became very good friends with Nina Ulanova, the Russian ice dancer who was paired with Steven Arnold. They went out of the competition early because Steven, bless him, was voted off. But little Nina was living with Matt in Hale, so I saw her frequently. I loved her Russian accent. She was always saying things like, 'Shall we go and have a walk in the willage? Denise can have a wodka in the willage. Where's Wanilla Ice?'

It amazed me that I was spending time with world-class skaters like Nina and Matt, because I would never have got to meet them normally. I almost had to pinch myself when they came over to my house.

'Are you sure you want us to come?' they'd say, because they were a little bit impressed by Tim and me and what we do.

'What? Of course we do!' I'd say, feeling bowled over that they would actually want to come and hang out with us. It was brilliant to have a new circle of friends from a completely different walk of life, and I found them incredibly interesting.

Luckily, I had a husband who was very welcoming. I'm a person who makes friends quite easily, because of my personality and the job I do, the places I go and the people I meet, and I randomly give out my number left, right and centre. I love having people round and I was always bringing my new friends home, where Tim was unfailingly nice to them. Looking back, I can't help reflecting that I expected too much of him.

I would say, 'Nina and Matt are coming over tonight. Can you make a pie?'

Now, if Tim had said to me, 'Steve and Joe from the pub are coming over tonight,' I would have said, 'No, they're bloody not! What do you mean, Steve and Joe are coming? I don't want Steve and Joe here.'

Yet when I told Tim that Matt and Nina were coming, it was already a *fait accompli* and he accepted it as such. It was probably quite selfish of me to expect him to go along with my plans. Still, he allowed it and never complained. I never said, 'Is it OK if . . . ?' because he never said it wasn't OK. It was always fine with him.

Conversely, he might say, 'I'm going to Keith's to play snooker tomorrow night.'

'You can't', I'd say, 'because we're going out for dinner with Julie and Robin.'

Now, if he had said that to me, I would have retorted, 'We are going out to dinner with Julie and Robin? Who said we are?' With hindsight, I can see that I was being unreasonable, but at the time I wasn't aware of it.

Now I think that perhaps Tim didn't mind having people over constantly because it deflected attention from our relationship and meant we didn't have to be together on our own. We'd become closer again over the summer and could still have a brilliant time together, especially when we went out of an evening or were on holiday. But the day-to-day grind of domesticity and long-term marriage had begun to get us both down, I think.

Like most couples, we often clashed over the kind of minor domestic details that can escalate into major frustrations over the years. It's the little niggly things that tend to build up. For instance, when Tim cooks, in his mind the kitchen is utterly pristine when he's finished. He thinks he's cleared everything up. The reality is something different, because there's gravy down the Aga, the sink is covered in grease, and the dishwasher is stacked in a completely impractical way. But after years of being married, as you re-stack the dishwasher and wipe down the Aga for the umpteenth time, you reach a point when you can't be bothered to complain any more. Instead, you think, I'll just let him believe he's cleared up!

Tim is brilliant at looking after people, especially in a crisis. But although he likes to think of himself as a nurturer on a day-to-day basis, he really only does the things he enjoys doing. So whenever I used to leave a list of things to be done when I went to London, they might not be done when I got home, but there would be a meal on the table, regardless of whether I had already eaten or not. Tim likes to cook, but that wasn't necessarily helpful if I wanted him to call the plumber to unblock a sink, or an electrician to mend a light socket. To me, the meal was far less important than getting things sorted around the house.

I flare up very quickly, like my father – I have the famous Welch temper – whereas Tim may look like a bulldog chewing a wasp, but that's where the resemblance ends. He's not the least bit aggressive. However, he has a gruffness about him that sometimes comes across harshly. For instance, in the morning, if he's sleeping in the big bedroom and there's something in there I need, I'll creep in to get it.

Rather than saying, 'Darling, I'm not getting up yet. Will you just shut the door after you?' he yells, 'SHUT THE DOOR!'

I find it hard not to fly off the handle and say, 'I'm just getting my knickers from the drawer and then I will shut the fucking door!'

Tim tends to bark orders at Matthew just when Matthew is in the middle of doing something important, like recording a song.

I've said to him, 'Try saying, "Matt, are you upstairs? Listen, can you come down for a moment?" Just try that.'

But it comes out as 'Matt, come outside and do such-and-such!'

If Matthew calls down, 'Dad, I'll do it in a minute,' Tim shouts back, 'You will bloody do it now!'

'Just let him finish the recording and then he'll do it,' I say. 'Yes, I know his bedroom is untidy, but let's deal with that later and deal with this now.' Like every mother, I do my fair share of mediating.

Tim is a world champion at losing things and it drives me crazy. Other people would say to me, 'Don't have a go at him about losing the keys. We all lose keys.' Yes, maybe we all do lose keys every now and then, but with Tim it's every time he leaves the house. Every time! It's an ongoing problem, which can be very stressful.

I can't count the number of times I asked him to leave the key out for me and I came home at midnight to find no key. Not there. It's lucky the neighbours have a spare key and didn't tell us where to shove it. Once I'd got into the house, there would inevitably be another key catastrophe before I left. At six in the morning, in a rush to get to the station, I'd go to find the jeep keys and they wouldn't be there.

Then it would be a mad dash up to sleeping Tim. 'Where are the jeep keys?' I'd shout frantically.

'Are they not downstairs?'

'No, they're not! My train goes in five minutes. Where are the jeep keys?'

Of course, when he can't find something, it's everybody else's fault. 'Where is the letter that was there?' he'd say accusingly, pointing at a side table.

'I don't know. Where is it?'

'Well, I left it there.'

'But if you left it there, it would still be there, because no one has moved anything from there.'

'Somebody must have moved it! I left it there!' Later, he'd find it in the place that he really put it, but not until he'd pointed the finger at each of us in turn!

Conversely, Tim was always moving things and not owning up to it. A minor example of this occurred one day when I was filling in some forms using the only black biro in the house. I left them on my desk for an hour, and when I came back, the biro was gone. 'Tim!' I called out. 'I left the biro here. Where is it?'

He came to find me. 'You didn't leave it there,' he said.

'I did. I've put two things down today and they've both gone,' I replied, seething with frustration.

An hour later, I saw him with the biro. It made me so angry. I tried to explain how the frustration and inconvenience of the lost biro had caused me anguish and put me in a right state. 'You just put me through all this angst about that biro, the only black biro in the house, and it turns out that you have taken it!'

A little later, some friends came round. I was still furious and not speaking to him. 'It's about a bloody biro,' he told them.

'Oh, Denise!' they said.

'It's not about a biro!' I screamed. 'You have no idea what this is about,' I snapped at Tim. But he never accepted that it wasn't about the biro. It was a kind of dishonesty and it made me angry.

Although day-to-day irritations grind you down in a marriage, it's quite possible to put up with them as long as everything else is fine with the relationship. However, in the early part of 2011, I found my tolerance evaporating, and I became very difficult to live with because I was angry a lot of the time. I think it was because I was in a relationship I didn't want to be in – and nor did Tim, although neither of us consciously acknowledged it.

My frustration came out in the form of constant exasperation. Everything Tim said irritated me; all his foibles drove me mad. We started wanting to see different friends. Our differences regarding parenting were becoming more prevalent. I was annoyed all the time. 'I'm not angry like this when you're not here,' I said to him on several occasions. 'I hate being so angry.'

I stopped wanting a physical relationship with Tim, but even then I wouldn't admit that I wanted out of the relationship, not even to myself. Some people say, 'You can't stay in a marriage if you don't have sex.' Well, I'm sorry, but loads of people do. Some just stop doing it, without ever discussing it. Other people might feel in the mood now and again after a bevvy at the local social club, when it's a case of 'Go on, then! Pull my nightie down when you've finished.' There are lots of people living like that who don't admit it. There are also those who decide that celibacy is the way forward and find that it improves their marriage. There's a multitude of different situations and different kinds of marriages.

I accepted that we didn't have a conventional relationship, so the lack of sex didn't seem a reason to leave. I worried that Tim still wanted sex, though. I'd think, It's been some time now. Perhaps I should initiate it. But I never felt in the mood, so I'd rush off to my bedroom to avoid it.

While getting changed for bed, if I heard his footsteps on the stairs I'd hurry to put my nightie on, just in case, God forbid, he caught a glimpse. I'm not flattering myself, because when Tim saw me naked, he'd say, 'I don't know what you're wearing, but it needs ironing!' But I felt the pressure, all the same.

Still, it didn't seem like an overwhelming problem. I think you can convince yourself that if you don't hate each other and you aren't arguing all the time, there's more reason to stay than to leave. I believed this and I guess I thought that if I wanted to have a dalliance now and again, I could, as long as I kept it to myself. I'm sure he thought the same.

But then we started to argue a lot more, and our rows always seemed to go round in circles. Perhaps it was partly because we weren't having sex, which would have counteracted the petty irritations of daily life. Sex is a great way to unbottle pressure, I think. Our arguments weren't the kind of dramatic drink-fuelled rows that we'd had earlier on in our marriage; it was more a case of a couple of glasses of wine at dinner making it possible for us to talk about stuff we were usually too inhibited to discuss. I wanted us to be more open about the fact that there had been infidelities on both sides, not just on mine, and I found it very frustrating that Tim refused to accept that I knew certain things *had* gone on with him. I didn't want to discuss the details or anything; I just wanted us to be honest with each other.

The public point of view was skewed because of the way the press has portrayed me. The affair with Steve Murray was mentioned practically every time my name came up, and the papers were always implying that I was 'up to no good' (usually with one of the gay men I was papped with). I didn't care, but it bothered Tim. However, whenever he said, 'I'm sick of this!' it would trigger an argument, because I knew he wasn't living a blameless life, either.

I would have been fine with Tim talking to the press about our marriage and giving his side of the story, and it wouldn't have bothered me if he'd admitted publicly to a few indiscretions himself, but I didn't feel it was my place to voice what I knew about that side of things. When we talked privately, I would say, 'Look, just admit this. Just admit that.'

Confessions would come out in the heat of the moment and I would discuss them without any anger or resentment. But when I tried to take the ball and run with it the next day, he would go into denial. I found it very frustrating.

'But last night you said you did!'

'No, I didn't.'

'Yes, you did.' It always felt like we were back to square one.

The press didn't follow Tim and I didn't say anything about what he might be up to, because I choose to be candid about my life but I respect that he wants to be much more private about his personal life. I'm an open book and one of my jobs is to talk about myself: people know that I wear terrible underwear; they know all kinds of things about me. On the other hand, Tim is an actor, not a TV personality. He can't bear the press and will only do limited publicity for his job. He certainly doesn't want to invite journalists into his private life. As a result, the press made assumptions about our marriage. As I've said, he was always cast as the long-suffering husband and I was his wild, good-time wife.

At times it has made things difficult for us that I've been so open and we have argued about press intrusion in our lives. 'I'll give everything up, then,' I've snapped, tired of taking the flak for it. 'You support us.'

It's easy to forget that I'm putting myself in this situation because we have to earn money. I'm the one who diversifies to pay the bills. Like most actors, Tim may have to wait six months between one great job and the next. Roles like the transvestite Les/Lesley in *Benidorm* don't come along every day, yet we still have to keep the household cogs turning for those six months, and one of the downsides of my work is the press attention on our private lives.

An even bigger downside is that I miss the children horribly when I'm away. The way I deal with it is to go into my work zone. I'm quite good at separating work from home in my mind, so it almost feels as if I'm living two lives. Having said that, I find it hard to shake off the guilt of being away from the kids, especially Louis, and he's very good at playing on that.

Louis is extremely bright, funny and switched on, which means that he can be quite manipulative when he wants to be. He may be having a brilliant time playing football with Matty, but when I ring up, he'll come on the phone and whimper, 'Hi-i, Mu-um,' putting on a faltering, tremulous voice that intensifies my maternal guilt. Then, as soon as he puts the phone down, leaving me in bits, he happily goes back to playing football!

'Mum, please don't fall for it,' Matthew says.

'But I feel so guilty about being away,' I say.

'Listen, Mum, you were away just as much when I was a child, and for longer stretches. Yet of all the things that I look back on in my childhood, I never remember thinking, Oh my God, my mum was absent in my life!'

It's true that when I was filming *Soldier, Soldier* in Germany and Cyprus, I was often away for two weeks at a time. Then I'd maybe come back for five days and go away for another two-week stint. Matthew was only five at the time, so sometimes he could come over for a visit, but Tim was often working, so it wasn't always possible. Nevertheless, either his dad was there or I was there or he was left with people who loved him. Neither of my children has been left with a host of nannies or people they don't like very much. They've always been with trusted people, and Tim or I have been with them most of the time.

In the last few years, we have sometimes relied on Matthew to take over when we aren't there. He's old enough and responsible enough to take charge, and he adores his little brother, so we've been able to leave Louis with him since Matthew was eighteen. Matthew appreciates the fact that he lives at home and we support him, so it's only fair that he looks after his brother sometimes to help out, and he is marvellous with Louis; in some ways, he's like a third parent.

He doesn't resent having babysitting duties, but he does occasionally resent it when one of us comes back and tries to take over when he's already laid down the rules. 'Shush, I'm dealing with your brother now,' Tim will say.

'No, Dad, I've said that he has to go to bed at nine, so it's not helpful when you tell him it's OK if he watches something until half past nine. I set the rules when you leave him with me, so don't push me out because you're back.'

'You have to accept that, mate,' I told Tim the last time it happened. 'If we expect Matthew to get Louis to school or babysit him in the evening, we have to hand over the reins to him.'

Of course, it drives me a bit mad that Louis will listen to Matthew or Tim, but not to me. It's a mum thing, though, isn't it? If I've been away, Louis will complain, 'You haven't been here to take me to school!' So I'll get up and get everything prepared, only to be faced by total noncompliance when it's time to walk out the door. We're always late for school when I'm there, more often than not because Louis won't put his shoes on. I'll shout and threaten and he'll take no notice of me whatsoever. Then his dad walks in and barks, 'Shoes on now!' Done.

Fury!

Matthew has a similar effect. If Louis is being cheeky with me, Matthew says, 'I never talk to Mum like that. Don't talk to Mum like that, ever!' And Louis will look up at him adoringly and stop right there.

I wish I had this blooming talent of snapping my fingers and getting things done. It seems so easy when Tim does it. 'Up, breakfast, shoes, out the door now!'

Tim says, 'It's because you're too bloody soft with him. It's because you let him get away with it.' Actually, that's not the reason he behaves differently with me. Talking to other mums, it's clear that it is simply because you are the mother.

My screaming is water off a duck's back to Louis. He doesn't even notice. It's so frustrating, especially when Tim has been away and I'm sorting everything out. Then Louis moans that he's been told off for being late, and it's all my fault. 'I won't take you any more, then!' I say.

It's even more infuriating when Tim gets back and says, 'Well, it doesn't happen when I take him.'

But despite the day-to-day hiccups, I think Tim and I have done a good job of bringing up our children. As I said to Tim the other day, 'Whatever we have done wrong, and by God we have made some mistakes, just like every other parent, you only have to look at them to see that we've done something right.'

Our children have always had a voice. When I'm in a mixed environment of grown-ups and children, and a child has a valid point to make or a valid question to ask, one thing I really hate is when other grown-ups don't hear or don't attempt to hear what the child is saying. I'm not talking about a situation where a child's pulling on your skirt while you're in mid-conversation, whining, 'Mummy, Mummy, Mummy!' My children don't interrupt, because if they do, they're told not to. But when they try to make a valid point and another grown-up ignores them, I will always say to the adult 'Actually, he is asking you a question.' I think it's wrong to disregard children just because they're children.

Like most parents, I'm incredibly proud of my kids. They are very open and funny and talented. I don't know whether or not they will utilize their talents, or whether they will make any money from them, but they are both talented in many different ways. Most importantly, they have a very well-developed, well-honed sense of humour, which I think is essential to getting through life. It's good to be able to laugh, especially when things go wrong.

People from all walks of life tell me what a great guy Matthew is. He gets on with everyone and I like to think that's partly down to our parenting. He and I have a very close relationship. In many ways, he understands me better than his dad does, and I have a strong sense of what's going on with him. Matthew is his own man and he doesn't want me to talk much about him, but I am aware that he has a slight leaning towards the dark side, although not to the extent that I do. I can always tell when he's not in the right zone.

Tim isn't perceptive of him in that way; I'm more connected with Matthew's moods and how to deal with them. Whether that's a mum's intuition or it's just because of the special bond between us, I don't know. That's just how it is. Still, Tim is a fantastic dad. He's always been very hands-on and he was amazing when the kids were small. He had to be, as I was lost to him because of my depression. As a result, he has an incredible bond with Matthew, which has strengthened over the years, although they can drive each other up the wall, too!

Life was probably easier for Matthew when I was at home than when he was just with his dad. He loves and worships his dad, but I think he found things less bumpy when I was there, partly because I'm a soft touch when it comes to my children, but also because I moderate their relationship.

At occasional low points in our marriage, I did think vaguely about splitting up with Tim, but I couldn't bear the idea that it might mean we couldn't do things together, like go to see Louis in a school play or watch Matthew in his band. I hated the thought that one of us would have to go on the Tuesday and the other on the Wednesday, as that's how most of my separated friends run their lives. 'You have him this Christmas and I'll have him on Boxing Day. One of us will have to miss the present-opening.'

I think of separation like this because I see it with so many of my friends. What's more, we have an eleven-year-old who is still a little boy at Christmas, and who will be appearing in the school play and going to senior school soon. I couldn't bear the thought that I wouldn't be taking him to his new school on his first day because of access arrangements. The idea terrified me.

Despite the arguments, I still wanted to be married to Tim, because I loved him. I also knew that I would never leave Tim for someone else. If the marriage ended, it would be because we had come to the end of the marital road, not because there was someone else involved. Our relationship was just too strong for another person to come between us in that way.

And so we muddled along. Neither one of us was able to acknowledge that our problems were getting worse. I just pretended everything was fine, because the thought of life without Tim scared me.

4

'This Is Lincoln Townley'

To a degree, it was easier for me to stay in the marriage than leave because I was away from home so much. I could deal with all the frustration because I'd dip back in for a few days and then come away again. I think it was hard for Tim that I coped so well away from him. He found it more difficult to be alone than I did.

For the weeks I was doing *Dancing on Ice*, my whole world was focused on training at Altrincham ice rink. I relished the feeling that I was living in a different world. It was like being in a protective bubble away from reality. On a show like *Dancing on Ice*, you have a reason for disappearing and that's very liberating; you can't see people or even ring them, because so much of your time is consumed with ice skating. You live, eat and breathe it. Even when you're doing other things, you're thinking about that tricky axel jump or crucial slide chassé halfway through your routine.

Obviously, I had to do *Loose Women* and keep up my other obligations, so at the beginning of the competition I was learning to skate, appearing on *Loose Women* and being a mum. By the seventh week, I was also filming an episode of *Casualty* in Bristol and a short film in Wales. My days were jam-packed. When I look back, I think, How did I do it all? Meanwhile, some of the younger contestants were just doing *Dancing on Ice*.

Somehow, I still found time to have the occasional, much-needed night out, and I remember one absolutely brilliant evening in the midst of all the work madness. It was a wet and windy night in the middle of February and it turned out to be memorable for many reasons. A group of us met up for drinks at Soho House, a private members' club in the heart of Soho. I was with Matt Evers, my *Dancing on Ice* skating partner; Sadie Pickering and Reece Douglas, whom I'd worked with on the TV series *Waterloo Road*; Sadie's mum and Markaiu, my bisexual Turkish friend (more on him later).

Out of the blue, my magician friend Paul Lytton phoned up and said, 'Are you in London?'

'Yes!' I said. 'I'm in Soho House with a bunch of friends. Come along!' It was a really nice surprise as I hadn't seen him in ages.

I've had an obsession with close-up magic for as long as I can remember. I adore it. For me, it's absolutely fascinating to watch somebody creating illusions right in front of my eyes. When a magician with a pack of cards goes around the tables at a restaurant, I can't wait for them to reach me. As they flick the deck and fan out the cards, I feel like a child again, bright-eyed with wonder. I sit on the edge of my seat, bursting with excitement, desperately trying to work out how they do it.

I can't do a single card trick myself, but I can spot a good close-up magician, and I instantly saw the potential in Paul when I watched him working the tables at a do at Newcastle United FC around fifteen to twenty years ago. He made a few mistakes, but he was extremely good for someone so young. Says me, like I'm a connoisseur of close-up magic! I'm just a fan, but I told him, 'I'm going to keep an eye on you, because I think you're going to be very good.' He went on to win awards for his work and he's become a good pal.

When Paul arrived, I thought, I'm not going to do that cringe-making thing of asking him to do a trick for my friends. It's like asking a comedian to tell a joke; it's not fair. You wouldn't ask an accountant to work out your tax liability on a night out, or expect a gynaecologist to take a quick look at your insides.

I was just happy to see Paul and meet his new wife. But then he said, 'I've been working on something new. Would you like to see what I've been doing?'

So I told my friends, 'I'm so proud of Paul. You just have to watch him!'

It was pouring down with rain outside and the windows of the club were tightly closed. Paul took out a deck and asked Reece to pick a card. When Reece gave the card back, Paul threw the entire pack at the window and we watched the cards flutter to the floor. Just one card remained stuck to the window, facing us; it was the card that Reece had picked. 'Oh my God, that's just amazing!' Reece said. But it was much more amazing than any of us had imagined, because when we went over to the window to inspect the card, it turned out to be on the other side of the pane! We had to lift the window up to get to it, and when we brought it inside, it was soaking wet. How did it get there? I really have no idea.

Paul's next trick was equally mystifying. Matt picked a card, which then disappeared from the pack. 'Do you have your mobile phone on you?' Paul asked Matt.

'Yes, but it's switched off, because you're not supposed to use phones in here,' Matt replied.

'May I see it?' Paul said.

Matt took his mobile phone out of his pocket and handed it to Paul, who carefully took the back off. There, inside the phone, next to the battery, was the missing card. We were stunned. That, to me, is magic. In this age of quick-access celebrity, when people with no talent become famous for doing nothing, I love the fact that brilliant people like Paul are still hugely in demand.

That evening happened to be the night of the Brits music awards and I had been invited to the after-show party. I've never been that interested in going to the Brits, or any other awards ceremony for that matter; I really only go to that kind of event if I'm presenting an award or getting one, and clearly that wasn't going to happen at the Brits! Well, you never know, I suppose. Some hip rapper might suddenly decide to sample the single I released back in the 1980s, or rework my classic cover of 'You Don't Have to Say You Love Me'. I can see it now: 'Denise Welch "feat" Tinchy Stryder'!

Actually, I can't bear the way that people never seem to make records these days without featuring another artist. 'Why can't any of you do it on your own?' I asked Pixie Lott when she came on *Loose Women*. 'You always have to "feat" somebody.' Adding, 'When I did my single, I didn't have to "feat" anybody!' I was only pulling her leg, but I do wonder sometimes.

Anyway, I had two tickets to the Brits after party, but I was with a group and I wanted them all to come. I'm not going on my own, I thought, so let's just go along and see if we can all get in.

Off we trooped to the Brits, where the guy on the door said, 'Den, you can come in with one other person, but not the whole gang.'

'Well, I want to stay with them, so never mind,' I said, turning to go. Alex Reid happened to be trying his luck at the door right then, and he was also knocked back. Of course, the next day the papers were full of the news that I had been publicly and embarrassingly kept out of the Brits party, along with 'my entourage' and Alex Reid.

The evening didn't end there, though! Markaiu, Sadie

and her mum and I piled into a cab and headed to Jet Black in Soho. Now, I have no idea where Jet Black is, because I've only ever been there at ridiculous o'clock when I'm happily pissed. That always seems to be when I get into a taxi and say, 'Jet Black, please.' The taxis know where it is, but I couldn't find it myself, by night or day. It's the perfect place to go if you're not ready to go home.

When we arrived, I went for a quick wander, and five minutes later, I walked back into the main room, but to my surprise I couldn't find any of my friends. They later told me I'd been gone for an hour, although I swear it felt like a few minutes. God knows what I was doing! Chatting, probably. Maybe I bumped into an old mate. Either way, I came back to find that everybody had deserted me. They said they'd looked everywhere for me and assumed I'd gone, so they left. A couple of hours later, Markaiu woke up on a park bench in Watford or somewhere crazy, having gone in the opposite direction to his home. He has no recollection of how he got there. It was one of those nights.

Meanwhile, I was still at Jet Black. Fortunately, I spotted my friend Noel, who's a model and nightclub organizer. He had a friend with him, a smartly dressed man with a lovely smile. 'This is Lincoln Townley,' he said. 'Lincoln runs Stringfellows.'

'Hi, Lincoln,' I said, and we started chatting. We immediately got on, and we both had a strong sense that we liked each other, but at this point it was absurdly late and I had to get home. Nevertheless, we exchanged numbers before I left.

Feeling a little the worse for wear the next day, I was glad that I didn't have to do any skating. After several weeks of being in the competition, I was trying to fit so much into my life that I was beginning to feel really tired. Tiredness leads to stress, and then I started worrying about getting overloaded. It was scary, because I didn't want to risk becoming poorly. As I've said, my depression is mainly endogenous, which means that it can't be attributed to external factors like emotional trauma or stress, but it can be reactive to certain triggers, and I'm definitely more vulnerable to it when I'm run-down.

Much as I loved appearing in *Casualty*, it added huge complications to my life. The problem with TV drama is that the schedule is unpredictable. They can call you at seven in the morning and assure you that your scene will be finished by two in the afternoon, but there's nothing you can do if the scene runs over. If you have to stay until seven in the evening, so be it. You can't argue. Unsurprisingly, the *Dancing on Ice* team were finding it very hard to work around that.

Casualty was already in my diary before I agreed to do *Dancing on Ice*, and I was determined that skating wasn't going to prevent me from doing my real job, which is acting. It was a one-off episode and I was playing Goldie, a haulage-company owner. It was great because it had been a while since I'd done a part on television and I love doing TV, but

I worried that I might not finish in time to get back to the skating rink for rehearsals and that put a lot of pressure on me.

Not only was I rehearsing for my own routine, they then threw the group skate at us, so that meant another set of rehearsals. Sometimes I was getting to Shepperton Studios at six in the evening and having to work on the routines until ten at night. Then there were all the extra bits of filming that needed to be done. They'd say, 'You're doing a rumba routine this week, so we're going to send you to a rumba class in London.' How wonderful! Except that it took up a whole afternoon in a week that was already bursting at the seams with things to do.

As with everything in life, you don't know how you do it. You just do it because you have to. But I think my skating suffered because I was becoming exhausted, and that really bothered me. Perhaps the public would have voted for me even if I had messed up and fallen down, but it didn't make me try any less. It was really important for me to be as good as I could be, and it bugged me when I didn't do as well as I should have done.

I spent most of the competition convinced that I was a terrible skater. There were certain moves that I just couldn't master, however hard I tried. For instance, I could never do a hockey glide, even though it's one of the simplest moves. I was also rubbish at arabesques. On the plus side, I was good at stopping, while other people were very good skaters but found it hard to stop. Matt comforted me by saying that everybody has their strengths and weaknesses, but I still felt under-confident. Sometimes I wondered whether I should just bow out gracefully. Was I making a fool of myself by soldiering on? I wondered.

I don't really like watching myself back on TV, but I've peeked at a couple of the routines I did and thought, Actually, I wasn't that bad! I certainly wasn't as terrible as Jason Gardiner said I was.

I've told Jason that I thought he was out of order on the show. It wasn't so much his comments about *me*, as they had very little effect, it was some of the things he said about other people that bothered me, because they overstepped the mark. I understand that there is an element of comedy in him being a pantomime villain, but I don't like the way TV companies appear to condone and even encourage nastiness on television. A lot of the time, what Jason was saying didn't feel like pantomime, because there wasn't any wit or creativity in his comments. I think it's possible to be cutting and scathing on the show, but it only works when it's combined with a sense of humour.

Off screen, Jason is a really nice guy and we had a good relationship, but I was appalled when he told Laura Hamilton, 'Your legs are rather stumpy.' On the same show, he said to Jeff Brazier, 'It's almost like you are missing a couple of chromosomes,' which is a totally unacceptable thing to say to anyone. Another week, he told Karen Barber, the head coach, who had been a judge in previous years, 'If your opinion still mattered, you'd be on the panel.' That upset me more than anything else; it was unbelievably rude.

He also said some awful things to me, but I barely noticed them. Did I care what Jason Gardiner and Emma Bunton thought of my skating? Not bothered. As one of my friends texted me about Emma, 'This is someone who used to dress up as a toddler for a living!'

The only judge whose opinion mattered to me was Robin Cousins, because he was the only skater on the panel. Jason is an amazing dancer, but he's not a skater. Neither is Emma, who would say things like, 'When you did that backward spiral . . .' Meanwhile, in the wings, they were saying to me, 'You didn't do a backward spiral! It's not even called a backward spiral!' It was like having two Alesha Dixons and one Len Goodman judging us. And yet I absolutely adore Emma Bunton and I think she was a good asset to the panel.

Although I was unconcerned about Jason's comments, I knew they wound Tim up. 'That Jason Gardiner,' he used to growl, 'he deserves a good punch!'

Tim and Louis came to watch me every week, but Matthew couldn't stand the tension. In Week 1, he surprised himself and everyone who knew him by jumping out of his seat and punching the air when he heard I was through to the next round. Matthew is a laid-back kind of dude who doesn't normally do things like jump up and punch the air; he never came again after that. 'I hope you understand,' he said apologetically. 'I can't bear to see Jason Gardiner trashing you, either.'

Mum and Dad came one week, which really touched me, because it was a huge effort for Mum to come all that way. She had been living with oral cancer for just over three years by then, receiving only palliative care. Although her cancer appeared to be no worse at this time, her emphysema made it difficult for her to breathe sometimes. It was a massive thing for her to come to London and sit around for hours in a TV audience. I was very concerned about her and felt jittery all evening. Her breathing problems had recently become much worse and she needed lots of attention. Still, she said afterwards that she'd loved seeing me skate live, so it was worth all the trouble. 'Don't take any notice of that silly bugger Jason Gardiner!' she said. 'You were brilliant.'

As the weeks passed, Tim became more and more inflamed by Jason's criticism, until he finally reached boiling point. In Week 9, Jason went too far after Matt and I did a slow routine to 'Alone' by Heart. It seemed to go well, I thought. Certainly, it was better than my skate to the Jennifer Lopez song the week before, which Jason seemed to think was the worst thing he had seen in his entire life.

Chris Dean praised our routine to 'Alone', and the judges gave us a combined score of fifteen, which wasn't bad. Robin Cousins and Emma Bunton said some quite nice things . . . and then it was Jason's turn. 'It was a marked improvement on last week's abysmal uptempo,' he said, stressing the word 'abysmal'. Apparently, unbeknownst to me, this made my little Louis fill up out in the audience, and Tim saw red.

'For me, though, what I would like to say is that it was a little bit like watching two people play Twister,' Jason continued in the face of increasingly loud boos.

I wasn't really taking any of it in because, as I've said, Jason's critique tended to go over my head. Once Robin had given his comments, I switched off. It was all happening *over there*, as far as I was concerned, while I was *over here* on the podium with Matt. So I was totally unprepared for what happened next. Just as Jason was explaining how my moves didn't flow, blah, blah, blah, Tim stood up, stormed the stage, dodged a bouncer and appeared by Jason's side. He just couldn't restrain himself any longer.

I nearly died of shock. 'Don't!' I yelled. 'Sit down!' I was petrified Tim would hit him.

'Who the bloody hell do you think you are?' Tim said, his face right up close to Jason's. 'She's fifty-two and she's got four jobs! How many jobs have you got?'

As well as being angry about the effect of Jason's words on Louis, he really felt for me, because he knew how hard I'd trained during the week. I'd been stretched and pulled every which way but loose, and now Jason was gleefully dismissing my efforts.

Jason obviously wasn't clever enough to think of a comeback, and seemed taken aback by what we now call Tim's 'pitch invasion'. His pathetic response was, 'Oh my God, your breath,' while waving Tim away, as if Tim was boozed up and breathing out alcohol fumes. Tim had probably had a fag, but the audience are not allowed to drink – and they are in the studio from four until seven o'clock, so they don't have a chance to get a bevvy in. There's no way Tim's breath smelt of drink.

Holly intervened by saying, 'Back to you, Denise . . .'

'Oh my God, it's only the transvestite off of *Benidorm*!' I joked, trying to smooth the situation over.

After Tim was escorted back to his seat by security, Matt and I went off to do our post-skate interview. When we skated back to sit in our allotted seats near the judges, I saw Jason Gardiner smile at Tim and mouth the words, 'Hysterical!' and, 'Great television!' And that was the end of that, or so I thought.

It seemed the viewers weren't going to let Jason get away with his offensive behaviour. Before long, he was being criticized on Twitter for being rude to Tim and for saying nasty things about my skating. This time, his response was even more deplorable, bearing in mind that if you say something on Twitter, you may as well say it on television, because the press pick up on it immediately. 'Those who say I was rude to Tim Healy can shove it,' he wrote. 'He got in my face with breath that smelt of stale piss n alcohol whilst I was talking.'

I was horrified. That was my husband he was talking about! It was then that I fell out with Jason; I couldn't bear the low-down hypocrisy of it. First he insulted Tim; immediately afterwards he chummily congratulated him on a great TV moment; and the next day he told the world that Tim stank. I felt deeply hurt the following morning when

Phillip Schofield made a joke of it on *This Morning* by squirting breath spray in his mouth before Jason's segment as the show's fashion correspondent. I felt it was wrong to respond on a family show to something offensive that had been said on Twitter. I also felt hurt because the bosses of *This Morning* are in charge of *Loose Women*, and they should have been protecting my feelings as well as my husband's. I'm a respected member of the ITV team and have always been very loyal to the channel. At the time, I was bringing a lot to the table, particularly by being a rubbish skater managing to stay in a big show courtesy of the public vote, thereby generating quite a bit of income.

I was told that Phillip and Holly would address it on *This Morning*, so I sat and watched it in my dressing room, thinking they might question Jason. I didn't expect them to ask about the Twitter stuff, because it was too vulgar to air on television, but I expected them to say, 'Do you not think Denise's husband had a right to do that?' In the end, they didn't question Jason at all and I was very disappointed. I was almost ready to walk out of the studio that day. Even though Tim and I are separated now, it still incenses me that someone can say my husband smells of stale piss and get away with it. And it didn't end there, because I couldn't let Jason off the hook. When a journalist from the *Mirror* rang to ask for my comments, I said how upsetting I had found his tweets. And the following day there were head-lines like, DENISE: MY FURY and JASON'S A COWARD.

It's a shame, because Jason and I had a really good relationship off screen up until that point. I'm not saying we're enemies now – of course we're not; when we found ourselves on the red carpet together at the Pride of Britain Awards later in the year, we had a hug, because life's too short to bear grudges – but I don't think unkindness should be condoned, a view that is perhaps shared by the *Dancing on Ice* producers now that Jason has left the show.

I left *Dancing on Ice* the week of Tim's pitch invasion, after losing the skate-off to Johnson Beharry. To be honest, I was ready to go. It had been a fantastic experience and I was very proud to have done nine weeks out of a possible twelve. What's more, I thought the right people were in the final five and I was just so proud of them all. Johnson Beharry, Jeff Brazier, Chloe Madeley, Laura Hamilton, Sam Attwater and their partners had all worked so hard and produced amazing results. By then I was getting really stressed about all my different commitments, and we were about to go into props week, where you have to skate round a table or hold a blooming umbrella or something, so it was a huge relief not to have to do that.

In the days leading up to my final show, I kept thinking, I cannot skate solo with an umbrella and do *Casualty* and *Loose Women* and try to see my children all in one week! I was freaking out, so I wasn't pretending when I told Phillip and Holly that I was relieved to be leaving. It was exactly the right time to go.

Most of all, I was glad not to have to rehearse the results show ever again. Every week, I dreaded it! We skated on, we stood there, and Phillip did this long pause before he told you who was through. Why do we have to rehearse it again? I thought. We had to practise it every weekend, when we all knew exactly what to do after the first run-through. The studio rehearsals on the Saturday were becoming a little arduous as well, because they're all about the cameras. Stop, start, stop, start. Boring, boring, boring.

Of course it was disappointing to leave the show, because it was the end of a short era for me, which had been a great experience, and I knew I would miss everyone. However, when I woke up the morning after my final skate and went on shows like *This Morning* and *Daybreak* to talk about my experience, I didn't think, I want to be back in the competition. I wasn't *loving* it any more – and by then I knew I was going to be doing the *Dancing on Ice* tour, which took the edge off my disappointment.

It was fantastic to go home to Cheshire and spend time with my children without having to rush off every other day. After a couple of weeks, I ran out of my oestrogen gel, but it didn't worry me, because I was feeling well. It was a bit like when you don't bother to finish a course of anti-biotics. 'When I go to London next, I'll get some more EstroGel,' I kept saying. But I didn't and I didn't and I didn't – and I didn't have a period, either. That could mean only one thing, as far as I was concerned, because EstroGel suppresses periods. It meant that I had been through the menopause and come out the other side! Joy! My menopause was done, and it had been aided and abetted by the EstroGel.

Strangely, my body temperature has changed since my periods stopped. Now I'm like a proper Geordie, who doesn't need a coat and wanders around in all weathers wearing a sleeveless top. It's great! It was a massive relief to have survived the menopause without hormonal havoc dragging me into the breakdown I thought would accompany it. I felt like a huge burden had been lifted as my dread of the future disappeared into thin air.

'Leave my bum alone, Denise! Stop it now!' Chris Dean snapped, trying to sound cross.

He said the same thing every night on the *Dancing on Ice* tour, because I couldn't resist giving his bum a quick nip as we skated down to the middle at the beginning of the show. When I used to watch Torvill and Dean in the Olympics, did I ever think I'd be in a situation where I would be tweaking Chris Dean's bottom on the ice? Not in a month of Sundays, and that's why it made me laugh so much.

I wasn't going to do the *Dancing on Ice* tour at first – not everybody does and Karen Barber makes the decision about who goes – so I was thrilled to be asked, but decided it wouldn't be fair to my family to be away from home for nearly four weeks. I hadn't been on a theatre tour for over twenty years for the same reason, and acting is my real job, so I didn't see how I could justify doing a skating tour.

However, if I didn't do the tour, Matt couldn't do the

tour, which seemed unfair. And as Tim, Matthew and Louis said they could manage fine without me for a few weeks and encouraged me to go, I thought, Go and do it! You'll be on tour with Torvill and Dean!

A record number of tickets were sold, which was fantastic, and in April and May, we toured the arenas of Nottingham, Wembley, Sheffield, Newcastle, Manchester and Birmingham, although not in any particular order. You might be in Nottingham one night, Wembley the next four nights and then back to Nottingham again. I loved every second of it. It was like going back to my old days of being on tour as an actress, but on a much bigger budget. Just getting on the tour bus was a thrill. It was like being a massive rock star, because we were playing arenas. Of course, it wasn't rock and roll in the sense of partying all night, because you're not allowed to go on the ice with a hangover, obviously. That would be dangerous.

I broke the rules only once by going to rehearsals with a sore head, and boy, did Matt punish me for it! 'Just lie down on the ice,' he said once I'd laced up my skates.

Obediently, I lay down; then Matt took hold of my feet. 'What the hell are you doing?' I asked, suddenly struck by a premonition that something bad was about to happen. Well, the next thing I knew, he had me in a headbanger, which meant he was holding me by the legs and I was whizzing round in a circle, my head perilously close to the ice. 'Stop!' I begged. 'Argh!'

I wasn't actually sick, but I came close. Immediately

afterwards, I had to do an interview on *Sky News*, which wasn't a lot of fun. Needless to say, I was never hung-over for rehearsals again! That was my first – and, I hope, my last – headbanger.

Fortunately, you didn't need to drink to have a great time on the tour, because there were so many fantastic people in the group. As well as Matt and Nina and all the other skaters and contestants, we had Christopher Biggins, Robin Cousins, Chris and Jane, and a guest judge on the panel. Biggins and I have been friends for a hundred years, so we had a lot of fun together, even when I was on the ice. As I skated past the judges, I'd go into a roll uplift on the top of Matt's shoulders and shout rude words at Biggins. He and Robin would be crying with laughter as they watched me sail past, mouthing obscenities. Some of the other skaters would improvise every now and then, so I thought of it as my way of adding a flourish to my performance.

Our first night was at the Sheffield Arena on 9 April. Everything seemed to be going smoothly until we came to the group skate, where two teams compete against one another. I was wearing a tiny, gorgeous black costume that made me feel like a proper skater – until I came down off a roll and Matt said, 'Oh!' in a very startled way.

'What?' I whispered.

He was staring at my chest. I followed his gaze and, oh dear, my black backless Lycra dress had come undone and my boobs were showing! Ten thousand people were goggling my boobs, and for once I hadn't even meant to show them off. It was only for a fleeting moment, but it was hysterical and the audience was in fits. Fortunately, Matt was quick thinking enough to pick me up, squeeze me close and swing me round to spare my modesty. He took me to the end of the rink while I looked around fratically for help. In the end Hayley Tamaddon skated over and fastened me up. Phew!

The audiences were brilliant, giving us the most amazing reception. I have never known any audience reaction like it. 'We had Bon Jovi here last week; we had Guns N' Roses here; but *Dancing on Ice* always gets the biggest reaction, by far,' the arena staff told us. I couldn't believe it the first time I saw hundreds of screaming people waiting outside after the show. Seeing 400 hardcore *Dancing on Ice* fans crammed in front of a gate made me feel like a massive rock star. It was just ridiculous. We had the best time ever.

One of my favourite parts of each show was watching Nina and Matt doing their professional skate. You don't get to see very much of the professionals dancing at their best on the television show, but on the tour they present the most stunning showcase of what they can do. Every night I'd be glued to the giant monitors, gazing in wonder as they swept across the ice. More often than not I'd be in tears by the end of their routine because it was just so beautiful. I can't believe they're my friends, I'd think. The ex-American champion and the ex-junior world champion! I marvelled at the fact that they had actually been to my house. Their grace, talent and ability blew me away.

During the tour, I received a text from Lincoln Townley, the man I'd met at ridiculous o'clock on the night of the Brits. 'Hi, it's Lincoln. We met at Jet Black. Fancy going out for a drink in London with some friends?' I wasn't in London at the time, but the next time I was, I texted him and some other friends and we all went out.

Lincoln and I got on really well, just as we had the first time we'd met. I found him very easy to talk to; we laughed at the same things; we had quite a few friends in common; and I was sort of attracted to him, although he wasn't really my type. I've always been a lover of long hair, so you would have thought that after being married to Tim for so many years, the next person I'd be with would have flowing, Samson-style locks. But no – and now, of course, I think Lincoln is the most gorgeous man in the world.

It was a slow burn with Lincoln. A month or so after we went for a drink, I was on my way to north London to visit somebody when I remembered that he lived nearby in Hampstead. I sent him a text asking if he was around. It was midday and he texted back, 'I'm on my way home now. Would you like to go for lunch?'

'Yes, why not?' I said.

He took me for a lovely lunch in Hampstead and we talked about our children. It was the first time we'd talked properly, one to one – the first time we weren't in a group on a night out – and it was lovely.

I was surprised to hear that Lincoln had a twenty-year-old son. After all, he wasn't even forty. He was very young when he married his ex-wife, Beverley, and his son, Lewis, was born. Back then, he didn't really have any money, so Beverley went back to live with her mother. After that, she moved to Spain, making it very hard for Lincoln to see Lewis. He used to go over every other weekend, which was tough, I think. He and Beverley were only together for about three years. It didn't last because they were so young, but they're still in touch because they share Lewis, and at our lunch Lincoln spoke very highly of her.

His next relationship was with the mother of a three-year-old girl and he was with her until the little girl was eleven, so he kind of brought her up. His subsequent two serious relationships ended because he didn't want more children and his girlfriends did. It was very upsetting for all concerned, because it's heartbreaking to split up with someone when you still love them and want to be with them. But if you can't agree on a subject as fundamental as whether or not you want children, there's nothing else to be done.

Lincoln's most recent relationship was with a woman in her twenties and, once again, they had split up because she wanted to get pregnant.

'Maybe you'll change your mind?' she said.

'I won't,' he said sadly. 'It's just not going to change for me.'

He told me that he has always been faithful to his partners, and I liked the way he spoke highly of the women with whom he'd had the three main relationships of his life.

He is very respectful of women, even though he has worked at Stringfellows, around lap dancers and pole dancers, for some years. I don't see a conflict there, actually. I have friends who are lap dancers, and I used to work in a topless bar, for God's sake! Only, I didn't make any money because I had horrible tits, even at nineteen. Argh! Just the thought of it makes me come out in a rash.

'Oh, "Stringfellows Lincoln",' a couple of people said dismissively when I mentioned him. But I wasn't bothered about his job.

When our lunch was finished, I felt strangely reluctant to leave. However, I had a *Dancing on Ice* show at Wembley Arena that night and I was due at the venue for a rehearsal. 'I'll drive you to Wembley,' Lincoln offered.

'That would be nice.' I was really enjoying his company and it was an excuse to go on chatting.

As he dropped me off at the arena, I said, 'Maybe we could do this again sometime.'

'I was thinking exactly the same thing,' he said, giving me a lovely smile.

I've made a new friend, I thought happily, as I made my way into the arena.

5

Denzie Does Düsseldorf and Other Mad Moments

I'm lucky enough to love what I do, so it's not often that I wake up and think, I don't want to go to work today. But on the rare occasions when I feel like I can't be bothered to drag myself out of bed, I simply have to remind myself of the job I had in the summer of 1976. That's all it takes to make me count my blessings, because it was the job from hell.

It was the summer after I sat my A levels, before I went to drama school. I was broke and desperately needed to earn some money in the holidays. My old school friend Jill Hewitson also needed a job, so we both applied to be waitresses at a holiday camp. The camp isn't there any more as it's been closed down. And let me say now that I'm sure it wasn't and isn't in any way representative of holiday camps generally, because I know loads of people enjoy their holidays at these places. It was just this particular camp that was horrendous. And it was a long time ago.

As waitresses, Jill and I did more than just serve food. When people came in for their breakfast in the morning, the tannoy system would play 'Save Your Kisses for Me' by Brotherhood of Man, or the Sailor song 'Girls, Girls, Girls', and we'd have to wave table napkins in time with the music. It was cringe-makingly awful. 'Girls, Girls, Girls', flap, flap, flap. Sometimes the guests would pick up their napkins and wave them along with us. At dinner, we had to serve soup in time to the music as well. We felt ridiculous in our uniform of a white polyester pinny worn over a black nylon dress that crackled with static every time you moved.

Some of the guests were devoted to their holidays at this camp. They'd tell us stories of how they'd ventured out and gone to another location one year, but had to come back because it was so much better. They praised the food, its quality and variety. What they didn't know was that it was a set menu every week. Mondays were always the same; Tuesdays were always the same; on Wednesdays, rice pudding was always served.

Most of the people who worked in the kitchens were ex-cons. They were migrant workers who did one job in the winter and another in the summer, and they all had massive forearms and scarred faces. Every one of them was tattooed from head to toe, like Rod Steiger in the 1969 film *The Illustrated Man*; quite a few of them had 'LOVE' and 'HATE' tattooed on their knuckles. They were incredibly intimidating and I was terrified of them.

One day, Jill and I went into the kitchen to find six guys

standing around a huge vat of rice pudding and weeing into it. We were horrified, especially as we then had to serve the rice pudding to the guests. We squirmed as we watched people raise their spoons to their lips and happily say, 'We wouldn't go anywhere else! We've tried other places, but you don't get rice pudding like this there.' I had to look away to avoid seeing all those poor, unsuspecting people tucking in. All the while, 'Girls, Girls, Girls' was blaring tinnily through the little speakers in the corners of the room. Wincing, we rhythmically served out seconds.

We all know the restaurant rule: don't complain about your food, because the kitchen staff will play football with it in the kitchen. But here people weren't complaining. They were happy with their piss pudding and everything else. And yet I still came across a bunch of the 'chefs' playing football with the guests' steaks one afternoon. It made me sick to see. I had to turn a blind eye, even though I felt incredibly sorry for all the trusting people who ate the contaminated food. Today, I would of course report the kitchen staff if I knew something like that was going on, but I was eighteen and terrified at the time. What's more, I had no prospect of getting another job and I needed to earn some money.

The staff chalets were awful, a grey, grim version of the brightly painted guest chalets. So many of the workers were ex-cons that there were security guys with air rifles patrolling the area in case there was any trouble. Jill and I shared a cabin and it felt like we were living in Colditz.

Unlike Colditz, though (to the best of my knowledge), the place was a complete shagfest, with staff shagging the guests left, right and centre.

One night, about two weeks into the job, Jill and I each had a boy back and did a bit of snogging and feely-boobies into the night. The next day, I was walking back to the chalet after lunch when Rob, my boyfriend from home, appeared out of nowhere. 'What are you doing here?' I asked. I was appalled, having had some ugly nerd who worked in the Garden Tropicale Café in my chalet the night before.

'Surprise!' he said with delight. 'I've got a job in the kitchens so that we can be together in the holidays.'

I was pleased to see Rob, but I was also a bit gutted, because the only bonus of working in such a terrible place was the possibility of having the odd snog with somebody else here and there.

A few days later, my mum and dad came down to visit. I tried to put a brave face on things, but they immediately realized how miserable I was. My mum cried when they left. It was so depressing and I was having such an awful time. She said afterwards that it felt like she was leaving me on a lifer's stretch in Holloway. 'You have to get out of here!' she told me, tears streaming down her face.

You were supposed to give a fortnight's notice before you left, but although I'm not afraid of hard work and I've done some crappy jobs, I couldn't stand it any more. Seeing the aghast look on my mum's face brought home to me how terrible it was. 'We have to go,' I said to Jill.

We'd been told that there would be terrible consequences if you went without giving the full two weeks' notice, but I couldn't stay a moment longer, so we booked a taxi to take us away. So frightened were we of getting caught, and the retribution that would follow, that we hid on the floor of the taxi, trembling with fear under a tartan blanket, as we were driven away past the guys with air rifles. It was unbelievably scary. Rob left the same day, I think, but not under the tartan blanket with us. He must have found another way to escape Colditz!

I've had some rubbish jobs over the years, but nothing comes close to waitressing at that camp, not even the time I worked as a very successful topless hostess in Soho while I was in drama school! I'm so lucky that work opportunities haven't dried up as I've grown older. I've done some of my best work in recent years and I'm hoping that the future holds even more exciting projects.

My teenage self would have found it hard to believe some of the things I get up to these days. In fact, my fifty-something self sometimes has trouble keeping up with the twists and turns my life takes! One of the wonderful things about my work now is that I never know what my next adventure is going to be. I mean, I could never have predicted that I would one day be taught how to skate by an ex-world-champion figure skater, who would go on to become one of my best friends. And when I first started my *Dancing on Ice* journey, there was no way of foreseeing that within six months I'd be in Düsseldorf presenting a piece on the Eurovision Song Contest for *Loose Women*, flanked by two Eurovision-mad producers and my Turkish friend Markaiu, whom I mentioned in the last chapter.

How did it happen? Well, it all began with Markaiu, who I met at the tail end of 2010 when I'd just started training for *Dancing on Ice*. I was with some of the *Dancing on Ice* gang at the Shadow Lounge, a gay private members' club in Soho, when he came up and introduced himself. I was immediately struck by how beautiful he is – he's very pretty, with long, dark hair – and we instantly got on, even though he's only twenty-three. I don't know why it is that young gay people are fascinated by me. I think it all started when I played a bit of a vixen in *Coronation Street*, giving me the beginnings of gay-icon status. Gay men love *Loose Women*, too, although, as I've said, Markaiu's bisexual, not gay.

We'd all had a few sherries and I kept telling Markaiu how beautiful he was and we ended up having a laugh. 'Hey, I have a place in Hisaronu in Turkey!' I said.

Markaiu frowned. 'Where?'

'Hisaronu!' I said, launching into the story of how Tim and I went to Turkey eleven years ago with our friends Jayne and David Gilbert, their kids and our kids. Louis was five months old at the time. One day, Tim and David went out to buy a shirt, got pissed and came back having bought a six-bedroom villa off plan. They were full of how Turkey was about to enter the EU and Hisaronu was the place to buy; the villa was an absolute giveaway and we had to buy it, they said.

Well, we still have a six-bedroom villa in Turkey and, more than a decade after we made our brilliant investment, it's worth about four and a half Turkish lira. In fact, it's worth so little it's simply not worth selling, even though it's a stunning place and would probably be valued at around £2 million if you transplanted it to the Algarve in Portugal. However, I have no regrets, because for years Mum and Dad spent six or eight weeks there every summer, which was fantastic for them. For that reason alone I'm grateful we bought it.

Markaiu was born in the UK, but both his parents are Turkish, so you'd think he would have heard of Hisaronu. He hadn't, though, or so he claimed. 'You've made it up!' he teased. 'Hisaronu must be the Brigadoon of Turkey; it only appears when you go there.' This became a standing joke with us. 'I've never heard of it! Nobody in my family has ever heard of it,' he kept insisting.

In turn, I took the mickey out of his job fronting a holistic clinic in London, where people pay thousands of pounds for their cupping therapy, in which a therapist places hot cups on their skin. We enjoyed making fun of each other and struck up an unlikely friendship. Despite being so young, he's quite old for his years.

A few months later, in February 2011, we were having dinner and he said something about the Eurovision Song Contest. 'You know, I don't think I've watched Eurovision since Cliff Richard was in it,' I said. 'It's not really my thing.'

Markaiu looked amazed. 'You don't watch Eurovision?

I don't believe it!' he screeched. 'How can you be a gay man trapped in a woman's body, then?'

'I don't watch it, I really don't,' I said.

It soon became apparent that Markaiu was obsessed with all things Eurovision. Apparently, it's as big as the Olympics in Turkey. It's absolutely massive; Turkish people throw Eurovision parties all over Europe. 'My dream would be to go to Eurovision,' he said, his eyes misting over.

'God, how sad are you?' I said with a laugh.

The following day – and I mean that literally; it really was the following day – Antony Costa from the boy band Blue left a message on my answerphone. 'Den, can you ring me?'

I rang him back. 'I just want to ask your advice,' he said. 'Blue have been asked to represent the UK at Eurovision and I want to know what you think.'

'That's a coincidence,' I said, telling him the story of the previous night. 'I think you should do it – if I can come and bring my friend Markaiu with me.'

'Hang on, I'll find out,' he said. He rang back a little later. 'I've spoken to our manager and she's spoken to the organizer and yes, you can.'

You cannot imagine the response when I phoned Markaiu to say, 'Guess where we're going in May?' He didn't believe me at first. It was like someone saying that their dream was to have tea at Buckingham Palace and the next day the Queen rings to ask you round for a cuppa!

That's how the Eurovision ball started rolling for me. A

couple of days later, I went into work and was telling my producers, Billy and Steve, all about it. 'I hope that *Loose Women* can get behind the Blue boys and support them,' I said.

Steve's face took on a green hue of envy. 'I can't believe you're going to Eurovision,' he muttered. 'I'm so absolutely gutted!'

'Honest to God, I had no idea that so many people aspired to go to Eurovision,' I said. 'Why don't you go and pitch it to the boss?' I added flippantly.

I heard nothing more about it until, about two weeks later, Steve came up to me looking considerably happier. In fact, he was beaming from ear to ear. 'The boss has gone for it. She wants you, me and Billy to follow Blue at Euro-vision for *Loose Women*.'

'Wow! Denzi Does Düsseldorf!' I squealed. It became the working title of our trip.

The four days that Markaiu, Steve, Billy and I spent in Düsseldorf turned out to be the campest days of my life, and that's saying something. We had a ball, despite the fact that by the time we'd arranged to go, all the posh hotels were booked up. There was some massive sports event in the city at the same time, along with about twenty-seven conferences, so we were in Hotel Crapsville. It was so bad it had an empty swimming pool that was knee deep in sludge. We had great fun taking silly pictures next to the muddy pool and sending them back to the UK.

Markaiu and I shared a room, which was hilarious. He

is so precise about what he wears that he does spreadsheets to plan his wardrobe. I looked at them: there was his outfit for the airport; what he wanted to arrive in; his clothes for the first Eurovision rehearsal, everything planned down to the last detail. When we had a change of schedule and missed the main dress rehearsal, he was totally thrown. His spreadsheets had gone out of sync and he didn't know what to wear! It was ridiculous. (I realize now that this was preparing me for Lincoln, who likes to iron seventy-five hankies before he goes out to the supermarket.)

Steve had a special phone number for the trip and it was in my phone under 'Steve Euro'. It remains his nickname to this day. People come to meetings with him at ITV thinking he's called Steve Euro!

I had to interview quite a few of the acts before the show, and meeting all these wacky people completely played to my strengths as a presenter. There were loads of funny moments. I never thought I'd hear myself saying things like 'You can't bring Greece in now! I haven't done Bosnia Herzegovina yet!'

At one point, I went up to the entry for Romania and said in very slow, clear English, 'Hell-o! It is a pleasure to meet you!'

'All right! I'm from North Shields,' he said. He was a Geordie! It was fantastic. He'd married a Romanian girl and lived in Romania.

The Azerbaijani couple, Ell and Nikki, who went on to win, had actually been formed for the competition. Nikki was from Azerbaijan, of course, which neighbours Turkey – Markaiu loved that about her – but she'd also lived in Palmers Green for years, near where I used to live, so we chatted about that and became quite pally.

It was wonderful to be with the Blue boys, because they're all my friends. They gave a fantastic performance. OK, they came twelfth, which was disappointing, but when you're there, you realize the competition is very much geared towards the Baltic states. I don't know why. You have these ninety-year-old pensioners who dance and sing a bit and come third. It's very bizarre. The following year, there was all this talk about Engelbert Humperdinck being a little old for the competition, but he would have been a whipper-snapper the year I went! In fact, some ancient Russian dancers came second in 2012, which just goes to show. People kept tweeting me to say, 'The Loose Women are on!'

Then, of course, mad Jedward were running around everywhere. It wasn't until I went into the crowds to inter-view everybody that I realized how massive their fan base is in Ireland. There was so much green there for Jedward! It amazed me to see how many people come from all over the world to support their countries. The most joyous part of it for me was watching the expressions on Markaiu and Steve's faces as they waved their British flags. It was hyster-ically funny. It made me wonder why Eurovision isn't big in the UK. It was, back in the day, when Lulu, Clodagh Rogers and Cliff used to represent us. Perhaps several years of *nul points* have put the mockers on our enthusiasm.

Back in the UK, our Eurovision film was edited and went down very well on *Loose Women*. A few days later, on 22 May, it was my fifty-third birthday and, instead of bringing on dancing men in underpants like they normally do, who should walk on but Nikki from Azerbaijan! The girls had flown her in for my birthday. Fantastic. My gay fans loved it. It doesn't get better than being friends with the winner of Eurovision. I'd love to go again one day.

As well as the many adventures I have *Loose Women* to be thankful for, I'm also grateful for the wonderful friendships I've made on the programme. I like all of the Loose Women. They're a great bunch. People sometimes say, 'You're all women together. There must be loads of backbiting?' But it's a complete myth and fallacy that an all-female environment creates conflict. It's so horrible that people think that.

I love being surrounded by women and I distrust people who say they don't get on with other women. I hate it when someone says, 'I'm a man's woman.' I would immediately steer clear of anybody who didn't have a good circle of girl-friends. Of course, we have our niggles on *Loose Women*. But we've got to the point now that we've known each other so long, we can speak plainly to one another without causing offence.

For instance, I can say to Carol McGiffin, 'Shut up, you miserable old cow,' and she won't bat an eyelid!

Actually, although Carol can occasionally be a miserable old cow, she's hysterically funny and incredibly intelligent.

A talented journalist who held down her own radio show for years, she has a huge amount of knowledge stored up in her brilliant brain. Understandably, she despairs of me every time I block my ears and sing, 'La-la-la-la!' when I find something boring or don't understand it.

Loose Women isn't a very political show, but we do talk about issues that affect our viewers, like money, tax and education. Funnily enough, I love listening to Carol talk about these topics, because she's very much a political animal. She knows everything about politics and manages to convey complex ideas in simple terms when she talks about them. Because of her, I've realized that politics isn't that difficult to understand; it all starts with being interested in your community and where your money's going.

I've learned more about politics from Carol McGiffin than anyone else. She's also helped me to take an interest in personal politics and how government policy will affect me and my family. Carol can't bear the fact that I don't know how much money I have. I don't know if I have none or lots, because I've handed over control of my finances to other people. Carol probably knows her finances down to the last penny, whereas I would never know if someone was creaming money off me. In fact, it's quite possibly happened over the years.

When my dad, who looks after my finances, says, 'You want to know what you've spent? Let me show you,' I say, 'La-la-la!' Unfortunately, I'm never going to be 'Spreadsheet Denise'!

Carol makes a very strong case for simplifying politics. She says that if policy were explained more clearly, it would make more people want to vote. But because we see the House of Commons buffoons yelling at each other like a bunch of idiots, we lose interest.

Certainly, my night at the House of Commons bar in May 2011 showed me that you can't take a lot of these people seriously. The evening began when I was invited to a do at 11 Downing Street, on behalf of various charities I work with. I was allowed to take somebody with me, so naturally I took Carol, my political friend. Cilla Black had also been invited separately and she asked us for drinks at her flat, which is very near the Houses of Parliament. It was a great start to the evening.

Later, as we were driving through the gates of Downing Street, the randomness of my life came home to me when I answered the phone to Joey Essex, one of the stars of the TV series *The Only Way Is Essex*. How ridiculous is that! I thought.

That night, I was wearing a little purple dress that came just above the knee, because I hadn't planned ahead and had nothing else in my suitcase. Carol, meanwhile, had turned up looking like Miss Marple, because that's how she thought she should dress for the occasion. She deemed my outfit totally inappropriate! Perhaps she was right, because when we went into 11 Downing Street, George Osborne came over to speak to me. He'd apparently heard about my compulsive flashing disorder and, while we were having a photo taken with some other people, he said, 'Put your leg up!' So there I am in my short purple dress looking like an off-duty dancing girl next to George Osborne.

There were a few charity speeches and then my friend Nigel Evans got up to speak. I met Nigel, who is a deputy speaker of the House of Commons, through another friend, Kevin Horkin, who used to provide the pets for *Coronation Street*. Yet more randomness! Whenever they needed a cat or a turkey on set, Kevin sorted them out. He also wrote books about animals, including *Star Dogs*, featuring celebrities and their dogs. We became quite friendly when I was doing *Corrie* and have kept in touch ever since. Kevin is openly gay; he knows everybody and I love meeting his friends.

I'm going off on a tangent here, but a few years ago, Kevin and I had a couple of memorable nights out with his good friend Cynthia Payne. It was brilliant listening to her talk about life as the madam of a brothel. At one point, she showed me a photograph of a man covered in mud.

'That's Terry,' she said, without a hint of irony. 'He was a lovely slave. He used to clean my house from top to bottom. All he wanted was to wank over my shoes and leave my house spotless.' What an incredible woman, and so interesting!

Around two years ago, Kevin called me and said, 'Are you in London? Would you like to come to dinner with me and my friend Nigel at the Ivy?'

Well, I was in London and I was with my gay friend

Steven, who's one of my oldest and best friends. 'Yes, that would be lovely,' I said.

Kevin's friend Nigel turned out to be Nigel Evans, who as well as being one of three deputy speakers of the House of Commons is also Tory MP for the Ribble Valley, where Kevin lives. He was about to come out publicly, and he and I got on like a house on fire at dinner and went on to become friends.

Now suddenly, I was at 11 Downing Street with Carol, listening to Nigel talking about the merits of charitable giving. Towards the end of his speech, he said, 'And I would also like to thank my dear friend Denise Welch . . .'

'I can't believe it,' Carol muttered under her breath. 'I just can't believe that a deputy speaker of the House of Commons is talking about you.'

'. . . for being there for me when I was coming out as gay,' Nigel went on.

Of course, the next day at work, I was jokingly dubbed 'Denise Welch, political adviser to the deputy speaker of the House of Commons!'

Another friend, Lucien Laviscount, was also there that night. I got to know the beautiful, mixed-race Lucien when he appeared in *Waterloo Road* with me, and he's also well known for being on *Celebrity Big Brother* in the same year as Kerry Katona. As we came out of number 11 and moved to 10 Downing Street, Lucien picked me up for a photo, which I asked someone to take with my camera. My dress had ridden right up my thigh, of course. That dress was probably a mistake.

A few days later, I was showing the night's photos to Garry Bailey, the lovely man who sometimes drives me and has become a good family friend. 'Ten Downing Street?' he asked.

'Yes. I was there for a do last week,' I said.

'I heard he was over,' he said, looking at the photo of me in Lucien's arms flashing my bare thigh. 'He looks like a really nice guy.'

'Who?' I asked.

'Him,' he said, pointing at Lucien.

'But you know him. You've driven him on *Waterloo Road*.'

'Oh, I thought it was Barack Obama,' he said.

As if!

Anyway, the night didn't end there – of course it didn't! – because afterwards Carol and I were invited to the House of Commons for a drink in the terrace bar, and of course we said yes. How brilliant! When we arrived, there was a mix of Tory, Labour and Lib Dem MPs, and it was very interesting to see them in their downtime. Some, I have to say, were totally hammered. What fascinated me was that the party rivalry in the House disappears when they're drinking in the bar. They're just people on a night out.

I was pacing myself with the sherries, because I felt a little awestruck by my surroundings. Carol, on the other hand, isn't easily intimidated and she really went for it. By the time we left, she was ranting furiously about the hypocrisy of politicians and Nigel and I virtually had to carry her along the corridors of power on our way out of the building. It was hilarious. Once outside, we hung around with a posse of policemen until Carol ran off and jumped into a cab.

A police van drove past. 'Will you take me back to my hotel?' I asked the driver. Suddenly, I found myself inside the van with the entire posse of House of Commons policemen, being driven to my hotel just over Westminster Bridge. I couldn't help asking the cute ones, 'And your name is . . . ?'

It was a fantastic night and I have never in my life woken up with so many people's cards in my handbag! I had a whole range of politicians' numbers. Funnily enough, it didn't take the shine off my opinion of politicians, but I didn't feel I had to be as reverent or fearful of them as I had been before.

All in all, it was a fantastic, fascinating, unforgettable evening and one of those nights that made me realize that, for all the downsides of fame, I'm very fortunate to have such a diverse and varied life.

6

Suddenly, the Future Seemed Unsure

The summer of 2011 was an unsettled time for me and some of the people around me. The unpredictable weather seemed to mirror the volatile courses of our lives. One minute the sky was bright with sunshine, the next it was stormy and dark, and the summer's events seemed to follow a similar course. Suddenly, the future seemed unsure; nothing was fixed; everything was up in the air. I don't know if something weird was going on with the moon and stars, but it was definitely a time of uncertainty.

There were big changes announced at *Loose Women* after the arrival of a new executive producer. Understandably, she wanted to make the show her own and so she made some adjustments. Now, I'm not in a position to question those adjustments and it wouldn't be my place to dispute executive decisions, because I'm sure that the management had genuine reasons for making those changes, but I couldn't help reacting on a personal level, because the overhaul affected my friends.

I'm a great believer in the saying 'If it ain't broke, don't fix it', but daytime TV is about constant renewal; they need to shake things up all the time. Sadly, Kate Thornton and Zoë Tyler were the casualties of this 'reorganization', and I really felt for them both. I realized, though, that when these things happen, it's not about whether the people in question are good at their jobs or not, it's often more about new management putting their own stamp on things.

I haven't forgotten how it felt to be sacked from *Loose Women* in 2002, back when the programme was filmed in Norwich. It wasn't the high-profile show that it is now, but I loved doing it and I thought I made a worthwhile contribution to the panel, so I was filled with self-doubt when I was suddenly replaced, without one word of explanation from the hierarchy. My agent was told, 'We're just having a little switch around this week,' and the next thing I knew there was somebody sitting in my seat when I turned on the television. I've never found out what I did wrong, but it was a cowardly way to sack somebody and I still feel resentful about it, even all these years later.

When something like that happens, you can't help but think it's your fault, not only as a performer, but also as a person. I remember feeling paranoid about my abilities as a presenter for some time afterwards, as well as thinking there must be something wrong with me personally. Because nobody tells you why they've got rid of you, your imagination runs riot and you end up thinking it's because you're rubbish. I would rather someone said to me, 'We just don't like you,' than give no explanation at all. If you're a boss, you should be big and ugly enough to say why you do things.

I felt for Kate when her contract wasn't renewed, because she'd endured a very public sacking from *The X Factor*, which had of course affected her career and her self-esteem. You could see the doubt in her face: What am I doing wrong? She hadn't assumed it was a job for life, but she had no reason to think she wasn't doing a great job. Suddenly, she was faced with headlines like SACKED AGAIN! and it made her doubt her ability as a presenter. That's terrible, because she's an incredibly good presenter. What's more, she loved *Loose Women* and it was the perfect job for her as a single parent. She could get her son, Ben, to nursery before coming to work and be home nice and early, three days one week and two days the next.

I thought Kate was a great member of the panel and I got on extremely well with her. The anchors on *Loose Women* tend to be more reluctant to talk about their personal lives than the other presenters, but eventually things happen and they start opening up. Andrea McLean took her time to become a Loose Woman, but she made the final transition long before her marriage unravelled. She started off as 'Snow White', then she became 'Snow Grey', and now she's 'Snow Barely Black'! She and I feel that latterly we've become something out of the film *Freaky Friday*, which is about people swapping bodies. She's drinking more and has a tattoo, while I've calmed down. She's now thoroughly embraced the wicked ways of *Loose Women*!

When Kate first came on the show, she was in a relationship with Darren, Ben's father, but then that relationship went downhill and they separated. She didn't slag him off at all, but she was much more open about her personal life after that. In my opinion, we'd just got to the point where Kate had become a Loose Woman when the axe fell. I thought it was a real shame and felt it was the wrong time for her to go.

It just so happens that I've known a lot of the Loose Women from before we got together on the programme, and I'd known and liked Zoë for fifteen years; she's always been a good pal. Zoë was upset about leaving the show, but less so than Kate, because she hadn't been a central figure on *Loose Women* for some time, although she was very popular and always made a fantastic contribution whenever she appeared. Zoë is a brilliant voice coach and singer, which means she has a lot to fall back on, so even though I hated losing Zoë from the programme, my real concern was for Kate.

I was told that a lot of people didn't take to Kate. Well, a lot of people don't take to me! I've seen the *Loose Women* forums. I don't look at them any more, but I'm well aware of the fact that for every person who loves me, there are just as many who want to see me dead, but that's par for the course when you're on the telly.

I've no doubt that the management had genuine reasons

for letting Kate go, but no one's told me those reasons, so I saw two friends feeling very vulnerable, particularly Kate. Kate's a survivor, though. She went on to present *An Evening With Will Young* and the *Strictly Come Dancing* tour, and I'm sure she'll be fine, because she's very good at what she does.

With the departure of Kate and Zoë came the announcement that new people had been recruited to the show. I was intrigued, of course. I have to say that I was slightly worried about the choice of Carol Vorderman, because we all know how good she is at maths, and I'm terrible at maths! I felt a bit intimidated at the thought of this really brainy person turning up. Carol and I had met each other over the years, as you do when you're both on the telly, but I'd never worked with her. She'd done a couple of shows as a panellist, but I hadn't been there, so I didn't know what to expect.

When I found out she was coming in as the anchor, I felt a little bit disgruntled because of my loyalty to Kate. I don't want a new person, I thought. But, to be perfectly honest – and I will now, at my age, always speak as I find – I get on brilliantly with Carol. She's hilarious. My standing joke with her is that she may be good at maths, but she's totally thick at everything else! Of course, it's not true at all, but it makes her laugh. Best of all, when Louis comes down to London and I take him into work, Auntie Carol does his maths homework with him!

Vorders gets a load of flak in the papers because she's a game girl, but we've been on a couple of nights out together and she's much better behaved than I am, let me tell you. I adore her, I really do. She's a very bright, warm woman, and there's nothing I don't like about her. Whatever anybody else says, I won't have a bad word said about her and she won't have a bad word said about me.

Again, as with all of us, there are people who love her and people who don't. But if Carol wants to go out in a tight dress, showing off her great butt, so what? It amuses me that the misogynistic female press, who you'd expect to support successful women, just want to slag her off, but she has more male suitors lining up at her door than any of her critics will ever have, so she has the last laugh. She has a great relationship with her children, who adore her, and she's having the time of her life. So what if people don't like what she wears? So what if she wants to wear dresses that people think are inappropriate? She doesn't care now. We've both reached that age when, if our kids aren't upset by it, then people can say what they like.

We have great fun together. We send each other little messages during the show when we have something to say about an audience member or a guest. 'How big do you think his willy is?' we ask each other, and then we draw secret diagrams of what size we think it'll be. I hope this doesn't stop any guests coming on in future! It's just a bit of fun and it doesn't happen very often – honestly.

'I really miss you when you're not on the show,' she says. 'You've made me get the iron rod out of my knickers about certain things.'

When it was first announced that Carol and Sally

Lindsay were joining the show, Carol texted me to say, 'I'm thrilled to be on board. I'd love to have lunch with you and catch up beforehand.'

So Sally, Carol and I met for lunch at Scott's in Mayfair. Carol had tweeted where we were going, so the paps were there when we arrived, but it didn't matter. We went in and had a real laugh. Sally had to leave to be with her twins and then Carol and I went outside, because it was a sunny day and I wanted a cigarette.

Suddenly, all these paps jumped out of nowhere. 'Oh my God, there's so much interest in us!' we said, amazed and rather flattered. Then Pippa Middleton walked out of the restaurant, which was slightly deflating.

'Oh!' said Carol jokily. 'Here I am, Rear of the Year, watching my runner-up getting into her car!' Because, of course, Pippa Middleton came second after Carol in Rear of the Year 2011.

We had a hoot that day and got on really well. Yes, she's a very brainy girl, but she's not remotely arrogant and she doesn't play the intellectual. She's a sexy woman who loves a gossip and girly talk. Like me, she's gone from one relationship to another all her life. And believe me, she's not without a choice of companions now that she's single!

Jane McDonald said something funny after a night out in a restaurant with Carol last year. Apparently, every straight man in the room swooned at Carol Vorderman, and every gay man swooned at Jane McDonald!

Of course, we were all thrilled when Jane came back.

She'd left the show to focus on her relationship with Ed, her true love, whom she first met when she was nineteen. It hadn't worked out all those years ago and now she wanted to give it her everything. Ed also made a sacrifice by giving up touring with the Searchers, because when one partner has an international career, it's very hard to keep things together. He made the choice to stop touring, supported by Jane, because they realized how important it was to be together.

Jane was doing a sellout concert tour as well as *Loose Women* and she reached a point when she thought, I must prioritize this relationship. Since she's primarily a singer, she decided to give up *Loose Women*. She had a great time touring, but I like to think she missed all her friends on the show as well.

When the shake-up happened in the summer of 2011, I kept saying to the new executive producer, 'Please try to get Jane to come back!' She was a miss as a pal and a miss on the panel. The producer was big enough to try and woo her back and, in 2012, Jane took time out of her concert tours to join *Loose Women* again. It was fabulous to see her back on the show. She said on her first day that she felt like she'd never been away, and we were all thankful for that. She usually sits in the 'mad auntie' seat on the end of the desk, which is where I sit when Jane and Sherrie Hewson aren't there!

We'd lost Coleen Nolan the season before, which was a shame as Coleen and I were great on-screen mates. We often had a good spar and, as with all my good friends on the show, we knew how far to push each other. Our on-set arguments never rumbled on backstage. I understand why Coleen left the show: she'd done ten years and was sick of talking about Shane Ritchie! I miss her bubbly on-screen personality and she's a real miss as a teammate, but we work in the same building and live four miles from each other, so fortunately we can see each other as much as we like.

I love being on the show with Lynda Bellingham. Lynda has a lot of strings to her bow, as well as *Loose Women*. She has her Isme campaign, she tours with the play *Calendar Girls*, and she appeared in her first pantomime, *Cinderella*, at the Birmingham Hippodrome in 2011. It was a massive success and I think she's doing it again. Panto pays a lot of money if you're playing one of the lead roles, so it's definitely worth doing if you can.

I haven't done panto for the last few years because I've always been so busy in the run-up to Christmas that I need to prioritize my family over the holidays, but as I said to Lynda, I have some fond memories of doing panto over the years. I'm glad I wasn't drinking when I appeared in *Cinderella* with the Krankies in Darlington five years ago, because now that they have openly come out as swingers in the press, I wonder what would have happened if I'd had a few sherries! Of course, the 'swingers' word wasn't really used back in the 1970s and 1980s – that sort of thing was described more euphemistically then as 'dabbling' – when

Krankies tours were 'wilder than rock tours' (or so they told a newspaper). In those days, Janette would have an affair with a circus leopard tamer, and Ian would be with the leopard tamer's assistant. 'Oh dear,' my friends say, 'which Krankie would you have woken up with?' Fandabidozi! I love the Krankies.

Honestly, my life! From the Krankies to Liza Minnelli, who came on *Loose Women* in June 2011. It's not often I'm completely star-struck, but sitting next to Liza Minnelli was really thrilling. Even though she seemed like she'd landed on a different planet and wasn't quite sure what sort of show she was on, I kept thinking, I'm sitting next to Liza Minnelli! The star of *Cabaret*! She's Judy Garland's daughter!

Massive stars like Liza Minnelli are used to being protected by the industry. When they're doing a promotional tour, they're taken from one studio to the next and aren't always au fait with the programmes they appear on. It doesn't matter much, because talk-show hosts and audiences are always so dazzled by their presence that they don't need to do a lot. I didn't care what she was like or how well she sang, it was Liza Minnelli and I was sitting next to her. It was quite something to have her on the show: I could feel star quality emanating from her.

One of the questions I asked her was, 'If they were to make a film of your life story, who would play you?'

'Well, me, of course!' she said. OK! I'm not sure that she quite understood what I was getting at!

I'd taken my phone down to the set, and as she was

leaving, I said, 'Can I have a photo with you?' It was Liza Minnelli after all. I *had* to have a picture with her. Anyway, I've decided to do that sort of thing a bit more these days, because I'm sick of people being too cool for school. After-wards, I tweeted the photo and someone commented that it was like an image of the same person in positive and negative, because of our short dark/blonde hair! I can't say I've ever been compared to Liza Minnelli before; that's definitely a first.

When I started doing *Loose Women*, we were lucky to get Bill Snodgrass, who was presenting a show on Channel 74 at three o'clock in the morning – that was the calibre of guest we attracted. Now it's a big show and people *want* to be on it. As it's become more popular, we've attracted some great guests, such as Mia Farrow. She's a huge political campaigner, and no matter how hard we tried to draw her out, she stuck to her guns and her message, so she wasn't our usual type of guest. I still found myself thinking, Oh my God, Mia Farrow! She married Frank Sinatra! She's starred in countless Woody Allen films!

Of course, we have our own stellar actresses on the *Loose Women* panel, and my great pal Sherrie Hewson did her first acting job in ages when she joined the cast of *Benidorm*. Derren Litten created the part of Joyce Temple-Savage for Sherrie and she couldn't have done it better. She was brilliant. I love Sherrie, I really do. She's very intelligent as well as barking mad. Sherrie plays on her 'dotty Auntie Sherrie' side on *Loose Women*, and the public love it when she goes off on a random tangent about stuff. It gets the laughs, but it's only one side of Sherrie. She emphasizes that side of herself for the show, but she has an incredibly intelligent, thoughtful side, too.

I saw a lot of Sherrie in the summer of 2011, when I was over in Spain with Louis visiting Tim, who was also in *Benidorm*, playing Les/Lesley the transvestite.

Loose Women sent me over to visit Sherrie with a crew and we did a sort of 'Denzi Goes to Benidorm' feature. One day, Sherrie and I did a shoot on motorized mobility scooters. When it was over, we decided we wanted to go for a spin. It was hilarious to see the astonishment on people's faces as we zoomed past. You could see them thinking, Have I really just seen Denise Welch and Sherrie Hewson go whizzing along the Benidorm seafront on mobility scooters?

Seeing Tim wasn't quite as much fun, partly because he was feeling ill and low and having a wobble over his age. At fifty-nine, the age his father had been when he'd died, Tim was facing his own mortality, mentally and physically. It was a crucial moment in his life. Until then, he had been in denial about the state of his health and the risks of smoking. He'll probably resent me for writing this, because he's still in denial!

Something was definitely wrong with him, and had been for some time, maybe even as long as a year. Some days he couldn't walk more than fifty yards without experiencing agonizing pains in his legs. He refused to do anything about it, though. I kept telling him to go to the doctor, but he brushed the problem aside as soon as he felt a bit better. 'I'm running out of sympathy here,' I kept saying. 'There's nothing I can do to help you if you won't go to the doctor.'

I smoke and I know it's not good for me – I know I can knock years off my life through smoking, and I know my mum's throat cancer and emphysema were caused by fags – but Tim was always coming up with that one example that proved smoking wasn't necessarily harmful. 'Jimmy Williams smoked and lived until he was ninety-seven,' he would say.

'Yes, but your parents didn't,' I countered. 'Your dad died when he was fifty-nine, and your mum was sixty-one. OK, I accept that your dad worked very hard and that your mum died partly of a broken heart, but they both smoked, and your dad dropped down dead of a heart attack. You can't eat cigarettes to the extent that you do and expect to be OK.'

I didn't say, 'You are the same age as your dad when he died.' I'd just say, 'You're fifty-nine, Tim. You have to go and get this checked out.'

'But, flower, I had an ECG in 1923,' he'd say.

'It doesn't matter that you've had an ECG. You can hardly walk!'

Going to the fun fair in Benidorm with Louis and Grandpa Tim was becoming very boring. 'I don't want to be married to Grandpa,' I told Tim. 'I'm not ready for Grandpa yet. I'll look after you if something happens, but please go to the doctor!'

Eventually, he was diagnosed with blocked arteries in his legs. It was nothing to do with smoking, though – of course it wasn't! – but he was still admitted to hospital for a lifesaving operation. It was a horrible time, I have to say, and I was terrified he would die although I was probably over-reacting. He had a blockage from his heart to the top of his legs which was preventing the blood flow to his legs. At first the doctors thought it was more serious than it turned out to be, and luckily all they had to do was put in two 2-inch stents in the arteries running from hip to thigh, which opened up the blockage. Blocked arteries, left untreated, can lead to gangrene or even leg amputations, so I was very glad I'd put pressure on him to get checked out. Still, he's a stubborn sod and discharged himself from hospital four days early because he couldn't bear sitting around doing nothing.

'It's not doing nothing,' I told him; 'it's called getting better!' But he wouldn't listen.

Fortunately the operation was a complete success and Tim says he feels better than he has done in years, but the whole scare made me realize just how much I loved and valued him. I knew I couldn't bear it if anything happened to him, and I vowed to be a better partner and to work harder on our marriage, although my resolve weakened in the face of day-to-day irritations and arguments.

We always seemed to argue about the same thing. It reminded me of Mum and Dad, who always used to have the same argument. Eventually, my sister, Debbie, and I named it 'Maureen Clarkson's party', because it focused on a night, 35,000 years ago, when Dad had apparently snogged Maureen Clarkson's friend at a party.

For the umpteenth time, Mum and Dad would start arguing, and Debbie and I would say, 'Oh my God, it's Maureen Clarkson's party again!' I always said I was going to write a play called *Maureen Clarkson's Party*.

During some of the rows Tim and I had, I'd tell him, 'I'm getting out of here! We're doing "Maureen Clarkson's party" again. We're talking about something that happened fifteen years ago and we're not getting over it!'

It felt like the same argument every time, with the same accusations. It wasn't always about the same thing, but it centred around Tim's persistent denials. 'But you did do that! You did say that!'

'No, I didn't!'

'Just say you did it!' I'd ask.

But he couldn't, and instead he'd say, 'Ah, but you made me do it, because—'

'All I'm asking is that you'll say you did it!' I'd interrupt. 'It doesn't matter why, just say you did it. I just want the words "Yes, I did it" to come out of your mouth.'

But he wouldn't. It was pathological. He'd say, 'I didn't, because what I did was—'

'No, you did it! I'm not asking you why.'

He will never say, 'Yes, I did it.' Never!

I found myself having more and more 'Maureen Clarkson's party' conversations with Tim. I don't want to be like this! I thought.

But I wasn't sure what to do about it. I had the constant underlying sense that I was a bit unhappy, but I wasn't *desperately* unhappy, so I decided to plod on. I now suspect that Tim and I were both unhappy for a lot longer than we realized. We were putting up with it because we thought that if either of us ended the marriage, we would upset the other person. We were both scared of confronting it because we cared for each other so much. And we were comfortable with our lifestyle; neither of us wanted to rock the boat. We were reluctant to say, 'It's the end,' because it's a very big thing to say. But in my heart, I knew that the time was coming when we would have to admit to each other that it wasn't working any more.

One day, Matthew said to me, 'Mum, I love you and Dad, but you're not making each other happy any more. Why don't you just split up? If it makes you feel any better, my friends whose parents are together are in the minority.'

'I know you're right and we should confront it,' I said.

For some time afterwards, I would tackle the subject with Tim and he'd say, 'Oh, we're fine; it was just the other night that we had an argument.' Then I'd go away again and another week would pass; I'd be back for a couple of days and away for another week. We never did address it properly, but as life raced on, I couldn't help thinking, Is this going to be it? I'm only fifty-three. I might want to find love again. Tim might want to find love again. And if I do find love, maybe I'll want to walk down the street holding hands with someone again, instead of being furtive because

I'm having an affair, worrying that the paps could jump out from behind a corner at any point, or anxious that a friend might see me and think, Poor long-suffering Tim!

But however much I felt this inside, I'd then think about our children, our home and our friends, all the years of memories and experiences we'd shared. So much was invested in our marriage. How could I tear it apart?

7

We Didn't Have to Pretend Any Longer

'I love you, but I don't fancy you any more,' Tim said to me one day. He didn't say it in a horrible way – he was just stating a fact, and it was a relief to me. At last we could both accept that the physical side of our marriage was over. It didn't mean that we were going to split up, but we didn't have to pretend any longer. I didn't have to avoid or initiate sex because I felt guilty or obliged. Perhaps we can live like this, I thought.

I also noticed that Tim had stopped asking questions like 'Where were you when I tried to ring you at three this morning?'

In the twenty-four years that we were married, I never felt the need to check up on Tim. I didn't question where he was going or who he was seeing, I never went through his pockets or the messages on his phone; it just wasn't that kind of relationship. I felt totally secure with him, so I didn't suspect that he was seeing someone else. However, to be perfectly honest, I wouldn't have been bothered if he was, because I no longer felt any sexual jealousy. I even said to my friends that I'd be kind of happy if he had a lover, because I knew that sex was as important to him as it is to me.

'So you have an open marriage?' people asked.

'No, an open marriage is where you agree to sleep with other people and you might even discuss the encounters you've had,' I said. It wasn't like that with Tim and me, not at all. We didn't discuss anything; we just didn't ask each other any questions.

'Surely you'd be upset if you found out he was sleeping with somebody else regularly?' my friends kept asking.

But I wouldn't have been – or so I thought. I was sure I'd be fine about it. Little did I know how soon my feelings would be put to the test.

One morning in the autumn, Tim forgot to take his phone out with him. Later in the day, he rang up because he needed Derren Litten's number from his contacts list. 'Will you look it up for me?' he asked.

I found his phone and scrolled through the contacts. Derren's number wasn't there, but I had it on my phone, so I read it out to him. 'I'll put it in your contacts so you have it in future,' I offered.

'Great, thanks,' he said.

After I'd typed in the number, his messages came up on the screen. The first line of a text caught my eye; it was from someone called 'Bill golf' and it said something about making daisy chains.

Well, I knew immediately that it wasn't from 'Bill golf'. It wasn't a 'Bill golf' message. I mean, even if 'Bill golf' existed, he'd never have said that! I knew that it was from a woman.

Normally, I would never think of spying on Tim, but I was intrigued. Of course I was! I scanned through the list of texts to see if there were any more messages from 'Bill golf' and it became apparent that I was right: Bill was a Jill. I then looked at Tim's 'sent texts' folder to see what he had written to her. She was also under another pseudonym: 'Jenson'. Whatever was that about? The thinking must have gone: What shall I put her under? I know, I'll stick with the sporting theme and use the first name of a famous F1 racing driver!

Reading through the texts, I realized that there was a sexual relationship between Tim and Bill golf/Jenson. I waited for the information to hit me, for a surge of jealousy to sweep over me, but there was nothing. Not a smidge. The only shock I felt was when I realized that I didn't feel in the slightest bit threatened or hurt. If anything, I found it quite amusing. I don't know what to do with this information, I thought. I really don't know what to do with it. I couldn't believe that I wasn't even a little bothered.

I phoned Garry Bailey and told him what I'd discovered. Over the years I've known him, he has become someone I trust with my confidences. Everything comes out when he's driving me on long journeys – on both sides! – and I've also become pals with his family. 'What do I do? What do I say?' I asked him. 'Something is obviously going on, but whether it's an affair or a dalliance, I really don't know.'

'You'll have to say something,' Garry said. 'You can't just leave it.'

I spent the rest of the day trying to work out what to do. My overwhelming feeling was one of relief that it wasn't just me who'd been looking for intimacy outside the marriage. Maybe things are going to have to change, I thought. We can't go on like this, can we?

Around this time, my relationship with Lincoln Townley became physical. It was a now-and-again connection; just fun, nothing else. If I was in London and wanted to see him, I'd give him a call, and he did the same. I never lay awake thinking, I want to be with him! It was just nice to see him when I did. Still, I couldn't help noticing that we always had a great laugh when we saw each other. We seemed to find the same things funny and I didn't have any inhibitions around him, which was very liberating. I really liked the fact that I didn't have to turn any tricks or show off.

I also liked his impeccable dress sense. He's incredibly fashion conscious and always immaculately turned out. As I got to know him better, I started to realize that being with Lincoln was like spending time with a gay best friend I really liked having sex with. He has exactly the same sense of humour as I do – which I don't find with most men, apart from my gay friends – and he has a gay man's attitude to clothes.

We were walking through Soho together one day and a guy selling the *Big Issue* called out, 'Ay! A Loose Woman and the best-dressed man in Soho!' That summed it up for me.

As we got to know each other, it became clear that we were very compatible. Things were great in the bedroom, and then I found I was enjoying the time we spent outside of the bedroom, too. Being with him was exciting but comfortable; I could just be myself. Gradually, I started wanting to see him more and more.

Lincoln intrigued me in so many ways. I have friends who say proudly, 'My partner has only ever slept with two women.' But that's not the type of person I'm attracted to. I prefer somebody with a past. I want to be with someone who has lived, and Lincoln definitely has a past. He's wrestled his demons and come out the other side, overcoming, amongst other things, a gambling addiction and a tendency to drink too much.

I like a little bit of danger in a partner. I don't mean danger as in I don't know what they're up to. And I don't mean danger as in they have a criminal past, or horrendous skeletons in the closet. I can't bear the way some women are turned on by gangsters and the criminal world. I hate all that. OK, Lincoln may well have done some ducking and diving in his time; he had a haulage business in the north-east at one point, I know that much. I don't want to know all the details, but I did make sure that he wasn't in any way dodgy. 'I don't suddenly want to find out you're in with the Krays or that sort of thing,' I told him. Fortunately, there has never been anything like that going on for him.

He knew I was married, but he never asked any questions about Tim or my marriage, and I never explained anything. Some people would say that's a bad thing, but I was grateful to Lincoln for giving me the choice about whether to discuss that side of my life or not. It was obviously delicate ground and he didn't feel it was his right to intrude. Fortunately, this gave me the time and space to start thinking things through without added pressure from a third party. I was beginning to realize that I did want to separate from Tim, but I sensed that it wasn't the right moment, so for the time being, Lincoln and I couldn't be seen out together and we always went out in a crowd.

Eventually, I started wanting to see him every time I went to London. I didn't think I was going to leave Tim for Lincoln, but in the days and weeks after I discovered the 'Bill golf' texts, I started to re-evaluate the situation. I was seeing someone and Tim was seeing someone; it was no longer a case of having a discreet one-night stand occasionally. Was there really any point in staying together, unless we wanted to have an open marriage or started leading separate lives while living under the same roof?

While all of this was simmering in my head, there was another huge shadow hanging over me. Our accountant had calculated the tax I was due to pay in 2012, and I was totally unprepared for the size of the sum I owed. I know I should have seen it coming by estimating what I was likely to owe and putting the money away in a separate account, like other freelancers do. I know it's pathetic that I'm so rubbish with money, and it's unfortunate that I married someone who is also rubbish with money. We're both absolutely hopeless.

When I told my manager, Neil, about the tax bill, he seemed astonished that I didn't have the savings to pay it. I tried to explain that our outgoings were quite substantial, but he simply raised an eyebrow. 'It just happened, Neil,' I said wearily. 'Everyone knows I'm no good with money.'

As is often the way with financial matters, things hadn't gone entirely as planned. Tim and I had decided to pay off a chunk of our mortgage with a sum of money that we thought was coming in, but then it didn't come in. Our house in Turkey was on the market and we thought it would sell, but it didn't. Unhelpfully, whenever our finances dwindled, we blamed each other. 'It's your fault!' we'd yell. It was so silly. Still, there seemed to be nothing for it but to borrow money against the house again.

I'm sick of this, I thought. I work very hard, I'm away from the children a lot, and now I've got this tax bill. That means more years of hard slog. I felt tired and frustrated that there seemed to be little to show for working such long hours and missing my children all the time. I do count my blessings for everything that Tim and I have achieved materially; it's just that the pot of gold I was trying to build up for a rainy day, or retirement, was constantly getting smaller, and the effect was very demotivating. How many years do I have to go on working at this pace? I wondered. I'm not sure I can do it for much longer.

Aware that Matthew would soon want to move out of home, I started to think about selling the house. We have this lovely house, but it costs a lot of money to run, I thought, looking out of my bedroom window at the swimming pool that nobody really used. We don't need all this space; we can downsize. It would be nice to help Matthew set up on his own. In the back of my mind, I was also testing the idea of splitting up with Tim. Perhaps selling the house would give us each enough money to buy a small home of our own.

I kept quiet about my 'Bill golf' discovery for a little while, partly because I didn't want to jeopardize the relationship if it was something positive for Tim, and also because I didn't know how to bring it up. I sneaked a look at his phone from time to time, trying to find out how serious it was. There was no 'I love you' in any of the messages, but it was clear that they were emotionally involved. Then he didn't come home one night, which was very unlike him. The next day, he said he'd gone back to 'Clive-from-the-pub's house', but I was sure he *hadn't* spent the night at Clive-from-the-pub's house. That's not his thing.

A few weeks after I first discovered the texts, we had a drink together at home while the kids were out. We weren't drunk, but we'd had a drink. Tim said something that annoyed me and an argument started to brew: he accused me of spoiling Louis sometimes, which was a recurring theme with us. I didn't deny it, because I do spoil him occasionally when I've been away, but Tim's comments riled me, as they always did. He was pushing the button that says, 'Mother's guilt,' and I was bound to react.

'Well, if I'm so terrible, why don't you just go and live with your girlfriend?' I said.

'What girlfriend? What do you mean?' he said.

'I know you have a girlfriend.'

'I haven't got a girlfriend – don't be ridiculous.'

'I know you have. Whether or not you call her your girlfriend, I don't know, but I know you're seeing somebody.'

'Don't be silly.'

'I've seen the texts.'

'What texts?'

'I've seen the texts.'

He repeatedly denied the existence of any texts, which made me angry.

'I've seen them,' I said. 'I've actually seen them and I can point them out on your phone.'

I went to get his phone and found a text to 'Bill golf.'

Tim laughed nervously. 'Oh, man, that's my mate Bill from Sunderland. I send him those kinds of messages as a joke, because I'm playing a tranny in *Benidorm*.'

'I'd rather you just said, "Yes, I am seeing someone,"' I told him.

'But I'm not,' he kept repeating.

Tim has always been rubbish at lying. He's a great actor, but a terrible liar. I couldn't believe he was still trying to bluff his way out of it, so I stormed off to bed, not angry about the woman, just angry about the continual denial that's annoyed me for years.

The next morning, I woke up at the crack of dawn to catch the train to London in time for *Loose Women*. I was fine, but still feeling cross. Just before the show started, Tim rang and said, 'Right, listen. I was seeing somebody briefly a few weeks ago, but it's all over now.'

'Darling, I genuinely don't mind whether it is or it isn't,' I said.

'It's completely over now.'

'Well, if it is or it isn't, never mind.'

A few days later, we went to a party. After a few drinks, Tim started talking about what had happened, about how I didn't give him anything any more and so he had to look for it outside the marriage. I'm not going to argue when we've been drinking, I thought, but inevitably I was drawn in and we had a row. Still, at least I managed to get some more information about 'Bill golf' out of him in the heat of the moment, because he always denied everything when he was sober.

'OK, tell me what's really going on,' I said to him the next day. 'Are you still seeing this person or not?'

He shrugged. 'Man, I was drunk. I probably talked a load of rubbish.'

'It doesn't matter that you were drunk. You said all these things in front of our friends, so why won't you discuss them now? You say I'm to blame for you looking outside the marriage, but that's not fair. I don't blame you for doing it, but actually, you are responsible for seeing someone else. It has nothing to do with me.'

It was completely frustrating. 'You're married to somebody who gets it,' I told him. 'You couldn't be with anybody who gets it more than I do. All I want you to say is, "Yes, I did." It doesn't matter what the reasons were. Just say, "Yes, I did."'

It was difficult for him to admit anything, though. He seemed to be in denial about so many things, from cleaning the kitchen to having an affair. It's definitely part of his make-up, and I put a lot of it down to losing his parents when he was relatively young. He loved them so much. I think there's a connection between the absence of his parents and the fact that he finds it hard to square things with his conscience. Subsequently, it may be easier for him to think that anything he's done outside our marriage is my fault, especially as my infidelities have ended up in the press, so everyone knows about them. Perhaps he even started believing that he was 'long-suffering Tim'; he's certainly allowed that image to endure.

In my first book, I alluded to the fact that there had been infidelities on Tim's side, but the press didn't follow it up. If he had written a book and said the same about me, the press would have hounded me to find out more, but it seems they prefer me to be the adulteress and Tim to be my long-suffering husband.

Tim went on to pour out his heart about our marriage to our friends several times, always after a few drinks. It was only then that he admitted that 'Bill golf' was actually called Jo and she ran a café. My friends adore Tim, so they were always very sympathetic, but I couldn't believe that he kept going on about it to them. Eventually, I got hold of Jo's number and typed it into my phone under 'Café Lady'.

Then, one night after I'd been out for a few sherries with some friends, I texted her. It was a spur-of-the-moment decision, and a slightly drunken one, I admit.

'Hi, it's Denise. I have absolutely no problem with you seeing Tim. All I want you to know is that my children are the most important thing and as long as you know that, then whatever else happens is absolutely fine.'

The next morning, I woke up to a message from Café Lady. It totally threw me because it was so friendly, suggesting we should chat over a glass of wine.

Whoa! I thought. I don't want to be your best friend. It felt like an odd response, and made me think she might be under the impression our marriage was over, which was not the case, so I didn't get back to her.

Later that day, I said to Tim, 'I texted your girlfriend.'

'I don't have a girlfriend,' he said.

'Well, I've texted her and she's texted me back,' I said. 'I don't need to be friends with her. I just wanted her to know that I know about the situation.'

Finally, he opened up. He told me that he liked this woman and that she was a very normal person. She wasn't remotely in the industry and didn't know anything about it. A widow in her late forties, she had a grown-up son who still lived with her because he loved her so much. 'She's an incredible woman,' Tim said.

'If she nurtures you and makes you feel good, then you should be with her,' I said. 'All I want is for you to be happy.' I really meant it, too. I knew that if we broke up, I would be much happier knowing that he had somebody.

'I like her, but I don't necessarily want to live with her,' he said. 'I really don't know where it's going to go. She is very independent,' he went on. 'She doesn't want me to pay for anything and she doesn't necessarily want somebody to move in with her. She's a strong woman and I have a lot of admiration for her.'

'Have you met her son?' I asked.

'Yes,' he said, which suggested to me that the relationship must be serious. But he was adamant that it wasn't. I think, like me, he was thinking of Matthew and Louis and how they would react if we broke up. We couldn't bear the thought of hurting them.

Not long after this, I saw a couple of texts from Tim that said, 'Love you.' That told me all I needed to know about his relationship with Jo.

However, a few days later, he came back from an evening out saying it was all over. I was gutted. I didn't want it to be over. 'Why is it over?' I asked.

'Because I'm married,' he said. 'She doesn't want to be involved in the break-up of a marriage.'

'But she's not,' I said. 'Ring her! Tell her it's not like that.' I felt awful that I might have contributed to the break-up of their relationship, but I also respected Jo for standing by her principles. 'If and when you're single, then come back and we will see what happens,' she told him. She seemed like a good sort.

'Are you seeing anybody?' Tim asked.

'Kind of,' I said. 'But it has nothing to with what's happening with us.'

'Do you love him?'

'No, I don't love him, but I enjoy spending time with him. I have no idea how long it will go on, though.'

Tim didn't seem bothered and we left it at that. I went on rushing down to London for work and he got on with his stuff. We were spending less time together now and it was becoming clear to me that we had grown apart. Even our social lives were diverging.

I don't think anybody specific made a difference to where we are today; it's just that, given a choice, we wanted to spend time with different people. Tim has some friends he's known for a long time in the north-east. He loves them and they adore him. He loves the outdoors in the north and goes clay pigeon shooting with them, bringing a sense of humour to their outings. It's not that I don't like these people; they're just not my friends. And my friends are not his friends. He likes them and he sees them, but he would rather spend time with his friends.

Do I want to spend a whole weekend with his friends? No. Does he want to spend a whole weekend with my friends? No.

'Let's just accept that now,' I said to him. 'When I see your friends, I'll get on great with them. And when you see my gay friends, you'll get on great with them. But we mustn't feel forced to spend time with these people any more if we'd rather see someone else.'

When Tim and I were together, we discussed the children, day-to-day domestic issues and the pressing matter of my upcoming tax bill. 'We're either going to have to sell the house or take a loan out on the house,' I kept saying. What else could we do?

'I know you're going to say no,' my manager said, 'But think about it first.' It was October and he'd called me for a meeting at his office.

'Think about what?' I said.

There was a pause. '*Celebrity Big Brother*,' he said.

I burst out laughing. 'You must be having a joke!' I said. 'Are you kidding me?'

'Let me just talk it through with you.'

'Look, whatever you say, I'm not doing *Celebrity Big Brother*. I'd actually rather kill myself than do it.'

'Two reasons,' he said. 'One, they're offering you a lot

of money.' He named a sum that would more than cover my tax bill and my heart thumped.

'And the second reason?'

'If you did well in *Celebrity Big Brother*, it might open up new opportunities for you, especially at Channel Five.'

'OK, I'll think about it,' I said.

As a viewer over the years, I hated *Big Brother*. I tried to steer clear of it, but it's hard to avoid altogether because it's on so much and your kids watch it. What I disliked was the way people would come out of the house with a 'passport to fame' and make a fortune simply because they'd sat on a sofa for twelve weeks. However, I dipped in and out of *Celebrity Big Brother*, as I usually knew someone on the show, which made it more interesting.

I vividly remember the year Brigitte Nielsen was in the house and they brought in Jackie Stallone to surprise her. It wasn't a nice surprise, because there was no love lost between them. That made my mind up about *Celebrity Big Brother* once and for all. Not in a million years would I put myself in a situation where my ex-husband, David Easter, could walk through the door! I thought. Fortunately, there are very few people I hate in this world – I don't even hate my ex-husband – but I wouldn't want him to land on my doorstep like that, especially if my family were watching. It's an appalling thought.

When the show moved to Channel Five, it mutated slightly; it seemed gentler and less vicious. I watched it the year Kerry Katona and Lucien Laviscount were in it, and it just seemed like a bunch of people having a laugh, with no big fights or nasty twists. Kerry told me it was boring, boring, boring, but everyone in the house got on and Big Brother didn't try to create any conflict.

My pal Rula Lenska had been on the show in 2006 and she said it was bearable. She was involved in a cringe-making scene with George Galloway, when they dressed up in leotards and pretended to be cats, licking cream off each other's hands, but generally it wasn't too bad, she said, just very boring.

Perhaps it would be OK, I thought.

I thought long and hard about it. I had to, because the money Channel Five were offering would have taken a long time to earn any other way. Sadly, you can work your socks off doing a brilliant drama series without earning anywhere near as much as you can make spending three weeks in the Big Brother house, but that's just the way it is.

My family were even less happy about me doing *Celebrity Big Brother* than they had been about *Dancing on Ice*. 'You won't be able to stand three weeks in there, Mum,' Matthew said worriedly.

I'd recently suffered another bout of depression when I took Louis down to London to see *The X Factor*. It had been quite a long time since the attack in May 2010 in New York, which I was thankful for, and this time it came on the Saturday and was gone by the Sunday night. I realized that it was coming and going much quicker than it used to, which made it far more manageable, although I couldn't be sure that I'd be free of it if I decided to go into the Big Brother house.

I knew it would be a challenge to be stuck in a house with a bunch of strangers, and stress can sometimes be a contributing factor to my illness, but my friends kept saying to me, 'You get on so well with people, Denise. You'll be the person to sort out arguments and smooth out any antagonism.' I never imagined I would be the creator of conflict!

Tim had never seen the show in his life, but he knew what the format was and absolutely didn't want me to do it. He thought the pressure would be horrendous and hated the idea of how vulnerable and exposed I would be. However, he also knew it made financial sense for me to do it, so he was between a rock and hard place, really. Matthew felt the same way as Tim did, but Louis wanted me to do it because he'd heard that some Playboy girls might be among the housemates and that there was a chance he could become friends with them!

'I don't know what to decide,' I told my friend Pammy. 'I feel exhausted even thinking about it.'

'Your life is so ninety miles an hour that it might be a nice rest for you,' she said.

She was only half serious, but she had a point and I began to change my mind. I started to view the show as a little sabbatical. There would be no television, no phones, and my alcohol intake would be restricted. Admittedly, being a Gemini, I'm not good at being bored, but maybe it would be a welcome break from my busy schedule.

'OK, I'll do it,' I told my manager. 'What's the worst that can happen?'

Not in a month of Sundays could I have predicted just how awful it would be. Without knowing it, I was signing up to total hell.

8

Life's Too Long to Be Miserable

'I fell for you before you fell for me,' Lincoln tells me.

I can't remember a defining moment, but for him it was when he came to the Denise Welch and Tim Healy Charity Ball in November 2011. I invited him along because I thought it would be interesting for him to see what an amazing job Julie Arnold does in organizing the ball. By then, Lincoln had told me he was thinking of leaving String-fellows and setting up his own business as a party planner.

'You'll never have seen anything like it,' I said. 'You really need to come! And bring your mum.' He's very close to his mum, and just like every mum, she still worries about him.

It was our tenth annual ball and this year's theme was Ice Fantasy. It was an indescribably incredible night, and wonderfully camp. Tim and I arrived on real reindeer, to the accompaniment of a hundred-piece choir on the stage. The *Dancing on Ice* professional skaters put on a breathtaking skating display on an ice rink that had been decorated to look like a make-believe ice world. The Overtones had just gone platinum, but they very generously came and performed as a favour to me, bless them. Then David Gest tipped up to join all the other celebrities. It was completely mad.

Hosting a ball like ours is like being the bride at a wedding, only with 800 guests! I managed to say hello to Lincoln on the night, but that's all, even though he was sitting quite near me. Of course, he was blown away. Everybody's blown away by the ball. Julie Arnold has to be the best events organizer in the country.

'What impressed me the most was you,' Lincoln said later. 'I couldn't take my eyes off you as I watched you play the host and interact with all those different people. There was a huge swell of affection for you coming from all over the room. When I saw what people mean to you and what you mean to other people, I realized how much I love you.'

The next day, as they were getting in the car to go home, he told his mum, 'I want her for myself.'

'Well, you can't have her,' his mum said. 'She's married.'

'I know, but I'm going to pursue her all the same.'

It wasn't long after the ball that I told Lincoln that Tim and I were likely to separate. Understandably, he wanted to know when it might happen, although he never pressurized me. It must have been hard for him, because I couldn't put a date on it. I hadn't even discussed it with Tim at that point.

When Lincoln told a couple of close friends that he

thought I might be free soon, they told him not to be a fool. 'People always say that. She won't leave! She's leading you a merry dance,' they said, obviously being protective. No doubt they had Googled me and read about what happened with Steve Murray, whose name is often coupled with mine in the press, unfortunately.

Tim and I finally had the conversation at the Hemmel, our family house in the north-east, where we go for Christmas most years. Christmas is always a nightmare for me – I've never enjoyed the whole festive thing – but this year was ten times worse because I was also feeling anxious about going into the Big Brother house and I had a flu virus – and I don't mean that in a 'man flu' way. We arrived at the Hemmel the day before Christmas Eve, and that night Tim and I took a big group of family and friends to see *Legally Blonde* at the Sunderland Empire. Starring my friend and ex-Atomic Kitten Liz McClarnon as well as Matthew Kelly, it was a great show and everyone had a brilliant night.

When we got home, Tim and I went off to have a ciggy in the conservatory. We didn't actually go in there to chat, but it seemed as good a time as any to broach the subject of breaking up, especially as neither of us had been drinking. I always knew that I'd have to be the one to start the conversation and it seemed the right moment.

'I really think we should go our separate ways, don't you?' I said as he lit my cigarette for me.

'You're probably right,' he said, sitting back in his chair.

'There doesn't need to be any animosity,' I went on. 'We

don't have to sell the house yet or avoid each other. The way we live our lives means that if I'm away working, you'll be at home. And when we're both at home, we can have dinner together.'

He nodded.

'It means you can openly see your girlfriend,' I said. 'I want you to be happy with her. I don't need to know everything about her – it's up to you what you do and don't tell me – but just admit to me that it's happening.'

He breathed a visible sigh of relief. 'It'll be nice to be open about it, as I've never been able to take her out anywhere,' he said.

'I want that for you,' I said.

We went back to join my sister, Debbie, and a couple of friends, and Tim had a couple of drinks. When I say a couple of drinks, I mean a couple of drinks. He didn't get drunk, but he did get sentimental. 'Ah, I'm not sure,' he said, backtracking. 'Remember how in love we were when we bought this house?'

I steeled myself to be strong, because I can go down that route as well. There will always be happy memories and it's easy to romanticize the past.

'And the other day I walked past the shop where I bought your engagement ring,' he went on.

I felt tears pricking my eyes and tried to blink them away. 'Stop this now, because we can't go back to those days,' I said a little too harshly because I was trying my best not to break down.

I stood up and went to the window. Outside, the night was clear and black, and the sky was filled with stars. 'Look, I can't be the one who's instigating this; we both have to want it. And if our discussions are fuelled with even a couple of sherries, it's not going to work.' I paused. 'We're going to do this, Tim,' I said finally.

'Are we really?' he said, looking at me wistfully.

I turned to look at him, blinking back tears. 'Yes, we are, because it's what we both want.'

I said the words as firmly as I could, but I felt as scared as he did. After twenty-four years together, neither of us knew how it would feel to be apart. There was no going back now, though. Things were going to have to change, because we weren't in love any more. Tim wanted to go on seeing Jo, and I knew my feelings for Lincoln were intensifying. I wasn't in love with him, but I wanted to see how things would work out if we were officially girlfriend and boyfriend.

'Life's not too short,' someone said to me. 'Sometimes it's too long to be miserable.' And I thought, Yes, I might live for another thirty years, and I don't want to be miserable for all that time. I don't want Tim to be miserable, and I don't want the kids to be miserable, seeing us miserable.'

Christmas passed quickly and then the New Year was upon us. With my entry into the Big Brother house looming, I was beginning to get panicky. My flu was as bad as ever. I'd been in my dressing gown throughout Christmas, and after three changes of antibiotics I still wasn't getting better.

I was due to start my *Big Brother* adventure in two days. Oh my God, I thought. The last thing I want is to be in that house with flu.

One day, Matthew found me sitting on my bedroom floor in my dressing gown, crying my eyes out. 'I knew this was going to happen,' he said, looking at me anxiously.

'I feel so run-down,' I sobbed. 'How can I go into the Big Brother house feeling like this? It's going to be hard enough trying to be myself and stay strong, but it'll be so much harder feeling weak and vulnerable.' I was crying hysterically. 'And I really don't want to be away from you and Louis for three weeks . . .'

'Oh, Mum!' Matthew said, kneeling down to comfort me.

'I feel so ill and low,' I whispered. 'How will I cope?'

'Mum, if you want to pull out now, you can,' Matthew said.

But I knew I couldn't.

I didn't tell Matthew that there was something else weighing heavily on my mind, because Tim and I had agreed that we wouldn't say anything to the children about our decision to separate. We still weren't sure how and when we wanted to break the news. Although Lincoln knew about the decision, he felt a bit insecure about me going into the house and being away for so long, but as I told him, I wasn't going to be getting up to much while I was locked away for three weeks. And I wasn't going to change my mind about separating from Tim, either.

Luckily, I started to perk up a little bit as the day went on, and forty-eight hours later, the adventure began.

Everything is very cloak and dagger in the lead-up to the moment when you and the other housemates enter the house. It's an amazing exercise in subterfuge that's planned down to the very last detail to ensure that none of the housemates – or the public – see who their fellow house-mates are. We were code-named after various cocktails, and my alias was 'Daiquiri' because my initial is 'D'. It was a weird situation all round.

I was taken off to a hotel near Borehamwood, where I was kept apart from the other housemates. I'd heard rumours in the press about who they might be, but nobody would confirm or deny anything. I was fairly sure Kirk Norcross from *The Only Way Is Essex* would be one of them, because he'd hinted as much in a text he'd sent me. Natalie Cassidy's name had also been bandied about in the papers and I really hoped she would be a housemate. I already knew and liked Natalie, who's best known for playing Sonia Jackson in *EastEnders*. Soap opera actors and ex-soap opera actors tend to bump into each other every now and then, and she'd also appeared on *Loose Women* a few times. One week, she'd brought her little baby, Eliza, along. Such a sweet little thing! When a tiny baby reaches out its little arms to you, as Eliza did to me, it's impossible not to take to them and their mum! I looked forward to spending time with Natalie. She's very likable and very much liked, which is why her surprise departure from the house remains a shock, even now.

An American actor called Michael Madsen was another name that kept coming up. One of Quentin Tarantino's favourite actors, he'd had starring roles in *Reservoir Dogs* and *Kill Bill*, not to mention *Free Willy*. I didn't know him at all, but my sister, Debbie, thought she knew him from a film she'd worked on. 'I have a feeling he might be the guy who was meant to be in *The Tournament*,' she told me, 'but it didn't work out.'

The Tournament was a low-budget film that a couple of my friends, Scott and Nick, had made a few years earlier. It had such a great script that they persuaded Robert Carlyle to come on board, even though there was hardly any money. Meanwhile, Debbie had done beauty therapy for years and, now that her kids were older, she wanted to retrain and do hair and make-up for TV and films, so I offered her services to Scott and Nick. 'Debbie would do this film for nothing, just to have it on her CV,' I told them, and they were delighted to take her on for the final three weeks of filming in Newcastle.

'So, what else do you know about this Michael Madsen?' I asked her.

'Not much.' She made a face.

'Not a nice person, then?' I said.

'Not having met him, I only know what I've heard,' she admitted. 'Oh, and he's the brother of Virginia Madsen, who was nominated for an Oscar for *Sideways*.'

I tried to do some more digging at the hotel in Borehamwood the night I went into the house, when the make-up girls came to do my hair and make-up. 'I'm not asking you who the other housemates are,' I said, because I knew they'd all had to sign twelve-page MI6-type documents swearing them to secrecy, 'but can you just let me know if there are any other mums going in?'

I wanted to be around other mothers who would understand how hard it is to be apart from your children for three weeks, without any contact whatsoever. Although my kids and I are used to physical separation, we are constantly on the phone to each other, so I knew that not having any contact was going to be very difficult. I was dreading that part of things. I was going to miss them desperately.

Before you go in, you're asked what you would need to be informed about while you are out of contact with the world. For me, it was anything to do with my family. Anything at all. I also said, 'If my family are struggling to cope with me being in the house, I will have to leave.'

The make-up girls hinted that there might be other mums going in, but they gave the impression that, like me, they were all mothers of boys. 'Nobody has a girl?' I asked. Oh no! I thought, because I knew Natalie had a girl.

Fortunately for me, they'd got it wrong and Natalie was among the housemates. She made me laugh when she told me of the requirements she'd given the producers. Along with needing to know that her daughter and family were fine, she said that she couldn't bear it if anything were to happen to Bruce Forsyth or Ronnie Corbett, and she would like to be informed if it did.

For me, there was one other deal-breaker. 'I'm a snorer,' I said in one of the pre-production meetings, before I agreed to sign my contract. 'If I go into a situation where we're all living together and people don't like me because of something I do or say, then that's par for the course. But I don't want people hating me because I'm disrupting their sleep.'

It's no secret that I'm a terrible snorer. Tim has taped me on many occasions and the noise level is truly awful. Luckily, my friends love me enough either to deal with it or book themselves into another room if we're in a hotel. That's one great thing about snoring, as I usually get my own room if the girls are pairing up, and I love my own space.

I told the producers, 'If I'm pissing people off because sleep is important to them, I need to know that I can sleep in the lounge.' I was assured that I could, and I was also told that Big Brother reserved the right to make the house-mates nominate in front of each other, but that they probably wouldn't.

Oh God, I thought. I really hope they don't. Even before I went into the house, I sensed how divisive that would be.

I was the last housemate to go in, which meant that I was holed up in my hotel room with a chaperone for nearly forty-eight hours. Everything was taken out of my case and checked, and any vestige of branding was concealed with gaffer tape. All my cigarette packets were carefully scrutinized, which was a big job, because I had about a thousand cigarettes with me. A colleague who'd produced *Big Brother* when it was at Channel 4 had urged me not to even *think* about trying to give up smoking.

'There's nothing else to do apart from smoke,' she said.

'What's the worst thing about being in the house?' I asked her.

'It's the boredom that will get you,' she warned. 'And you have so much thinking time that you can't help but over-think everything.'

My chaperone didn't leave my side, almost to the point of coming with me to the toilet in case I wandered off or tried to smuggle in some booty. Luckily, he was a great guy called Will – you grow quite close to someone when you're with them for nearly two days! It's as if you're stranded on a desert island with them. They're there until you go to bed and there when you wake up in the morning.

I entered the house at ten o'clock on the second night, and it was like going into a party. I scoured the room and was thrilled to see Natalie Cassidy. Yay! But, apart from Natalie and Kirk Norcross, none of the faces was familiar. I don't know who anybody is! I thought with a slight sense of alarm, although I sort of knew Nicola McLean from having watched her in the eighth series of *I'm a Celebrity . . . Get Me Out of Here!*

My next thought was, Oh brilliant, there's Natalie and me, and everyone else is a bloody glamour model, with tits akimbo. OK, Natasha Giggs wasn't a model, but Nicola McLean was a successful page-3 girl, who subsequently became a WAG; there were Karissa and Kristina Shannon, the Playboy twins, who'd spent two years in the Playboy Mansion; and Greek-Irish glamour model Georgia Salpa.

Then I saw MC Romeo from the UK garage group So Solid Crew. Oh my God, he's gorgeous! I thought. Fityoungthing.com! Quite forgetting that I was on telly, I marched up to Natalie to ask who he was. Then I noticed a camera in the corner and reined myself in.

I knew who Frankie Cocozza was, even though I hadn't watched him on *The X Factor*. It was impossible to miss him at the time because he was constantly in the public eye. I assumed he was an idiot as that's how he'd been portrayed in the press – a teenage boy who went out taking coke and shagging girls the whole time. I should have known not to trust what the media says, because he turned out to be lovely.

Gareth Thomas, the retired rugby player, came straight over to me and said, 'My mum loves you,' which was very nice. He's a lovely guy. I also warmed to singer/songwriter Andrew Stone.

None of us knew that Natalie had been set a secret task the minute she arrived in the house and that she had to follow instructions through a hidden earpiece. She told Michael Madsen that she'd loved him in *Free Willy*, which of course she'd never seen in her life.

'Not many people say that,' he said, looking confused.

Natalie had to kiss Frankie on the lips twice, which was pretty unexpected. At one point, she came up to me in tears. 'I don't know if I can deal with this,' she said. I did my best to reassure her.

She was also told to come out into the garden area and confess that she'd been filmed making a graphic sex tape. I don't think we reacted as we were supposed to. 'Hmm, were you?' we said without much interest. 'Really?'

Then we all got into the hot tub with our costumes on. What a good bunch! I thought, relaxing into the water.

Nevertheless, it felt odd. I'd never been in a hidden-camera situation before, and there are hardly any *visible* cameras in the Big Brother house. There was a camera in the kitchen that would occasionally move around, but most of them were behind mirrors. While you're doing your teeth, you're thinking to yourself, I'm on *Celebrity Big Brother*! You're very aware that the show's been on for eleven years, and here you are. But – and I know everyone says this – you forget that you are on TV very quickly.

The only comparable situation I'd been in was when I filmed *Playing the Part*, a documentary at my old school in which I taught a class of children. There were sound and camera people trailing me, but I just got on with it and ignored them because I was confronted by a far more frightening prospect: teaching a classroom of pupils. There in front of me was a sea of faces all waiting for me to help them. Eek!

When I'd watched *Big Brother* in the past, I had always

looked on with fascination, thinking, How can you do that? How can you say that? Even though you might not be able to see the cameras, you know they're there! Now I know just how quickly you forget you're being filmed, especially when you're having a laugh. You are a gang of people and you just stop thinking about being filmed, even though you wear your mic pack at all times, except in the shower and hot tub.

There are no cameras in the shower or toilet, but there are microphones, which kind of freaked me out, because I'm sensitive about my toilet time. 'Can we take our mic pack off in the toilet?' I asked.

'No,' they said. 'We don't listen in to your ablutions, but if a gang of you girls goes into the toilet to look at each other's boob jobs, the mic will pick up what you're saying.' As it happened, the girls did go into the toilet to show off their boob jobs. I haven't had one, but I went for a look anyway!

'We don't listen to you going to the toilet,' they assured me. Why would they?

I was pleased to find that there were three toilets. 'Let's make the outside toilet the poo toilet,' I suggested, and everyone agreed. Interestingly, the Playboy twins always went to the toilet together, which was a bit weird. I kept my eye on the outside toilet and they didn't even go for separate poos! That's really strange.

When we got out of the hot tub on the first evening,

we went upstairs to choose our beds. The twins chose a double bed next to mine. They pooed together; they slept together; they did everything together.

Their funny habits didn't bother me, though. I was more concerned about the impact of my snoring than anything else. If it starts to annoy people, I'll go into the lounge after a few days, I thought.

As it turned out, Michael Madsen was the one whose snores lifted the roof for the first few nights. My own efforts didn't seem to bother anybody for the first week. In fact, it was hardly mentioned. 'Did I snore?' I'd ask every morning.

'You had your moments,' Natalie would say. 'I whacked you with a pillow a couple of times.'

'Yes, and we said, "Mama, Mama, Mama! Turn over!"' the twins said. 'And you turned over and stopped snoring.'

I quite enjoyed being a mother figure to the twins. I missed my children dreadfully, so it was good to have an outlet for my maternal instincts, however limited. I enjoyed talking to the girls about Hugh Hefner and the Playboy world they'd inhabited, because it was so alien to me. I was also interested to learn that, until they were in their teens, they'd been under the impression that their grandmother was their mother. It was touching to hear them talk about how much they loved their grandma.

It took us a while to tell them apart, and after that we wondered how we could ever have mixed them up, because they're actually quite different in looks and personality. I was fascinated by their incredible confidence. Their egos were massive! It was really entertaining, as they thought they were truly amazing. Wow! That's probably not coming over great, but I like them, I thought at first.

Their arrogance sometimes made me cringe, though. They often forgot they were on the television and sometimes I heard them talking and whispering in their double bed at night. They'd be saying things like 'We're going to look so hot tomorrow night. Those boys are so in love with us! It's crazy the way they look at us. Oh my God, they've never seen people like us before. They've never seen beauty like ours.' Those aren't direct quotes; it's just the sort of thing I overheard after lights out.

Contrary to expectations, I was the first in bed nearly every night, and the first up every morning. I never once had a hangover. I tend to wake early, because I'm used to rushing out to get on set first thing, or taking the early train to London. These days I never seem to have the time to sleep in. Ideally, I like to get up early, take the papers back to bed with me and drop off until three in the afternoon, but I don't get the opportunity to do that very often!

Our first full day in the house was quite fun. It hadn't yet sunk in how claustrophobic the house was. There's the lounge, the bedroom and the outside area, but that's it. If you wanted a bath, you had to have one wearing your swimming costume, because the bath was in the main domain. OK, I wasn't expecting privacy – that would be a joke – but I did expect the house to be more spacious.

Of course, this wasn't a worry on the first day, as we

all got on like a house on fire when we were set our first task. At this point, Michael was the dude. He was totally Hollywood and had the accompanying swagger, cowboy hat and Hawaiian shirts. Kirk and Frankie thought they'd landed in heaven. They knew his films inside out and hero-worshipped him. I now know that's what Michael wanted us all to do, but I got the measure of him early on and never joined in the adulation.

The previous night, I'd said to him, 'I'm from a place called Newcastle, up north. Were you in a film called *The Tournament*, which was filmed up there?'

'I don't think so; I can't recall it,' he drawled.

Wow! Perhaps he's made so many films that he can't remember, I thought. But now I wonder if he did remember; he just didn't want to admit it.

Everything was cool on the first day. I knew instantly that Natalie and I would be good friends. We got on really well from the start, despite the age difference. Although she was twenty-eight and I was fifty-three, she kept saying, 'I'm actually seventy-five!' And sometimes she did seem a bit like a seventy-five-year-old trapped in the body of a twenty-eight-year-old. She's an old soul and a very lovely person, and we had exactly the same sense of humour.

I got on well with the boys: Frankie, Kirk, Romeo and Andrew. They reminded me of my naughty boys at home. I enjoyed Frankie and Kirk's naughtiness, but I know it annoyed some of the others. It amused me when they joked, Keith Lemon-style, about 'smashing girls' back doors in' and that sort of thing. Romeo worried that young girls in the audience would hate them, but I think people realized that they don't disrespect girls; they were just trying to be funny.

I liked Gareth very much and also had a laugh with Nicola and Natasha, although they were both very different from me and I felt a bit uncomfortable if I was left in the room with just the two of them. Nicola had been quite outspoken in the press about her dislike of Natasha. Although they'd made their peace when they met in the house, there was still some bad feeling bubbling under the surface. I felt it was unfair on Natasha. I don't judge anybody because of who they've had an affair with; no one knows what goes on behind closed doors.

Our first task was to play a game that involved clipping yourself to podiums that revealed events from your past. The first podium that was unveiled read, 'I've been in a film that's been nominated for an award.' That was one for me, I assumed, and confidently attached myself to it. I knew that the *Big Brother* researchers looked exhaustively into every housemate's background, so they would know that a film I'd acted in called *A Bit of Tom Jones?* had won the Welsh Bafta. Although Michael's films are obviously more high-brow, I expected him to clip himself to this one, too, but he said he didn't know if any of his films had won an award!

Next, I was going to attach myself to the podium that said something about being in a gay magazine shoot, because I've appeared in *Attitude*. But as the game developed, you had to move around when you realized that you were in the wrong place or linked to a podium that didn't describe you. When the puzzle was finally solved, it transpired I hadn't been allotted the film-award podium or the gay-magazine podium. Horror of horrors, I was attached to 'I've done Class-A drugs' and 'I've had cosmetic surgery'.

Oh God, I thought. I mustn't react publicly to this. This information is out there, so they have a right to use it. But secretly I was dismayed.

You had to get the links right to light up the big buzzer at the end. If we lit the buzzer, we won a treat or our shopping list for the day. In a situation like that, it's completely counterproductive to lie. Firstly, you're part of a gang and you love everybody, so you don't want to be the one who ruins the final result, and secondly, you fear that if you don't do the task right, the people who already don't like you will dislike you even more, because you've lost the shopping budget.

I would have been happy with a bowl of pasta and grated cheese every night, game over. But somebody like Gareth Thomas needs his steak and veg, which is why he loved Nicola and Natalie so much, because they were the cooks. They made it quite clear at the beginning that they enjoyed cooking and loved to nurture. I think Nicola wanted to be seen as the best mother in the world, which is fine, because she's certainly a good cook and I'm sure she's a good mother.

I had recently watched *I'm a Celebrity . . . Get Me Out*

of Here! and noticed that there was quite a lot of conflict about who did the cooking, so I was happy to stay out of the kitchen. 'Please don't think we're taking over,' they kept saying.

'Take over and cook!' I said emphatically. It was absolutely fine by me. 'I'll do other things to help, but please let that be your domain, because you like doing it and I don't. The boys and girls will be much happier if you do the cooking.'

As nomination time approached on Day 4, I worried that we would be asked to publicly nominate people for eviction. I wasn't so bothered about people finding out I had nominated them *after* they left the house, but I felt it would cause tension to do it openly. The other rule that stressed me out was that we were allowed to talk about nominations, which wasn't the case in the eleven preceding years of *Big Brother*. I couldn't understand why they'd changed this rule. 'I don't want to talk about the nominations,' I said.

Other people wanted to, though. 'Isn't it better to talk it over?' they argued. 'Isn't it better to get it out in the open, rather than find out when you watch it at home afterwards?'

'No, I'll happily go home and watch it and find out,' I said. 'If we talk about it amongst ourselves, I think it will create conflict, because no matter what reason someone gives for nominating you, the bottom line is that they want you gone.'

Another rule change was that you couldn't give a flimsy

excuse for nominating someone for eviction. For instance, you weren't allowed to say, 'It's because I have less in common with you than some of the others.' But after knowing someone for just four days, what other reason could there be, unless you have a real clash of personality? We all appeared to like each other, so it was very difficult.

On Day 4, I nominated Georgia for eviction on Day 7. She was a really sweet girl and I liked her, but I didn't know her as well as I knew the others and she wasn't bringing anything to the house. She didn't say anything! I didn't want her to know I thought that, though.

The other person I nominated was Michael. 'I like Michael. I have a laugh with Michael,' I said. 'He's an odd bod, but I really like him. The thing is, I know what his wife and children are called, and how many children he has, and that he's a Hollywood actor, but he doesn't know a thing about me, because he's never asked me one question.'

Now, when you come from America to England, and you claim that you don't know anything about *Big Brother*, as he did, wouldn't the first questions you asked be, 'Why are you here? What do you do?'

And when someone asks you, 'Is your wife an actress?' wouldn't you ask in return, 'Is your husband an actor?' It's just conversation.

I said, 'Really, I like him, but he's not interested in me. I can't think of a reason to nominate anybody else, so that's why I'm choosing him.'

If Michael had known that I'd nominated him, I'm sure

he would have started hating me then. When I eventually told him I'd nominated him and explained why, everything kicked off.

Of course, after that I made it my mission to get behind the movie-star façade. I realize now that he didn't want that; he wanted to maintain his veneer. The reason he didn't like me was because he knew I'd got the measure of him on Day 1. He came in saying things like 'If I seeing any fucking bullying . . .' and yet he turned out to be the biggest bully of them all.

For our first shopping task on Day 6, we each had to take the role of a different fairy-tale character. Big Brother told Karissa to play the part of Goldilocks. It was also her job to cast the other characters. 'I've chosen Denise as Mummy Bear, because she's like our mom in the house,' she said. So I was Mummy Bear, Kristina was Belle, Gareth was Prince Charming, Andrew was the Beast, Georgia was Rapunzel, Michael was Geppetto, Natalie was Little Red Riding Hood, Natasha was Pinocchio, Georgia was Rapunzel, and Frankie, Kirk and Romeo were the three little pigs.

'And Nicola is the Big Bad Wolf,' Karissa said.

That was the first time I saw Nicola appear upset. She seemed to me to be looking at Karissa with fury in her eyes. Understandably, she was probably thinking, Why am I the Big Bad Wolf?

We were then told to get into our costumes. I was in a massive bear suit. 'You cannot take your costumes off for the next forty-eight hours, apart from sleeping hours,' Big

Brother told us. Now, I no longer have hot flushes, but I still get hot very easily, so being in a bear suit for hours on end was no joke.

The nominations were announced: Georgia and Andrew Stone. Georgia didn't seem surprised. I think she'd genuinely expected to be nominated, because she knew she wasn't saying anything. Andrew was gutted and I felt for him, even though it wasn't a huge surprise. He may be his own worst enemy, but he's a nice person and I liked him, so it was tough to see him go the next day.

Eviction night is horrible on many levels. Remember, you have no clock, no watches, no phones, no reading material, nothing. So you can only tell roughly what the time is, because you know that you're waking up at about nine in the morning and that in January it starts to get dark around four in the afternoon. We had a clock on the cooker, but they would put it forward or back during the night to confuse us, although sometimes only by half an hour.

I wasn't exactly sure when the first eviction night would be, but other people had done their homework and looked through the TV listings before they came into the house. During the day, we started hearing faint noises, which we thought might be the sound of scaffolding being moved. There was also the odd snatch of crowd noise from outside, although we couldn't be sure about that, because they mask any real noise with old crowd noise. It's a bit of a mind game, because the recording is on a loop and goes on for a long time.

They called us into the lounge area very early the next day, which was boring and incredibly hot for someone wearing a bear suit. I'd already sweated my socks off in the suit the previous day, when the garden had been out of bounds for four hours. Now I was roasting under three inches of fur again, in the blistering glare of the lounge lights, with the heating turned on full. Still, there was hilarity to be had from seeing So Solid Crew's Romeo dressed as a pig.

'I can't believe people are going to see me as a little pig tonight!' he said, looking pained, just before we went live.

'Romeo, they've been watching you play a little pig for the last two nights!' I said, laughing. 'Just because it's live now doesn't mean they haven't seen you like this before.'

I loved Romeo. We often joked that maybe nobody was watching the show. We laughed at the thought that, when we came out, there would be one solitary person with a board, yelling, 'Whoo, whoo, whoo!' We had no idea if the show was a hit. Perhaps it wasn't. Perhaps it was so boring that nobody could be bothered to switch on.

The only time we heard real crowd noise was when Brian Dowling said, 'You are now live on *Big Brother*. Do not swear . . .' My heart pounded as he listed the names of the housemates, triggering a crowd reaction of either cheers or boos. I had no idea what people outside the house were seeing in the edit, or what they were thinking as they watched. I listened with trepidation for my name.

'Kirk Norcross . . .'

'Hurrah!'

'Michael Madsen . . .'

'Boo!'

'Denise Welch . . .'

'Hurrah!'

'The twins . . .'

'Boo!'

'Gareth Thomas . . .'

'Hurrah!'

'Nicola McLean . . .'

'Boo!'

'Romeo . . .'

'Hurrah!'

'Natalie Cassidy . . .'

'Hurrah!'

God, what a relief. Even though we'd been told that there would undoubtedly be some professional hecklers in the crowd – the type who come down to *Big Brother* to vent their fury on the world – there seemed to be some logic to the general response. However, all your guesswork about what the outside noise means is just that, guesswork; you're clutching at straws, really, because those few minutes of sound are the only evidence you have to work with.

We were constantly being called into the diary room, where we were asked what we were thinking and what we thought other people were thinking. 'This is very stressful,' I'd say, 'but it's not like we're in Afghanistan or anything.'

It was very important to me that I shouldn't come over as one of those overdramatic housemates who moans and groans as if it's the end of the world being in the house.

It's not the end of the world; it's just psychologically weird. You don't realize how tough it is being trapped in a bubble until you actually try it. And I'm talking about the good days, the fun times, when things were still going OK. When things began to go wrong, it was psychological meltdown.

9

The Trouble Began on Day 8

With little or no contact with the world you're familiar with, your sense of self can very quickly be eroded. If someone is nasty to you, there's nowhere to escape to. You can't ring your sister or husband for reassurance; you can't cuddle your children; worst of all, you can't avoid the person who's been mean to you. So the nastiness stays with you. You can't get rid of it and it grows out of all proportion in your mind. You begin to wonder if it's your fault that someone has taken against you and you modify your behaviour just in case. Acutely self-conscious about every move you make, you stop acting naturally. That's when you start feeling lost.

I went into the house as I go into every situation, wanting to like everybody. So it still surprises me that I was at the centre of much of the conflict. My friends know that I will do anything to avoid an argument. My family say differently, because that's where all my conflicts happen; I argue like mad with my family, but generally I'll walk away from antagonism with everyone else.

Since I had never been the victim of bullying before, it took me some time to see it for what it was. I didn't expect people to dislike me, let alone victimize me, so the realization crept up on me very slowly. I kept thinking I was being paranoid, but I now know that I wasn't. I'm not saying I didn't become anxious and paranoid in the house, because I definitely did, but I was right to think I was being picked on.

Some people have said to me that in that first week I was completely under the radar and they thought, Oh, Den, you've got to up your game a bit! But I wasn't playing a game, so I didn't know how to up my game. As it turned out, I didn't need to. Suddenly, I was the centre of attention without even wanting to be.

The trouble began on Day 8. Until then, things were OK and everyone was more or less getting on. Even Michael and I had a laugh together sometimes: we were around the same age, so there was a shared perspective and we giggled at some of the antics of the younger housemates.

I enjoyed being the mum of the house, too. When Georgia got upset after hearing what she thought was the public's opinion of her, I loved the fact that the twins came to me and said, 'Mom, Georgia's really upset. She's in the toilet. Can you go in and talk to her?'

I quickly established myself as a mother figure to Romeo. He is a lovely guy and we really gelled. And when

Gareth was picking teams for a task one day, he said, 'I've got to have the house mum on my team!' Being the oldest woman in the house, it made sense that I was the maternal housemate, and I liked playing that role.

On Day 8, I was outside talking to Romeo about our children when I got on to the subject of when Louis was poorly, just after he was born. It's a dramatic story and I tend to relive the horror of it when I tell it, especially the part when I'm in an ambulance with Louis, willing him to stay alive until we get to the next hospital. Then Michael suddenly stood up and walked away, saying, 'I can't listen to stories about sick people.' Since Romeo was transfixed and I was only halfway through the story, I didn't think much about it.

Later that day, I was lying on my bed, whiling away the time as best I could. Michael was in the bedroom and I jokingly asked him why he kept disappearing off to the diary room. 'You were there for about an hour last time!' This was during the day, so it definitely wasn't a case of wanting to barge in there after a few sherries.

We were constantly reminded to use the diary room as a place to get away from everybody. 'Feel free to talk to us as you would to a counsellor if you are stressed,' they said. But most of us only went when we were called. Michael, however, kept going in there on a voluntary basis and staying there for ages, and I was curious to know why.

He came and joined me on my bed. I think I was putting

on make-up at the time. 'Why do you spend, like, ten hours in there?' I teased.

'Big Brother keeps calling me into the diary room,' he said.

'But really, why do you think Big Brother is so much more interesting than us?' I said.

His expression changed and suddenly he looked thunderous. 'You wanna know why? You wanna know the reason?' he snapped defensively. He went on to tell me that he was worried about someone close to him who was ill. His tone implied that I wouldn't understand, which annoyed me, because he had heard me talking about Louis's illness and was probably aware that I was coping with my mother being poorly, too, because I had talked about it to other housemates.

'Whoa, hang on a minute!' I said. 'You think that I wouldn't be concerned about that? You're talking to me as if I'm criticizing you for something. After what I've said, you don't think I would be sympathetic?'

'You have no idea,' he said dismissively.

That really riled me. 'Fuck off, Michael!' I retorted. 'I'm the person you could talk to about this.'

Unfortunately, the final edit didn't include what he had confided in me. So people watching saw Michael coming to sit on my bed and me asking, 'Why were you in the diary room so long?' and him saying, 'You have no idea,' and me getting angry and telling him to fuck off. It must have looked quite odd, although we didn't know it at the time.

The conversation upset me and stayed with me for days to come, although I didn't tell a soul about it. It concerned me that Michael hadn't said, 'I'm worried. You've had experience with something like this. How did you cope?' Instead he lashed out at me for no apparent reason. That's when I first realized that Michael could be very volatile.

About a day later, it dawned on me that the atmosphere in the house was dominated by Michael's moods. When Michael was in a good mood, we were allowed to be in a good mood. When he wanted to talk, we all talked; when he didn't want to talk, no one talked. People began pussyfooting around him and walking on eggshells, especially the boys. Who is this guy? I thought. He was very changeable.

I confronted him that night. I still maintain that the amount of alcohol Big Brother gives you doesn't allow you to get hammered, but as we all know, a couple of glasses of wine loosen you up a bit if you have something to say. And I had something to say, because when somebody doesn't like me, I need to know why. I'm not used to being disliked and it really upsets me. I'm not talking about someone who doesn't know me. I understand why people who see me falling out of a nightclub and flashing my tits might not like me. However, I don't care about those people, because I don't know them and I can reassure myself that they don't like me because they don't know me. It's different when someone I know doesn't like me. I need a reason. I have to know!

I went to find Michael. Now, Michael gave the impression that he wasn't drinking much, and he blamed everything that went wrong between us on *my* drinking. Whenever anything happened, he'd say, 'Oh, she drinks! She changes when she drinks.' It was very unfair.

On this particular night, I'd had a couple of glasses of wine – definitely no more than two, as any of my friends in the house would attest. I went into the bedroom and sat on Michael's bed. 'I was really upset the other day,' I said, 'so I want to have this out with you now, because I really like you.' And I did like him, when he wasn't being moody with me. We shared a sense of humour and I enjoyed the times we laughed together.

I haven't watched much of the footage of what went on, but I have seen this clip. I had completely forgotten that Michael was stroking my fringe and pushing my hair away as we talked. He didn't have a drink upstairs, so he was sharing mine. I suspect that he had probably downed a couple earlier on.

'I was really upset when you sat on my bed and confided in me,' I said. 'Don't get defensive,' I went on, because that was his usual response when anyone tried to break down his barriers. 'I just want to know why I'm winding you up. I don't want to wind you up. You heard me talking about what I had been through with Louis and I would have loved you to come and talk to me about your worries.'

I said that I hadn't told anybody about the discussion, even though I'd been upset by the way he had turned on me. 'The other thing is that we have been in here a week and a half now and you have never asked me a single question about myself. You show an interest in being with me and being around me, but you don't know anything about me.'

'Why are you trying to psychoanalyse me?' he asked, and then it all kicked off again, with him telling me to fuck off.

I couldn't help flaring up. 'You know what, Michael? You're a fucking twat! I don't want to know you anyway.'

It was the beginning of the end for us. We spent nearly three days not talking and I felt bad about the impact it had on the other housemates. 'I'm sorry, everybody,' I said. 'The last thing I want to be responsible for is causing conflict in the house.'

At that point, there were no other fights going on. There was the odd niggle between people, but nothing like when Michael and I were in a room, when you could really feel the tension. 'I can't bear this, because I'm never the cause of arguments,' I said. 'I'm usually the pacifier, the person people come to when there's trouble. And now suddenly I'm at the root of it.'

If Michael was outside having a cigarette with the boys, I would wait inside until he'd finished, even if I was desperate for one myself. Then when he came inside, I'd go outside. We were like a weathervane: the man goes in the woman comes out!

While he ignored me, he was overly nice to some of

the others, which may have been a calculated move to annoy me. Nicola only had to put some peanuts in a bowl on the table and Michael would say something like 'You are the best fucking woman in the world. Look at the peanuts she's given me. She is the best. She is the nurturer.' It made me want to smash the bowl over his head.

I felt very fortunate to have a friend in Natalie and, to a lesser extent, in Nicola. From the start, I was aware that Nicola was playing a game. Of course *Big Brother* is a game, and people are entitled to have a strategy because it's a game show, but I was very conscious that her game plan was to be seen as the perfect mother and cook. She wanted people to see beyond the booby, very attractive girl that she is, and I can understand why.

I also thought at the time that Nicola made it obvious that she liked Natalie more than she liked me. When Natalie, the twins and I emerged from a task involving charades, wearing very unflattering all-in-one white Lycra suits, the others applauded us because we'd done quite well.

Nicola said, 'Natalie, you was by far the best at acting! You was by far the best.' I didn't care who was the best at charades while wearing white sperm outfits, but why say that?

Natalie and I had a real rapport and I felt totally on a level with her. She was my partner in crime, my little soul-mate. I was also very grateful for her support whenever there was a drama with Michael, although I still went to Big Brother in tears sometimes, partly so that the other housemates didn't have to be involved in the drama. 'I don't know what I'm doing wrong,' I sobbed. 'It's really upsetting me.' One time, Michael went in after me and did a fifteen-minute rant about how annoying I was.

It seems pathetically trivial to the people watching, but it's your whole world when you're in there. It's not nice to live with that sort of tension, and I was always thinking about my kids, as I knew it would be unbearable for them to see this person being horrible to me for no reason and upsetting me.

There's one particular clip I've seen that really interests me. The scene took place around this time, when Michael was in the throes of hating me. He went into the bedroom with Georgia and the twins – my 'twin daughters' – and finally asked a question about me. 'Who is this woman? What does she do?' he asked them.

'She's an actress,' Georgia said.

'Yeah, I get that,' he said. 'What else?'

'She's on a lunchtime TV programme called *Loose Women*, which is a bit like *The View* in the US.'

'Like *The View*?' he asked. 'Is it as popular as *The View*?'

'Oh my God, yes,' they said. 'She's very famous in England.'

'What the hell is she doing here, then?' he said.

Surely he should have been asking himself the same question. What the hell was he doing there? He was supposed to be Quentin Tarantino's favourite actor!

Perhaps he was alarmed to find out that he'd been slagging off someone with a big fan base in the UK. I think he'd been wrongly working on the assumption that I was there because my career was on a downslide, possibly like his. He had no idea how much affection the public had for me, and neither did the twins. The Americans were generally at a disadvantage on this front, because they didn't know the rest of us from a bar of soap.

I didn't say it, but I kept thinking, I know who you are. I know why you're here. Don't tell me that you haven't seen or heard about this show. You're a big, famous Hollywood actor who's worked with everybody in the world. You don't get on a plane in Los Angeles and fly to London to be trapped with people you don't know when you haven't even seen the show! I said none of this, but he knew that I knew.

After three days of barely speaking to me, he suddenly appeared outside with a smile on his face, wearing my fake-fur coat. The girls said, 'Den, that's his way of saying sorry!'

I was pissed off that he couldn't approach me and make things up one to one, but I let it go. Oh well, we're all in this together, I thought.

So I went into the lounge and sat down next to him. He immediately put his arm round me and we went back to having a laugh together. We chatted about how we rubbed each other up the wrong way and discussed what our thought processes had been when we were avoiding each other.

'I'd sit there thinking, She's coming now; what do I do?' he recalled.

And I said it was the same for me when I saw him

approaching. I didn't want it to look like I was leaving because he was coming in, so it was hard to know what to do. Should I just sit here? I'd wonder. We had a good laugh about the psychology behind our moods.

The next morning, I got up with a palpable sense of relief that Michael and I were talking – for everybody's sake, not just mine. It's hard to deal with a falling-out in that environment. Michael and I were usually up first and I found him in the lounge area. 'Morning,' I said on my way to make a coffee.

No reply, nothing. He simply walked out of the room. His inconsistency drove me mad.

People kept telling me to relax, but it was difficult, because he could be very combative. One day in the lounge, a group of us were talking about something and he got off the couch and said, 'Well, you are the fucking hypocrite here!'

I looked around in amazement. Natalie seemed totally bemused. 'Hang on, when have I ever been a hypocrite?' I said, standing up to follow him to the bedroom. I pride myself on the fact that I'm not a bully or a hypocrite, so his accusation really stung. 'I want you to tell me when I have been a hypocrite,' I called after him. 'If I have, I will apologize for it.'

'Denise, you wind him up; just sit down,' I was urged. 'Don't wind him up!' So I sat down. Once again, this was during the day, so no alcohol was involved.

It was very confusing, especially as Michael was often

my best friend again when he stopped sulking. 'What am I doing wrong?' I kept asking Natalie and Nicola. 'I genuinely have no idea.'

They didn't seem to know, either, although I found out later that they secretly thought there was a sexual tension between us. 'I think Michael fancies Denise. Maybe Denise fancies Michael, too. You know she loves a bad boy. Perhaps that's why they've put two fifty-year-olds in here together.' It was all going on!

I can see why they might have thought that, because there seemed to be no other explanation. But I have another theory, which is that I sussed out Michael Madsen almost immediately, and he didn't like it.

He constantly blew hot and cold with me. One evening, we were in the hot tub together, chuckling about the absurdity of our situation. 'What the hell are we doing here?' we asked each other cheerfully.

'I don't want to dress up for the next task,' he confided.

'But, Michael, you've just been Geppetto for three days!' I said with a laugh. 'You've already lost any semblance of being cool. The Hollywood cachet is long gone.'

'I wouldn't want to embarrass my kids,' he said.

'Luckily, your kids aren't watching,' I said. 'But that doesn't detract from the fact that you've been walking around in a grey wig and false moustache.' We both giggled at that.

When he was in a good mood, he'd say something nice. 'You know what they said to me in the diary room today?'

'What?'

'They said, "If you were offered a romantic comedy when you came out of the Big Brother house, would you be able to do one with Denise?"'

'Oh yes?'

'And I said, "I could do anything with Denise, because I'm convinced she is a really, really good actress."'

'That was a nice thing to say,' I replied, and everything would seem fine between us. Then the next minute, I'd say, 'Do you want another glass of water?'

'Fuck off out of my fucking head, man. Fucking hell!' would be his reply.

'Just let it go. Let it go,' the others said, leaving me wondering why on earth things had kicked off again.

What I couldn't understand was that Nicola could say something like 'You're an ugly fucker who wears a stupid cowboy hat and I fucking hate you!'

And he would laugh and reply, 'Nicola, you're a gas!'

Inevitably, we were bored stiff a lot of the time. 'Let's play some games,' I suggested one day. 'How about charades?' Anything's better than nothing in my book.

'I hate charades,' Michael said, although he didn't even seem to know what it entailed.

'It's easy, for God's sake!' I explained how it worked, with all the different actions, but he didn't get it at all. I don't know if he was being deliberately obtuse because he didn't want to play, or if the concept was genuinely alien to him. Either way, it ruined the game and served up another reminder of how difficult he could be.

I'm not sure why, but around this time I began to snore more loudly and for longer during the night. Perhaps it was the stress of the situation with Michael. Either way, I started to worry about disrupting the other housemates' sleep, particularly Gareth. Sleep and food are integral to Gareth's demeanour, which is why he adored Nicola, I think, because she fed him.

I could see how the nightly disturbances were affecting Gareth's mood in the morning. Poor Gareth. Michael's snoring went on all night, and mine came and went in occasional violent blasts. I sensed that it was becoming very difficult for him, so I asked Big Brother if I could start sleeping in the lounge, as agreed. To my consternation, my request was declined. Apparently, the lounge was out of bounds during the night, because that was when they used to set things up for the following day.

'But I was told I could!' I protested. I now know that the person who assured me that I could relocate to the lounge had genuinely thought that I could. She wasn't trying to trick me into signing my contract, but I probably wouldn't have signed up if I'd known that sleeping in the lounge was not an option. I hated causing a disturbance, although Natalie kept assuring me that Michael's snoring was far worse than mine.

Although the situation with Michael was messing me up, I could just about cope with it as long as Natalie was around. 'Don't even think about walking out!' I told her when she said how much she was missing her daughter.

By now, Andrew, Natasha and Georgia had been evicted. After Georgia went, to my horror we were told to decide our next nominations right there and then and to explain them live and face to face. I hated the idea of doing it – we all did – but we had no choice.

You could have heard a pin drop as we wrote our nominations in chalk on mini blackboards then we had to stand up in turn and state our case. 'I'm nominating Michael because the constant arguing between us is causing an atmosphere in the house and I don't want to be party to that,' I said in a shaky voice. 'So if I'm not going, it has to be Michael. I rub him up the wrong way, as the actress said.' Although it was a high-pressure situation, I was careful with my choice of words and didn't lay the blame on Michael, much as I would have liked to.

'I'm also nominating the twins because they're beautiful, they're successful, they've got a fantastic career, but they're from a different world to me,' I added. I didn't have anything against them at this point, as it was quite funny watching them walk around being the hottest girls in the world, thinking that every man was in love with them and that those who weren't were idiots. It was a slightly flimsy excuse, but I managed to get away with it, despite the new nomination rules.

I was sure Michael would nominate me, but I hoped that he would be as respectful as I had been when I'd nominated him. He wasn't.

'I can't stand another minute in this house with Denise,'

he said bluntly. 'I'm not the source of the arguments; she is. I feel she's emotionally disturbed. Like she said, it's either me or her, and I feel the same way.'

'Thanks a lot, Michael,' I muttered, trying desperately not to cry.

I was stunned. I think everybody was, except the twins, perhaps. Like the bully he was, he had refused to take any responsibility for the conflict between us. What's more, I couldn't bear the thought of Matthew watching and hearing me described as 'emotionally disturbed', because I knew how much it would worry him. He had been very anxious about my depression recurring while I was in the house and Michael's words would feed his anxiety. I knew that Louis would be all right, because he wouldn't be allowed to watch most of it, but I spent the rest of the day worrying about Matthew. I felt that for Michael to say such a thing, knowing that my child would hear it, was horrendous.

'He will be so devastated, so worried for my health,' I kept saying to Natalie and Nicola. 'He'll want to speak to me. I wish there was some way I could reassure him.' Being mothers themselves, both of them were very sympathetic, or so it appeared. Although what happened next made me seriously doubt Nicola's concern for me.

Nicola had made no bones about the fact that she was going to nominate Michael. Like many of the others, she didn't have a problem with him herself, but she didn't like the problems he was causing me. However, when he nominated her on the grounds that she was missing her kids as much as he was missing his and he felt she needed to go home to them, she claimed to be nominating Michael for the same reasons.

You've just heard that man say something really horrible about your friend, I thought. If that had been me and he'd said that about one of my friends, I would have pulled him up on it when I nominated him. I would have said, 'That's a terrible thing to say about someone whose children are watching.' But instead she just told him what a lovely dad he was.

OK, I thought. I didn't say anything, because nominating is a difficult thing to do, but suddenly I wished I'd nominated Nicola instead of the twins.

Gareth was the only person who wasn't nominated. After that everyone thought he was going to win. I think even he thought he was going to win. If you said that to him now, he would respond, 'Don't be silly!' But I'm sure he half expected it at least. Anyone in his position would have thought the same. He's a very nice bloke and he was the only person who hadn't been nominated that night. When anyone was asked in the diary room who they thought was going to win, they'd say, 'Big Gareth!'

I was very fond of Gareth, but sometimes I wanted him to stand up for me against Michael, though he never did. Privately, he would sympathize with me, but he wouldn't say anything in front of Michael. My guess is that Gareth was reluctant to take sides, even though he saw the controversy and anger between us. Just like everyone else, he didn't know how we were being portrayed to the outside world. Meanwhile, Frankie didn't care. He liked me, so he stuck up for me. End of. Gareth sat on the fence because he was playing a game. Of course, *Big Brother* is a game show and you've got every right to play the game. I wasn't playing a game, though. If I had been, I wouldn't have behaved as I did in there!

The day after the live nominations, we were split into two teams for our next task. I was with Frankie, Gareth and the twins. My gang was sent off into one of the task rooms, where we found letters from home for the other team and a shredder. It was the same for the other team in another task room. Both teams had fifteen minutes to decide if they were going to let the other team have their letters or not. If we let them have theirs, we forfeited our letters, so if we decided we wanted our letters, the other team's letters would be shredded in front of their eyes.

Being the only mother in my team, I felt I should sacrifice my needs for the other team's. After all, Nicola, Natalie, Romeo and Michael were all as desperate to hear from their children as I was, and they were all in the other group. 'As long as I know that my children are physically safe, which they are, or I would have been told, I can wait another week for news from them,' I said. 'I think there are people in the other room who need their letters more than I do.'

Having said that, Gareth and Frankie were desperate to hear from their mums, and I knew that the twins would have loved to hear from their grandma. We all had a reason to have contact with home, but we made a group decision within seconds. Naturally, we expected the others to guess our train of thought and shred our letters, because there were more parents in their room, but I think we all assumed that they would wait a decent length of time before pressing the red shredder button.

We talked amongst ourselves for fifteen minutes and then our letters were shredded. Brilliant. End of story. We walked back to the house and met up with the others.

'I'm really sorry, guys,' Nicola said.

'That's OK,' we said.

'But I didn't wait!' she said, looking guilty. 'Romeo looked like I'd murdered someone.'

It turned out that Nicola had pressed the button to shred our letters after just one second. 'I'm really sorry, guys, but I want to know my kids are all right,' she'd said without consulting the rest of her team. 'Shred, shred, shred, shred, shred!' she'd yelled as she frantically pressed the red button. 'Why isn't it working? I want my letter! Big Brother, I've pressed it!'

In other words, Nicola gave no thought to the other team's needs and the needs of our families, even though I'd repeatedly told her how worried I was about Matthew after what Michael had said about me. That hurt me and it stayed with me. I couldn't believe she'd pressed the button so quickly.

'How could she do it?' I asked Romeo later.

'I didn't know what to do,' he said, looking pained. 'Me

and Natalie just looked at each other helplessly.' They were very embarrassed. Yes, it meant they received their letters, but it was a hollow victory in their eyes, I think.

To make matters worse, Nicola and her team went on to read out their letters from home in front of our team. Nicola wasn't embarrassed in the slightest and she cried as she read her letter. If it had been me, I couldn't have sat there enjoying my letter, knowing that I'd shredded hers within a second.

I couldn't help wondering why I'd been put in a group with all the non-parents. Why did they put me in this group? Why are they hurting me like this? I thought. I realized later that it had simply been a case of grouping us in alphabetical order. But of course Big Brother didn't tell us that was the case, because the show is about constant mind games. It's very clever, and I think Big Brother played it well. It was obvious that I would be thinking, Why am I the only parent not to have a letter from my children? It was so upsetting that I burst into tears and tried to run out of the room.

The next night was eviction night again. This time, there was nothing straightforward about it. There was a huge cheer for Kirk when the doors opened, and yet he was evicted. Frankie was devastated. 'How is that possible? He has thousands of followers on Twitter, he was given a massive cheer, and yet he was voted out!' he said. It didn't make sense.

Now it was a choice between Natalie and Michael. Later, Michael said that Natalie had looked at him as if to say,

'You're going, mate.' Not in a horrible way, obviously, but it seemed the logical outcome. We were all thinking the same, because Michael had been booed and Natalie was given a massive cheer.

Thank God! I thought. My experience of Natalie was that there was absolutely nothing negative about her for the public to dislike. I hadn't seen the way she was presented in the edit, but it seemed to me that there was nothing to warp. And I couldn't wait to see the back of Michael.

'Natalie!' announced Brian Dowling.

I have a line in the play *Steel Magnolias* that goes, 'I never, ever felt that words would fail me in my life, but I think this is it.' It describes exactly how I felt when Natalie's name was called.

How is this possible? I thought, with a surge of unease. What the hell is going on in the outside world? My soulmate has gone and I'm left with horrible, horrible Michael. What is the public thinking?

If you've been nominated for eviction and you're not evicted, the viewers probably assume that you think the public loves you. But that's not the case at all. Natalie's eviction was so counter-intuitive that it made me wonder what people thought of me. They must hate me, I thought. They love Michael Madsen so much that they got rid of Natalie because they want more conflict. It was unbelievably confusing, and a growing sense of anxiety and paranoia crept up on me.

None of us could think of any reason why Natalie would

be voted out. Not one reason. Some people suggested afterwards that it might have been because she and Nicola liked to look after the men. Natalie's very much of that mentality: 'You sit yourself down. I'll do it. I like to provide for my man.'

Before the eviction, I had told everyone, 'If Natalie or Nicola are voted off, I can cook. We can all cook! I'll do the scrambled eggs one day and you can do them the next day. But if you think I'm going to become the house nurturer, let me make it clear now that I'm not. We are all quite capable of making scrambled eggs on toast.'

Could the viewers have objected to Natalie's nurturing instinct? Somehow I think it's unlikely that hordes of feminists were picking up the phone to vote, but you never know. It's mostly young people who vote, so maybe they were registering their disapproval of traditional roles. I have no idea. Whatever the reason, as far as I was concerned, the soul went out of the house when Natalie left.

Natalie and I had talked about her problems with her partner, Adam. It's been well documented that he'd been violent towards her and that she'd been through some tough times. They got together again after *Celebrity Big Brother*; Natalie agreed to give him another chance because he admitted he was an alcoholic and stopped drinking. People who criticized her for taking him back missed the point, I think. She is totally against domestic violence and would never condone it, but alcohol was Adam's demon and he gave it up. I believe they got back together on the understanding that if she ever saw him with even one sherry, she and Eliza would be out of there. Personally, I think it's great that she gave the relationship another try, because she and Adam were very happy together when his drinking wasn't out of control.

None of this explains why she left the house, though, and it still remains a mystery. I was devastated, because she was my ally, and it was a huge shock. I'd thought that either Natalie or Gareth was going to win, so I'd assumed that they would be there until the end.

When it came to why Kirk had been voted out, the consensus among the younger people in the house seemed to be that it had something to do with him fancying Georgia, which had caused an argument when Big Brother put Kirk, Georgia and the twins in a boat in the bathroom. For some reason Georgia didn't speak to Kirk afterwards, which upset him. Since I hadn't been privy to what went on, I wasn't interested and didn't want to get involved. It was between Georgia, Kirk and the twins, and I think Nicola also got involved afterwards. I just stayed out of the way.

After Kirk was evicted, people started saying, 'I think it must have been the boat incident.' Frankie didn't say that, but some of the others did, and the inference was that he'd said something offensive to Georgia, which the public objected to.

The 'boat incident' became a big topic of conversation. You'd find yourself saying, 'It was all to do with the boat,' as there was nothing else to talk about. The boat was the thing.

We all asked each other, 'Did you go in the boat?'

'No, I stayed away from the boat!'

We were clutching at straws, though, because none of us really had a clue why Kirk and Natalie had been evicted. What the hell are they doing in the edits? I thought.

As an avid viewer of reality shows, and having appeared in several of them, Nicola knows her stuff when it comes to the psychology of these programmes. She told me that there's always a sadistic element to a show like *Big Brother*. It's boring to watch people sitting around a table smoking and getting on well. Viewers want to see fights and arguments.

Suddenly I remembered watching a few episodes of *Big Brother* one year with Matthew. There was a really bitchy girl in the house, one of those people who points her finger in your face when she's angry. As a viewer you hated her, but you also *loved* to hate her. It was compulsive television, because you couldn't believe anybody could be so horrible. Of course, you lost interest in the show as soon as she was voted out. You wanted her out, because she was horrible and that was her comeuppance, but you weren't interested once she was gone.

Perhaps the voters wanted Michael and me to stay in the house and quarrel. Maybe they hated us both and were enjoying the conflict. It was a terrifying thought. How on earth am I being portrayed? I wondered. From then on, I questioned every single thing I said and did.

10

Determined to Be Stranger and Wiser

My life may be many things, but it's not boring. I don't have time to be bored and I'm not good at boredom. Being a Gemini, I thrive on staying busy and having lots of different things going on, at home and at work. I'm not saying I never relax, because there's nothing better than putting your feet up in front of the telly after a long day. But given a choice, I'm happier doing too much than too little. It probably isn't a good idea to go at ninety miles an hour all the time, but I'm never going to be somebody who enjoys twiddling her thumbs.

Being in the Big Brother house was fatally boring, as there was nothing to do, meaning there was far too much time to think, just as I had been warned. I over-thought everything. When you don't have enough to occupy your time, your mind starts playing games with you. Trivial actions take on huge significance, and tiny things seem incredibly meaningful. Everything gets mixed up in your head. It's hard to distinguish between what's important and what isn't. Your behaviour is house behaviour, not normal behaviour.

Little gestures suddenly meant so much. There were huge profile photos of each of us in the bedroom and most people had somebody else's photo above their bed. Romeo had my photo above his bed and I would have been really upset if he'd taken it down. It seems ridiculous when I think about it now, even if we did get on really well – he's a twenty-four-year-old dude from So Solid Crew and I'm a fifty-three-year-old woman – but things like that seem crucially important when you are paranoid about shifts in mood and changing relationships. Everything is loaded with meaning.

Michael's profile photo was in the bathroom. When he and I were speaking, I would take it out of the bathroom and bring it into the bedroom, so that he didn't feel left out. I didn't put it above my bed – I was savvy enough to know what that would mean – but sometimes other people put it above my bed. In the same way, if I put a teddy on my bed, I might put a teddy on Michael's bed, or on Gareth's bed. After Natalie left, I started putting things of hers on my bed so that when she watched *CBB* on the TV, she could see that I was thinking of her. It sounds crazy and pathetic when I recall it now, but that's the way things were. There's nothing else to focus your mind on, so you go a bit mad.

After Natalie went, my time in the house was horrendous

and unbearable. Just after she left, I remember saying to Nicola, slightly pathetically, 'You won't go off with the twins and leave Nana out in the cold, will you?' It still amazes me that I said it, because it's so unlike me. It just goes to show that we were living in a different world, ruled by playground allegiances.

Since Nicola had spent the first week complaining about the Shannon twins' disgusting habits every time she found soggy strands of their hair extensions in the bathroom, I decided that she wasn't likely to pal up with them. Along with Natalie, Nicola was a proper cleaning fairy, so it irritated her that the twins lived like messy teenagers. Also, none of us had liked the way they isolated themselves with Georgia before Georgia was evicted. 'We're the clique of hot bitches,' the twins had said gleefully. They, in turn, were obviously not particularly fond of Nicola, as Karissa had cast her as the Big Bad Wolf. So, I reasoned, surely I didn't have to worry.

Inevitably, people talked behind each other's backs. I didn't mind at first. It was to be expected, as far as I was concerned. When you're living together 24/7, with all external stimulus removed – no television, no phones, no loved ones, no contact with the outside world and no knowledge of world events – even the people you like start irritating you. Some of us discussed this and agreed not to be upset if we got home and watched the clips back, only to find that somebody we liked had complained about us in a moment of exasperation. However, that was before the paranoia set in.

I wasn't aware how much the twins talked behind my back until I came out of the house. They took against me after I nominated them for eviction in the face-to-face nominations, even though I tried to explain that it was only because they were from another planet. I didn't do it maliciously; it was partly because I knew that it was unlikely I'd bump into them again after *Celebrity Big Brother*, whereas I'd probably come across most of the other housemates. I still liked the twins at this point – I liked everyone except Michael – and I was always asking them about life at the Playboy Mansion. It was fascinating to hear them talk about how they walked naked around Hugh Hefner's parties. I have friends who are strippers and I thought I'd heard it all, but the twins' stories were something else.

I liked them, but I began to question how nice they were on the morning of Day 11. The night before, I had been the first in bed, as usual. While Gareth, Michael and I usually went to bed quite early, the younger ones often sat up, with or without alcohol, until four in the morning, and they always made a real racket when they came to bed.

'What happened last night?' I asked the twins, because I'd heard some of them going into the hot tub.

'Oh my God, Nicola is just going to die!' Karissa said. 'Her husband is going to kill her. She was kissing Frankie in the hot tub.'

'Kissing Frankie in the hot tub?' I said, incredulous.

Knowing how much Nicola loves her husband, Tom, I found it hard to believe. 'What, tongue-kissing?' Karissa put her tongue in her cheek and nodded. 'Does Nicola remember this?' I asked, because Nicola often said she got drunk very quickly.

'No,' she said.

'What exactly happened?' I asked. She said that Nicola and Frankie were flirting and Nicola had leaned in for a kiss.

'Well, I'm going to tell her,' I said, knowing how terrified Nicola was of doing anything wrong.

Frankie was fast asleep, so I couldn't talk to him about it, and I was making coffee when Nicola came in. 'Did you have a good night?' I asked.

'Yes, although I can't really remember much about the tail end of it,' she admitted.

'Well, I'm telling you this now because you asked me to tell you if you ever did anything you shouldn't: the twins have just said that you kissed Frankie.'

She went white. 'No, no, no!' she said.

'Go and talk to the twins about it. That's what they said to me. I'm telling you now so that you can sort it out.'

She burst into tears and ran off to the diary room, where she banged on the door and demanded to go home. 'Don't go!' I said to her later. 'It'll be all right.'

When Frankie woke up, I asked him about it and he vehemently denied kissing Nicola. I've seen the clip now: Nicola swooped in jokily, but their lips didn't even touch.

They were flirting a little bit and he was saying, 'Would I be too young for you if you were single?' That sort of thing.

So why did the twins insist that they had kissed? Why didn't Karissa say, 'I couldn't really see, but it looked like they were kissing'? A few days later, I went in the jacuzzi with Frankie and Kirk, and it occurred to me the next day that maybe the twins would spread rumours about what I'd been up to with the boys! But that would have been too ridiculous for words.

When I watched some of the show back, I wasn't surprised at what Michael said about me to the others, but I was astonished at some of the things the twins said. They obviously saw me as a threat and plotted to get me out. One night when Gareth was asleep, they came into the bedroom talking loudly and noisily began to rummage through a suitcase. Their lack of consideration surprised me. When you go in a bedroom where people are asleep, you whisper, don't you?

'Girls, indoor voices,' I said softly, like I say to Louis when he's being too loud. It was one o'clock in the morning, after all.

'Indoor voices?' they said, utterly outraged. 'You keep us awake half the night snoring and you're telling us to use indoor voices?'

Frankie piped up, 'Excuse me, Denise can't help snoring; she's just asking you to keep your voices down.'

They went back into the lounge then and blew this very minor episode right out of proportion. Suddenly, it was a major incident; they told the others that I'd had a real go at them and yelled at them to shut up. Since this clearly hadn't happened, and the viewers would have known this, I can only assume that they thought the editing would favour them. Otherwise, why would they make up something so silly and leave themselves so exposed?

In a normal world, I couldn't have cared less if the Shannon twins talked behind my back, but what with Michael's nasty, inconsistent treatment of me, Natalie's shock departure and my worries about how the edits were portraying me, I definitely wasn't inhabiting a normal world. OK, the boys were sweet and lovely, and I still had Nicola to talk to, but her role in the shredding task was still playing on my mind as it really made me question her friendship.

It's difficult to cope when somebody says or does something hurtful and you already feel vulnerable. You can't walk away and see your real friends, so even the most ridiculous scenarios end up wounding you, as I discovered two days after Natalie left.

It all began when Big Brother came on the loudspeaker and said, 'Would the housemate who thinks that they are the honey of the house come to the diary room?'

If Natalie had still been there, I would have said, 'Obviously, I'm the honey of the house, because everyone fancies me!' People would have laughed and in I would have run. But in the post-Natalie house, I didn't dare do that, so I didn't say a thing.

'I'm the honey!' Frankie declared.

'Go on, go in there,' we said.

As a result, Frankie was selected as the spelling bee and had to correctly spell a range of words to complete the task. Depending on how well he did, he would win us alcohol for the night, a full party or nothing. Meanwhile, the rest of us had to dress up as bumblebees and run around the garden with buzzers on our bums. If Frankie spelled a word wrong, we would get an electric shock through the buzzer.

I would have loved to be the spelling bee, because the one thing I'm good at is spelling. Meanwhile, Frankie, the worst speller in the world, almost had a nervous breakdown when he discovered what he had to do. He had no idea that we were all watching him on a screen in the garden, dressed as bees. I was in fits because a few days earlier, Michael had given Big Brother a tirade about how his integrity was in tatters and he couldn't possibly dress up in a white leotard for a miming task. Now he was sitting on a flower in the garden dressed as a bumblebee.

The twins weren't happy, either. But they never were. They always protested when we were set a task. 'You're joking, Big Brother!' one of them would yell. 'I want my lawyer on the phone now!'

'Girls, girls!' I said placatingly. 'Let's just get on with the task. They've said that if we get ten points, we can have a party; if we get five, we can have alcohol. If we don't, we won't have a drink tonight. So let's just all be happy bees and be buzzed.'

As it turned out, the buzz was more of a sharp tingle than a shock. Anyone who has ever tried Slendertone or something similar would know just what it feels like – not pleasant, but not unbearable. At first, you yelled, 'Ah! Bloody hell!' But I've used Slendertone in the past and I know that you get used to it. After a while, it started hurting my throat to scream every time I was buzzed, so I stopped reacting.

The twins, however, were really creating, screaming as if they'd been stabbed, but I didn't bother. Frankie would get something wrong and we'd be buzzed. End of. When we finished, we were told we had five points, so at least we had alcohol coming later. Having some wine to look forward to is a major thing when you're in the house.

We went into the bedroom to take off our outfits. 'You wasn't getting buzzed, was you?' Nicola said to me.

'Yes, I was,' I said, perplexed by the question.

'No, you wasn't!' she insisted.

'I was being buzzed, Nicola. Why would I say I was being buzzed if I wasn't being buzzed?'

She smirked. 'Oh, Denise, I thought better of you,' she said. 'I thought better of you!' She turned to Karissa and Kristina. 'Twins, what do we say? We say she's a little bit of a liar!'

A liar? Oh my God, I thought. I need to get out of here. I said, 'I'm not lying, Nicola.' And I became a little tearful as I thought, Why is she saying this?

Frankie later told me that she then went into the lounge and said that I'd been telling 'porkies'. Frankie, confused, asked her what she meant, at which she admitted that since her buzzer hadn't been working and neither had Gareth's, she'd assumed mine hadn't been, either. At the time, she and Gareth hadn't said they weren't being buzzed. Meanwhile, I *was* being buzzed! Oh my God, I can't believe I'm recounting this story.

Seriously, putting the ludicrous buzzer issue aside, Nicola was calling me a liar and I was offended. The incident also made it clear to me that her allegiance had switched from me to the twins, although she would deny it, I'm sure. I didn't mind that much, except that it left me without a girlfriend in the house and I need a good girlfriend.

Is Nicola still my friend? I wondered anxiously as I watched her huddle up with the twins. I was a ten-year-old again, transported back to Appletree Gardens junior school, worrying whether Julie Jarvis was going to drop me for Audrey Wilson again this week.

By the evening, I was beginning to feel better. Although I was still upset about what Nicola had said, I was determined not to say anything, for the sake of the house. The boys all went to bed early, so for once we were all girls together: Nicola, the twins and me, all of us in our pyjamas. While I was in the garden having a cigarette, I heard the others yelling that some booze had appeared. Since we were always begging for more alcohol, which they didn't give us, it was a real turn-up for the books. We used to beg for music, too, but we only had music when we won a party.

Everyone brightened up after a couple of glasses of wine. Although we weren't drunk, the atmosphere was much merrier. While I was out in the garden having another cigarette, because there was nothing else to do in the house but smoke, 'Girls Just Wanna Have Fun' by Cyndi Lauper came blasting through the loudspeakers. The others started bouncing on the settee and shouting for me, so I ran in and jumped around with them. When I lifted my top up, they all thought it was hilarious. There I was, getting out my shit bra again. (Hasn't it occurred to anyone yet that I'd be perfect for an older woman's bra campaign, so I could show off some nice bras for a change? Honestly, I couldn't have tried harder!) Kristina flashed her bra, too.

Then I did something that would have been hysterical had I done it to any of my pals: I jokingly pulled down Karissa's pyjama bottoms. It was a stupid thing to do, but that's my sense of humour and any of my friends would have laughed about it. It's not like I revealed her bottom or anything: she was wearing knickers.

Karissa screamed and sat down. 'I don't know if I'm OK with that,' she said, looking to Kristina for her reaction. 'I don't think it's OK that she did that.'

'Oh, come on,' I said.

Both twins were laughing, then snap! They thought about the legal possibilities and the atmosphere changed.

'I'm not all right with this!' Karissa said. 'Apologize!'

'I'm sorry,' I said, wondering what all the fuss was about. What was the big deal? Hadn't she told me that she'd attended Playboy parties naked? Surely a quick flash of her knickers wasn't a problem.

But it was a problem, and everything kicked off from there. By now, the boys had wandered in from the bedroom. 'Denise just pulled my pants down,' Karissa told Romeo. 'No, don't fucking laugh, Romeo. It's not funny.'

'Karissa, I've said sorry. I'm not going to do it again,' I said, starting to get upset.

Karissa accused me of trying to pull her bottoms down twice, when I hadn't. As I explained, it was a joke; I didn't mean to upset her. And having upset her, I definitely wouldn't have done it again.

Things went from bad to worse when Kristina said, in all seriousness, 'Everybody in this house knows that Karissa is a little bit reserved.'

This statement really confused me as it certainly wasn't my impression that Karissa was reserved, especially after everything she'd told me about her life in America. In the heat of the moment, I objected and said something about her taking her clothes off for a living, which suggested to me that she wasn't all that reserved, at which Kristina freaked out. Frankie told her to calm down, which infuriated her further, and she shouted that he was acting like a typical eighteen-year-old boy. Then Nicola stepped into the fray and tried to take Karissa into the garden.

'Please step aside, Nicola,' I said. 'This is between Karissa and me.' But Nicola wouldn't get out of my face, and it made me see red.

The pressure of being in the house, Michael's nastiness, Natalie's absence, my fears about what the public thought of me, the shredding of the letters, the accusations of lying and the way Nicola was suddenly the twins' best friend had been simmering in my mind all day. Suddenly, it was all too much and I blew up. I went mad.

'Nicola, I haven't said a lot of things to you that I've wanted to say over the last couple of days,' I yelled at her.

Realizing I was shouting, I took a deep breath in an attempt to calm myself down. 'I'm not going to get into that right now, though,' I added, not wanting the row to escalate.

'Are you kidding me? Go! Say it!' she said.

I tried to stay calm, but the lid blew again. Why had she pressed the buzzer in the shredding task without consulting anybody else? I asked furiously. I turned to walk out of the room, very upset by now.

Ducking the question, she said condescendingly, 'Denise, go and have another drink, babe, and enjoy yourself.'

I turned back angrily. 'And I'm not a liar. Don't call me a liar!' I shouted. 'You don't know me well enough to call me a fucking liar!' She looked bemused, so I loudly reminded her of the buzzer incident before storming off.

I ran into the bedroom, crying my eyes out. I was shaking with emotion and felt very fragile. What the hell was going on? A bit of a lark had turned into a dark, horrible row and ended in bitter arguments and shouting. Why was

I at the centre of the conflict again when I hadn't wanted to quarrel with anyone? I'd just wanted to let off steam with silly jokes and laughter, but the game had become deadly serious and now I was the target of everybody's anger. It was awful. I felt very low. Knowing how the night's events would look to my family, it distressed me to think of how upset they would be to see it.

Frankie went to follow me. 'I'm really disappointed that you'd go in there,' Nicola said to him.

'What? And leave her by herself when she's really upset?' he said. 'If one of you had walked in there—' He stopped himself. 'No, actually, I probably wouldn't have, to be fair,' he said, making it clear what he thought of them all.

'Really?' Nicola said, sounding genuinely surprised. She subsequently stopped speaking to Frankie, who told her she had changed since Natalie had left the house.

Sometime later, Karissa went into the diary room to threaten Big Brother. 'She shouldn't have done that,' she said, referring to me. 'She knows I'm the most reserved woman in the house. I'm the classy woman in the house. I do not do that type of stuff and I'm going to sue you for it. So I want to leave now. This is a serious matter.'

It seemed a bit dramatic, but this was only the beginning of an even bigger disturbance. On a roll now, she and Kristina went on to complain about Frankie, presumably because they were angry that he had stuck up for me. 'I'm done with Frankie's sexual harassment,' Karissa said. 'He sexually harasses me every day and I want to go home.'

The next thing I knew, Frankie was standing in front of me ashen-faced, saying they'd reported him to the police.

'What?' I said, barely able to comprehend what he was saying. It didn't make sense, because earlier they'd described him as 'harmless'.

I was horrified to see the devastation in his eyes. To me, he was a young boy who wasn't in the least bit sexually predatory. Of course, he was always talking about sex, and no doubt thinking about it, but he talked about it in a Keith Lemon way, not seriously. He'd ask them to show him how to put a condom on, for instance. It was laughable stuff. In any case, he was no match for the Playboy twins.

Suddenly, it was as if he were my son, and I felt incredibly sorry for him. When the twins had finished complaining about him to Big Brother, I went in and said, 'I'm really being serious here. If the police come because of those girls and if they take Frankie, I'm going with him. Don't try and stop me if that happens.' I could not have stayed if he'd been taken away.

Thankfully, the police weren't called, but Frankie, Gareth, Romeo and I were locked in the bedroom, while the girls and Michael weren't allowed in until the situation calmed down and we were fast asleep. Michael hadn't played a role in the fight, but if the girls had stabbed me in the kitchen, he would have sided with them; there was no doubt whose side he was on.

I lay in bed crying until the early hours. Between racking

sobs, I kept whispering, 'I want my husband! I want my husband!'

I missed Tim so much right then. I missed Lincoln, too, but our relationship was very much in its infancy and our closeness hadn't yet been tested. In any case, on this particular night I wanted Tim, because he is the person I've always gone to for solace when I'm upset. I wanted to call him and say, 'They're being really horrible to me in here. Make them go away!'

I just needed him to say, 'You'll be fine.' But there was no way of contacting him.

Of course, no one in the house knew anything about Tim and me separating. In my mind, my marriage had been over for some time, but I had to keep it bottled up, because nobody knew. I had to keep so much inside. I was desperately worried about how the children would react when we told them. I hated the thought of them being upset, as I didn't know how being physically separated would pan out. Would we sell the house immediately? Where would we live? I wouldn't go and live with Lincoln, because we hadn't been together long enough for that; at this stage, I wasn't sure I would ever want to live with Lincoln.

It was scary to think that I would be on my own after twenty-four years of being married, even if I wasn't single. Anyway, who was to know whether I would be single or not when I finally emerged from this prison? Just as I didn't know how the public saw me, I didn't know what Lincoln thought about everything that had happened to me in the house. Perhaps he'd been put off by what he'd seen. I had no idea.

I knew I had to have faith that everything would be all right, but it was very difficult when I was feeling overwhelmed by anxiety and paranoia. That's why I needed Tim; I still needed to turn to him in a crisis. Although I often thought about Lincoln while I was in the house, he wouldn't have understood how I was feeling in many of the scenes he saw, whereas Tim would recognize every single emotion I was experiencing. So it was Tim I missed that night.

Finally, I fell asleep, drained and utterly exhausted. The next morning was horrendous, as the atmosphere in the house was awful. I got up red-eyed; Nicola got up red-eyed. She was doing the dishes when I went into the kitchen. I walked past without speaking and she didn't speak to me. I walked into the bedroom and the twins weren't speaking to me. Wow! This is going to be exceptional, I thought.

Big Brother called me into the diary room to talk about what had happened. I admitted that I was wrong to pull Karissa's pyjama bottoms down. It was an invasion of privacy and I had overstepped the mark. Part of the problem with being in the house is that you become close to people far quicker than you do in the outside world, because you're all each other has. So I sort of jumped five years with a friendship. As a result, I felt comfortable enough to do something I shouldn't have done to someone I didn't really know.

My friends would have screamed and said, 'Eee, you!'

But of course Karissa wasn't actually a friend. I was wrong and I apologized. I couldn't do more than that.

A little later, Romeo mediated between Nicola and me, and I made up with her for the sake of the house. 'I just want to apologize if anything I said upset you, and I'm sorry for the way I said it,' I said. 'It was wrong and I'm really sorry and I'd just like to be pals.'

It was never the same between Nicola and me after that. As for the twins, I couldn't have cared less about them any more. I was perfectly civil, so that we could all rub along, but the days dragged horribly, because I was constantly aware of people talking behind my back. I've never really had paranoia before, but this was intense. I'd be in the garden and I would dread going into the house because I was sure the group of people in the lounge were talking about me. It was awful and my anxiety levels rocketed. I'm not used to being in a situation where people clearly don't like me. Even though I make friends too easily and probably shouldn't allow certain people into my life, at least they've always appeared to like me.

Michael continued to be up and down with me. I stopped asking him questions, because he clearly wanted to be the lonesome, moody cowboy and didn't like people going deeper than the surface. I also stopped being pleased when he was nice to me. It struck me as pathetic that I had cared about how he treated me. It was annoying, though; some of my best laughs in the house had been with Michael, because we were older. But he was too changeable for me. We'd have a giggle and then, for no apparent reason, he would turn on me. It had become a pattern, but I still found it hurtful.

He was incorrigible. As the resident bad girl and boy in the house, both of us about the same age, we realized that the edits would probably portray some sexual tension between us. There wasn't any, not from my point of view anyway, but when we were having a laugh together about our spats, we were convinced that the conversation would be edited in a particular way. Of course, Michael misguidedly thought I fancied him. So, right at the end of our time in the house, I said to him, 'Michael, why don't we just have sex on the floor in front of the cameras and give them what they want?'

He claimed later that I had begged him for sex. Because of course I would beg somebody for sex knowing that my children were watching me on the television! It's so pathetic. No, we were in the front room, with other people there. And I was joking! It was a crazy thing for him to say and it made him look like a complete idiot, because everyone knew it wasn't true. If it had happened, it would have been broadcast, for God's sake! Michael definitely thought the public were keeping him in because they liked him, which was a bit deluded, I think. And the twins thought they were being booed by pantomime booers, when in fact people genuinely hated them.

During my final ten days in the house, I felt afraid to be myself. It was horrible. It wasn't just when I was around

Michael; I couldn't be myself with anyone, not even Romeo or Frankie. I felt that if I said anything funny, people would think I was trying to be funny for a reason, and I was terrified of the tasks. I was scared of doing well in the independent tasks, because I thought people didn't want me to do well as an individual, and I was scared of doing badly in the group tasks, in case I was the one who lost for everybody.

I felt my illness coming on two days after the fight with Nicola and the twins. I really thought I was going to be poorly, but thankfully it came and went very quickly. All the same, I was walking on eggshells and felt isolated and lonely, which is a very unfamiliar feeling for me. Usually, I like being alone and enjoy my own company, but I've never felt unpopular before, cut off from the love of friends and family.

I missed them all so much and thought about them constantly. After everything that had gone on, I kept thinking, My God, I'm so lucky to have so many wonderful, loving people in my life: my parents, my sons, Tim and my dear friends Pammy, Rose, Steven and the rest of the gang. These are the people I really love and trust. These are the only people I want around me. I don't care about anyone else.

My mum was constantly on my mind, too. I'd gone into the house knowing that her health was fading, but I also knew that if she'd become really ill, I'd have been told. Even so, I hated the thought that all the nastiness in the house would be upsetting her and contributing to her ill health.

Her doctors had said they would like to give her four sessions of radiotherapy, hoping to arrest her cancer and emphysema, and perhaps ease her breathing problems and soothe her awful sore throats. We weren't expecting a miracle, even though Mum had managed to pull off a fair few in the twenty years, having survived cancer once before, but I really hoped that she would be feeling better when I came out of the house. I was desperate to see her and give her a hug.

I thought about Mum and Dad's amazing circle of friends, many of whom they've known for most of their lives. The more I thought about them, the more it became clear to me what a huge gulf there is between real friends and the mates who are just acquaintances you have fun with from time to time. It made me realize that there's a lot of dead wood in my address book. As my manager said, when you come out of a nightclub and your new friends jump into your pap shot, they're not your friends. When they're tweeting everybody the next day to say, 'Have you seen me on the front of the *Daily Mirror*?' they're not your friends. I'm not saying I couldn't have a fun night out with them, but I needed to remember that they weren't genuine friends.

I don't really know these people I've been giving my number to, I mused. I don't love them or trust them. Why do I waste my time with them when I could have a far better time with my real friends?

It struck me that I sometimes try too hard to please people. I should listen to the old adage 'You can't please all of the people all of the time.' Look where it had got me in the Big Brother house! I resolved there and then to stay close to my old-school friends when I left the house. I knew I would continue to make fun acquaintances, but I wasn't going to bring random people into my inner sanctum any more. I've never doubted the friends who love me and want the best for me, but my experience in the house reaffirmed just how lucky I am to have them in my life. I couldn't wait to see them all and tell them just how much I loved them.

It turned out that there were advantages to having too much thinking time after all. Constantly turning things over in my mind made me realize with absolute clarity who and what was important in my life. I will never forget the lessons I've learned here, I vowed. Whatever the outcome of the final votes – and I certainly wasn't expecting to win – I was determined to emerge from this horrendous experience a stronger and wiser person.

11

'And the Winner Is . . . Denise'

What was the best thing about winning *Celebrity Big Brother*? Seeing the look of total and utter shock and disbelief on Michael Madsen's face.

But it was a hollow victory, because I had a horrible time in the house. Yes, I paid my tax bill, and I don't regret doing it, but there was nothing much to celebrate, because it was such an awful experience.

The final few days were hell. When Romeo was evicted on Day 21, my only remaining friends in the house were Frankie and Gareth. Looking around at the rest of the housemates, I thought, I might as well go over the wall now! Luckily, there wasn't long to go, and I felt I could just about bear another forty-eight hours – but only just.

Romeo's eviction was totally unexpected, and once again I thought, What's going on? How can Romeo be voted out when Michael and the twins are still in the house? It was a total mystery. I wasn't surprised when Nicola was evicted just before Romeo went. I was relieved, though. I couldn't wait to see the back of the people who had hurt me, and she was among them.

As she was walking up the stairs on her way out, she turned and said, 'Bye! Bye! Just to remind you guys, there's a shepherd's pie waiting to go in the oven.'

'Now, look at that,' Gareth said approvingly. 'She's going now and she's still thinking about us eating.' He was a bit naive, was Gareth.

Oh my God! I thought. She's not! She's thinking about how the public view her.

Now there were five of us in the house, if you counted the twins as one person. We were a very strange bunch. Never, under any other circumstances, would you have found us together, and somehow we had to keep going without killing each other.

The night before the finals, we were told to dress up for a dinner party. Subsequently, we were treated to a slap-up dinner that was known as 'the Last Supper', with all of our favourite foods. By now, I thought I could explode with anxiety and paranoia at any moment. I was on autopilot as I tried to make it through the final hours.

After exclaiming how delicious the starters looked, I sat down at the table and began to look through the menu to see what the main courses were. 'Tim Healy's home-cooked pie!' I read aloud. 'Oh my God, they've put my husband's pie on the menu!' I was incredibly moved. Though no one else knew it, Tim and I were separating, but it didn't mean he would stop baking pies for me.

'Do you think it really is his pie?' Frankie asked.

'Yes,' I said.

I looked at Gareth. 'I was talking to you about Tim's pies, wasn't I, Gareth?'

I was fond of Gareth and I really wanted him to like me, so I was desperate for him to like the pie. Finally, I was feeding him. I was a feeder by proxy! Equally, I wouldn't be able to bear it if he didn't like the pie, because Tim would be watching and he might be hurt. My feelings were so raw by then that even the slightest hint of rejection could pierce me to the core.

We poured out glasses of wine and clinked glasses. 'To the end of an awkward and annoying, horrible experience,' said Frankie.

'But lots of fun,' I said, like a mum at Sunday lunch trying to keep family arguments at bay. It was crazy: I couldn't have said anything I believed less.

'Average,' Frankie said.

'Average,' I agreed.

When Tim's pie arrived, there was a heart baked into the crust. I could have wept when I saw it. I knew that Tim was sending me his love and support, and it meant so much to me, especially at that moment. Fortunately, Gareth thought the pie was delicious when he tasted it.

'That's better than a letter, isn't it?' Michael said, making his first reference to the shredding incident. He'd never acknowledged how hard it had been for me to be the only parent in the house not to get a letter from her family.

'Yes, it's very sweet,' I said, trying my best to keep calm. I had no interest in talking to Michael.

The final day in the house was one of the longest days of my life. The knowledge that we would all be leaving soon created a different atmosphere: the relief was tangible. The order in which we left had become irrelevant, certainly to me. I just knew I was going and I clung to that thought like a drowning man to a matchstick. There was no task, no intervention; Big Brother hardly spoke to us. Everybody was watching the clock, because each minute that passed took us closer to the exit doors. It felt as if we were standing around waiting for a kettle to boil for twelve whole hours!

Halfway through the afternoon, a light on the pantry door went on. 'Your cases are now available. You may start packing your clothes,' said Big Brother. At that, it was as if we'd all had a simultaneous multiple orgasm. Our suitcases! We really were leaving! In an attempt to make the hours pass more quickly, we stretched out the packing by placing our belongings in our cases one item at a time.

I felt sick and nervy. We'd been cocooned for three weeks and I had managed to keep at bay most of my worries about what was going to happen when I went out into the world again. But now my mind was working overtime. Was I going to be booed? Did everybody hate me? What did Tim, Matthew and Louis think? How was my mum? Would

Lincoln still want to see me once I was out? Would I want to continue seeing him?

The minutes crawled by so slowly that it sometimes felt as if time had stopped altogether. Finally, Big Brother called us to the settees. This was always a nightmare time, because we had to sit there for ages while they sorted out the camera angles. We were bored and hot, and every time we left the settee area, they called us back. The garden was closed off, so we couldn't even go for a cigarette. Frankie had been told off for having a cigarette in the toilet some days before, so on this last night of rebellion, he thrust a cigarette lighter sneakily in my hand and winked at me. I duly went off to the toilet to have a couple of puffs, feeling like I was back at school.

The twins left the house to the sound of loud boos, and the same happened with Michael. I don't get this at all! I thought. Why were they still in the house if everybody hated them?

Three of us remained: Gareth, Frankie and me, all holding hands. To me, it didn't matter who had won, but since I was sure it was Gareth, there was no tension. Then Gareth went. It was so random! I think he was surprised – I would have been if I'd been in his shoes.

Frankie and I looked at each other in amazement. What was going on? We sat side by side, barely saying anything, because we just couldn't believe we were the last two finalists on *Celebrity Big Brother*!

Wow! I'm actually in the Big Brother house! I thought, almost for the first time since Day 1.

'I am so proud of you,' I whispered to Frankie. 'Everybody hated you when you came in here – you were the dickhead from *The X Factor* – and now you've come either first or second on *Celebrity Big Brother*. You've turned public opinion around!' I felt proud of him like a mother would and I genuinely would have loved him to win. He had grown up a bit during his time in the house and I was glad the public had realized he was a lovely boy.

'And the winner is . . .' Now came the epic pause that I had experienced every week on *Dancing on Ice* the year before. It was painful.

'Denise!'

I can't really recall what I did next and I've only seen still photographs of the moments that followed. I remember that it seemed ridiculous. I started cuddling Frankie and then Big Brother said, 'Frankie, leave the house.' He walked up the stairs and the doors shut behind him.

I was left on my own, wandering around the house, talking to Big Brother. 'What's happened?' I kept asking.

'You've won,' I was told. But it still didn't sink in.

It was a surreal few minutes. I kept looking around the house and thinking, I'm in the house and I've won *Celebrity Big Brother*! I don't know what to do!

When Brian Dowling said, 'Denise, you may leave the house,' the doors at the top of the stairs didn't open, so I wasn't sure whether to go or not. He kept saying, 'You may leave the house, Denise,' but I was rooted to the spot at the bottom of the stairs!

When the others had left, they were encouraged to go up the stairs by the people remaining in the house. 'Go on, up you go. Kiss, kiss, bye!' But I was on my own and there was no one to kiss. All the other evictions had been different, so I felt a bit stumped. 'Shall I go up the stairs?' I asked finally.

'Yes!' came the slightly exasperated reply.

Then, of course, bang! Out I went. It was time for another of life's surreal experiences. I stood outside the house, looking around manically for my family and friends, surrounded by a crowd of cheering people. People were holding up Frankie boards and Gareth boards, but I couldn't see any Denise boards. How have I won? I thought. There are no Denise boards! Who voted for me?

I looked to the side and saw three of my pals from the production team of *Loose Women*. They were shouting, 'You've won, Denzi!'

'Course I did!' I yelled back, because that's what we always say when something totally random happens.

For instance, I may say to them, 'Last night I ended up in a transsexual bar with so-and-so from such-and-such a programme. It was just a normal Tuesday.' And they'll say, 'Course it was!'

I talked to Brian for a couple of minutes and then I was taken indoors. I was still looking for Louis, Matthew and Tim, but they weren't there. Then I saw my dad, my friend Pammy and Neil, my manager. It turned out that Pammy had become a professional *Big Brother* Denise commentator while I'd been locked up.

My dad mouthed, 'I'm so proud of you.' Relief washed over me. It meant that whatever I'd done in the house was OK. As it turned out, it wasn't OK with certain people in my family, but at that point it was reassuring to know that Dad was behind me.

Dad explained that Louis hadn't been able to come, because children weren't allowed for insurance reasons, and Tim had decided to stay with him. I understood, but I was disappointed. I wanted to be with people who loved me. Matthew wasn't there because he wanted to avoid the publicity of being the son of a *Celebrity Big Brother* winner – it didn't really fit with being a cool young musician on the brink of a record deal!

'I told you! I said you'd win!' my manager kept saying.

I was whisked into a chair opposite Brian and he began to recap on the events in the house. I was nonplussed when he focused on the time I went into the jacuzzi with Frankie and Kirk. To me, it had been a fleeting moment of fun, but suddenly there were massive newspaper headlines blown up on the screen: DENISE GOES TOPLESS WITH FRANKIE and DENISE CAVORTS TOPLESS.

What? I thought. *Cavorts?* It was just a bit of larking around!

There's a pool at home in our log cabin in the garden, and many times my friends and I have whipped off our tops and jumped in, with the children present. It's the kind of thing you do after a drink on holiday. After all, topless sunbathing is legal in most countries.

I could understand there might be a furore if I had jumped in with no top on and flirted suggestively with someone. But, believe me, if I was going to flirt suggestively with someone, my top would be stapled to my tits! Under no circumstances would I get them out to flirt with anybody. I whipped my top off because I was jumping in the jacuzzi completely innocently with Kirk and Frankie, having a laugh, holding my tits up. As my sons said later, 'That's just a Tuesday night round our house.'

I was amazed when I saw comments in the papers like 'How could she do it?' and 'What a slapper!' The truth was, I could barely remember doing it, not because I was drunk but because it was so inconsequential.

'And what about Pantsgate?' Brian asked.

'What about what?'

Up came a tabloid headline on the screen: PANTSGATE!

What on earth is Pantsgate? I thought. I was totally and utterly in shock. It had always been in the back of my mind that the show might have bombed, that nobody was watching and that the press weren't interested, but now I was being told I'd been front-page news more than once for doing insignificant things that had been blown way out of proportion. I was horrified. What on earth had my family been through while I was in the house? Tits out in the jacuzzi and Pantsgate! I couldn't believe how awful it was.

It was very strange, because I'd stepped out of what had been my temporary home for three weeks and suddenly I was backstage at Elstree. I went from nothing happening to total madness. Half of So Solid Crew were lifting me onto their shoulders, and MC Harvey was yelling, 'Denise in da house! Den from da block!' Then I saw Matt Evers zoom past on a golf buggy, having just come off the set of *Dancing on Ice*. Whoa, I'm in another world! I thought. Get me back in the house! It's weird!

People kept saying, 'Hooray, you've won!' and handing me glasses of wine. So by the time I arrived at the studio for the live show *Big Brother's Bit on the Side*, I was decidedly merry, as well as being on a high, horrified by the newspapers and in shock. It was such a bizarre mix of emotions that I don't know how I managed to string a sentence together.

As I entered the studio, I could see Emma Willis in the interviewing chair and all of the other housemates on benches ahead of me. Romeo and Frankie put their thumbs up when I walked in; Nicola and Michael were talking together and pointedly didn't look up. I took all of this in as I came into the studio. Then I noticed Jamie East, one of the presenters of *Big Brother's Little Brother*, wearing a hat wih a picture of my tits on it. I knew he had been championing me to win, so I thought it was hysterical. My stomach turned slightly when I heard that John McCririck had been interviewed wearing my tits on his head, though!

There are pictures of my tits on people's hats! I thought. It was all very odd; it felt a bit like being in a modern-day *Alice in Wonderland*.

Emma started to interview me. She was being very nice

and, as far as I could tell, she seemed glad that I had won, but it was all going in one ear and out the other. I don't remember what I was asked: questions, questions, questions. Then I was aware that while I was speaking, Michael was making snoring sounds. 'That is so rude!' I said. He laughed in his horrible, nasty way and I couldn't help myself – I said, 'Oh, fuck off, Michael!' I didn't give a shit that I was on the television. I just thought, Go away, you sad, jealous, horrible little man!

When the interview finished, I was escorted from the interview area to where I was going to sit on a panel with Pete Burns and some other people. Nicola joined me on the walk over; she was all over me like a rash. 'We're all right, aren't we, Den?' she kept saying.

Just then, Michael Madsen walked past me and nipped my bum, as if to say, 'I was only joking. We were having a laugh. It's only a game show!' I was very nearly sick.

Never mind, I told myself. When I get out of here, I will never have to look at Michael Madsen's face again – in real life, anyway.

I rang Tim, Louis and Matthew to tell them I loved them. I was feeling highly emotional and becoming merrier with every glass of wine that was thrust at me. After the post-*Big Brother* chat was finished, we went to a party at the hotel in Borehamwood where the housemates had been holed up before we went into the house. That night was carnage, and I'm embarrassed to say I remember very little of it. I didn't have much sleep and woke up in the morning with several people on the bed in my room. It was like being a teenager again! I had to do some interviews that morning and my friends scurried around the room hiding bottles before the journalists arrived.

After the interviews, I had to do a shoot for *OK!* magazine at a fantastic house in Hertfordshire. I'd done shoots there before and had become quite friendly with the owner, Sina Capaldo – course I did! – but I didn't know where we were going or what the shoot would entail until I arrived there with my management team. We were horrified to discover that we were in the same house as the other finalists, including Michael bloody Madsen and the twins, who were wearing skirts halfway up their bums. Frankie was my only pal there. It was awful! Meanwhile, the twins' manager was in the kitchen saying to me, 'I've looked back at the footage and they were only having a laugh, you know.'

'Oh yes?' I said. I wasn't that bothered about the twins at the time, because I hadn't watched the footage and seen how horrible they'd been behind my back.

About half an hour later, I heard that Michael Madsen had been talking to a paper about me, apparently saying that I had begged him for sex. Incensed, I tried to find him in another part of the house, because I really wanted to wallop him, but they wouldn't let me at him.

Frankie and I did some photos lying down on a Union Jack. It was all a little surreal and we were desperately hung-over. We just wanted to leave and get away from everybody. Just then, my phone rang. 'There's a story breaking tomorrow about you having an affair with Lincoln Townley,' my manager told me.

'What?'

My first thought was, Oh no, not again! I couldn't believe it. Had I been publicly betrayed by another boyfriend? I didn't think my heart could sink any lower that day, but I could feel it dropping like a stone. My life was turning into a nightmare. Not only was I being attacked in the press for behaving inappropriately for my age, but I was doubtless about to be condemned for my private life yet again.

'Sorry, Denise, but it's in the *Sunday Mirror*,' he said.

'Who's behind the story?' I asked him, my heart thumping furiously.

'I don't know for sure, but I think I can guess,' he said. I knew then that he thought Lincoln had sold a story on me.

My friend Pammy spoke to Lincoln before I did. She rang him in a sort of 'PR Pammy' capacity. 'Do you know about this?' she asked him.

Lincoln was on a bus with his son, Lewis, and Lewis's friends when she called him. He instantly thought she was accusing him of selling the story and he was furious. Bearing in mind that I hadn't spoken to him since coming out of the house, it's not surprising he was cross that the first call he received was saying, 'Have you done a story about Denise?'

I was very much looking forward to seeing him, but we really didn't know each other that well at the time, so I couldn't help having doubts about him. I'd been betrayed before by someone I loved and trusted, so it didn't seem far-fetched that Lincoln might have sold a story. I didn't know him well enough to trust him implicitly, especially when people were saying, 'Who else would have known some of the details in the piece?' I also realized that the photo used to accompany the article had been taken by one of Lincoln's pals when we'd been on a night out.

I can't remember if I spoke to Lincoln after Pammy did, because people were constantly topping up my glass and it's all a bit hazy. Everyone wanted a piece of me; people were playing everybody off against each other; it was chaos.

Finally, I crashed out in the back of the car on the way home. While I was asleep. Lincoln phoned Pammy and said, 'Don't ever again phone me up and accuse me of something like that in front of my son.'

'I don't know if I like Lincoln,' Pammy said to me later. They're best friends now, but they got off to a bumpy start that day.

Meanwhile, people were telling Lincoln, 'Well, it's all right for Denise. You've been thrust into the spotlight with no one to support you, but she has her team to protect her.'

He was appalled by the story. As a party planner setting up in business on his own, the last thing he wanted was to find his face on the front of a newspaper in connection with an adultery scandal. Discretion is an important part of his work, because the parties he organizes are often private and the party planner's role is very much behind the scenes. I tried to explain this to my friends, but they didn't know him, so they weren't sure whether they could trust him. Since I was still suffering from anxiety and the aftermath of the paranoia I'd experienced in the Big Brother house, I didn't know who to believe, either.

Feeling terrible, I went straight to bed at home and had a lie-in the next morning. I would have stayed in bed all day, especially as it was a Sunday, but it was Tim's sixtieth birthday and I wanted to celebrate with him. At last, I got up and spent some time with the kids, which was really lovely. It was only then that I fully realized what absolute hell Matthew had been through while I was in the house. It was far worse than I had anticipated and he was traumatized by my experience. He had been on the phone to the *Big Brother* producers every day and had spoken daily to my manager. Twice he'd said that he wanted to pull me out of the house, but they had cajoled him and persuaded him against it. He really struggled for me in there. It was so hard for him.

'Look at this,' I said to Tim a little later, handing him the newspaper article about Lincoln and me.

'Flower, I don't give a fuck. It's my birthday,' he said. He glanced down at the picture of Lincoln and me. 'I thought he'd have more hair, though,' he joked.

The article didn't matter. We knew where we were with each other, even if other people didn't. Tim knew about Lincoln and it wasn't a big deal. We put the paper and the story to one side and I brushed off people's questions about it. The kids didn't see it and we all had a great time. It didn't matter that Tim and I were separating; it was an important birthday and I was full of love for Tim.

My dear friends Trisha Penrose, Julie Arnold, Gaynor Morgan and Lesley Wheetfield had all planned a day in Alderley Edge to celebrate Tim's birthday and my freedom. At lunch in one of our favourite restaurants, I learned that they had set up a Facebook page supporting me, and that Trisha had championed me and criticized Nicola in front of Nicola's husband when she appeared in a spin-off *Big Brother* programme after the shredding incident. It was bizarre: Trisha couldn't look at me without filling up. 'We'll never let you go through anything like that again!' everyone kept saying. I looked around at them and thought how lucky I was to have them in my life. After everything that had happened, I appreciated them more than I had ever done before.

I hadn't realized how many times I'd been upset in those three weeks, and how hard it was for my friends and family to see. When you're in the house, you forget that you're on television, but people reminded me of the time I was in the garden, crying my eyes out and pleading with Big Brother. 'Please get me out of here. I want to go home.' I don't remember it, but it was heartbreaking for my family.

My sister wasn't speaking to me because she believed what the press had said about me being drunk in the house, and she's always had a problem with my drinking. Fortunately, my boys made it clear that they were proud of me, although Louis had only been allowed to watch bits of the show. When I asked them if I'd embarrassed them, they said, 'Mummy, we would have been much more bothered if you'd been horrible to someone in there.' Tim was also very supportive of me, and I felt extremely grateful to have such a wonderful close family unit. I vowed that they would always be my top priority, especially the boys, whatever life threw at me. If they were OK with what I did, I didn't care about anybody else.

Meanwhile, people kept coming up to me in the restaurant as if I was the prodigal daughter, lifting me up, giving me high fives and saying, 'Well done!' It felt like I'd just come out of prison – 'the Alderley Edge One' had been released! I lost count of the number of people who said they'd been on the verge of going down south to break into the house and get me out. I couldn't believe it; it was so hard to take in.

I was knackered and didn't know what was going on with the world. Everything seemed to have gone mad. Alderley Edge hadn't seen a pap presence like it, not since the days when Victoria and David Beckham lived there. There are usually a couple of stray paps wandering around, but suddenly there was a pack of them coming at us. It wasn't great for me, because one of my teeth had fallen out the night before. Still, I happily flashed another of my fantastic bras at the photographers and walked along the street, arm in arm with Tim, trying to disguise my missing tooth by putting my hand over my mouth and smiling lopsidedly. Safe in the knowledge that all I had to do the next day was go to the dentist to have the tooth put back in, I was determined to relax and enjoy myself.

Loose Women had told me that I didn't have to go in on the Monday, so we all had a drink and celebrated. So I was pretty taken aback when I got a phone call saying I did have to work the next day, after all. But what about my tooth? I thought.

I left the house the next morning at six o'clock, as usual, but my train to London broke down and I was so badly delayed it looked like I wasn't going to make it to ITV in time for the show. To save time when I arrived in London, the *Loose Women* producers sent a motorbike taxi to pick me up at the station. I wasn't wearing make-up and hadn't bothered to bring my make-up bag, because I was only down in London on a day-return ticket and had assumed that I would get to the studio in time to have my make-up done. I comforted myself with the thought that at least I wouldn't be recognized as I zoomed through the city streets on the back of a bike wearing a helmet. The toothless wonder rides again! But no such luck: people kept waving to me as I went past. They were doing it in a nice way, but I was still mortified.

The fourth part of the show was about to start when I arrived at the ITV studios. Someone gave my lips a quick dab of lipstick as I rushed through the building and hey presto! This toothless, make-up-free woman ran onto the set. It was crazy. I hadn't seen any of the girls since I'd left the Big Brother house! We rated two million viewers, but in hindsight I'm cross that I went on *Loose Women* looking like the Wreck of the *Hesperus*. Afterwards, Neil had to field a thousand calls from people saying, 'She's obviously lost it; she's gone under. She went on television with no make-up and a missing tooth.'

It felt very weird to be on the show after spending three weeks in complete isolation.

I didn't know what they had talked about while I was away or what people had seen of *Celebrity Big Brother*. There had been no time to reflect on everything, or to prepare myself to go on television and talk about it. I wasn't ready and I shouldn't have been there.

I think it was Vorders who asked, in reference to the article in the paper about Lincoln and me, 'What has Tim thought about this?'

I wasn't expecting the question, because I thought we'd be focusing on *Celebrity Big Brother*. 'Everything's fine at home,' I said. 'We celebrated Tim's birthday yesterday, so we're all a tad worse for wear, as you can imagine. It's amazing how, when you're not around to defend yourself, people will want to make a fast buck out of you, but there's nothing that's gone on that my family aren't aware of.'

I was accused afterwards of lying and saying my marriage was fine, but that's not what I said. I said that everything was fine 'at home', and it was. We'd had a fabulous day celebrating Tim's birthday. Tim and I knew that, at some point, we might announce that we'd gone our

separate ways, but it was up to us when we told people. I
didn't have to talk about the state of my marriage if I didn't
want to, so I said that everything was fine at home and we
moved on.

All week, the papers kept up the attack, regurgitating
what had happened in the house, repeating the rumours
about Lincoln and trotting out a lot of old news. They just
couldn't get over the shock-horror image of me going in
the hot tub with a couple of teenagers without my top on:
'She's fifty-three and she's leaping topless into hot tubs with
nineteen-year-olds!'

If I had my time again, I probably wouldn't do it, just
to avoid all the media outrage. I tried to make a joke of it
by saying that it wasn't perhaps my best moment, but I
didn't want to deprive the nation of my natural assets!
However, the condemnation continued in the papers and
online. It was upsetting, as well as annoying, because nobody mentioned that it wasn't the first time I'd got my
tits out on television. Just a couple of months earlier, I'd
had a mammogram live on *Loose Women*. I volunteered to
do it because I wanted people to see that a moment's
discomfort can save your life. That's all a mammogram is,
a discomfort. It's not even painful.

I thought it was important to show what it's actually
like, so I strongly disagreed when it was suggested that
my nipples be pixelated. In fact, I refused to do it if they
were going to pixelate my nipples, because that would
imply I was showing my saggy old tits squashed into a

mammogram machine for some kind of titillation. 'You don't have your nipples pixelated when you go for a mammogram!' I said. 'Please let's show it how it is.'

I had to fight quite hard for that and I'm glad I did, because it soon became evident that the feature had struck a chord with a lot of people. Hundreds of viewers emailed, rang in and wrote comments on forums afterwards, saying things like 'I'm going for a mammogram now that Denise Welch has shown it's not the worst thing that can happen.'

It's strange that people think it is OK for me to show my tits in that context, but people rant and rave when I flash my bra or get in a hot tub topless on reality TV. I've never had a big thing about tits. I don't get it, although I do think it's funny to flash them when I've had a drink. Why? I think it's because other people find it so shocking.

It's all a question of context. I don't understand people who walk around the house in a bikini all day, but if you accidentally catch them in their bra and knickers, they scream, 'Get out! Get out! I'm not dressed!' In the same way, nobody would have thought twice if I'd been seen topless on a beach. Not one journalist mentioned that I'd had a mammogram on live TV, either.

There were only a couple of journalists who defended me. Jane Graham wrote a piece in the *Belfast Telegraph* saying that she had originally cringed at my lack of dignity when she saw me in the hot tub with Frankie, but that her opinion had changed.

'I've concluded that the problem with her behaviour

isn't that it was unacceptable or "disgusting", it's that I have a stick up my backside about the importance of maintaining one's dignity at all times,' she wrote in early February.

'Actually, I've concluded, the ability to say, "Sod dignity, I'm going to get drunk, loosen up and enjoy myself – even, gasp, when I'm 53," is a rather admirable thing,' she went on. 'And I, like lots of other people in this judgmental country, could do with relaxing a bit.'

Polly Hudson at the *Mirror*, who is known as quite a caustic writer, stood up in my defence, without any prompting from me. It meant so much to me, especially as Jane and Polly were lone voices in a pack of press wolves baying for my blood, none of whom had a good word to say about me. I was called so many awful names, you would honestly think I'd killed someone. I was really hurt by it all.

I didn't feel as though I had done anything wrong and I felt persecuted. Hang on a minute, what have I done? I thought. Did I bully anybody in there? Was I horrible to anybody? Did I embarrass my husband or family by trying to get off with somebody? No! I jokingly took my bra off in a hot tub with a nineteen-year-old boy and his pals, just like I would have in front of anybody if I was on holiday with them. And I had a laugh with some girls who turned it all on its head. Now I'm an adulteress and Tim is 'long-suffering Tim' again. I've had enough!

I spoke to Tim. 'I'm sick of this, babe,' I said.

'So am I, darling,' he replied. 'I hate the way you're

being treated. You went into that house for the sake of the family and you don't deserve this.'

'Mum, you made a huge sacrifice by going in there,' Matthew said. 'We had a tax bill to pay and you put yourself through hell to pay it.'

This is what was being said to me privately. Fuck you, press! I thought. You have no idea what my family really feel. Tim and I had spoken to Matthew and Louis about our plans by now. Matthew felt we were doing the right thing. In fact, he had thought we would be happier apart for some time now, but I used to argue that there was too much keeping us together for us to break up. We had also sat down and talked to Louis and he understood, as well as he could at eleven. He was very used to his parents being apart because of our work, and we reminded him about that, as well as reassuring him that we still loved each other.

So everything was fine at home, but I felt the media had no right to put me through this.

I needed to face my critics head on and take the power back from the media. I weighed up my options. I can do an interview with a paper, but they will choose their own headline, I thought. It won't work, because I won't have any control over how they spin it.

Then it came to me. I knew exactly what to do. I would tell my side of the story on live TV. I would announce the end of my marriage on Monday's episode of *Loose Women*, and the press couldn't do anything about it.

12

'I Just Hope That You'll Support Us'

Tim and I sat down and talked about the idea of me announcing our separation on *Loose Women*. 'I think it's the perfect opportunity to do it,' he said. 'I'd like to know what you're going to say.'

'Well, it's live television. I'll be emotional,' I said. 'How could I not be? I don't know exactly what I'm going to say, but I can sketch out what I'll be saying, in theory.'

I didn't involve my wider family in the decision, as in my mum, dad and sister. They knew we were going to separate, but I didn't inform them I was going to announce it on the television. That was because I didn't want to be dissuaded from doing it. I thought my dad might worry about what people would think. I love that about him, but I was at the point where it was more important to me to explain the situation than it was to care about what people thought. I thought Dad would say, 'Oh God, this is a massive can of worms!' And I didn't need to hear that, because it might sow seeds of doubt, and it had taken a lot out of me to make the decision.

I decided the issue was between me and my immediate family. Much as I needed my parents' approval for many things, this was about Tim, me and the two boys. Everyone else was going to have to deal with it, because this was about us. I spoke to the children and I said, 'This is what I'm going to do.' I found strength in our quartet, which seemed stronger than ever after my experience in the Big Brother house.

On Monday, 6 February, I announced the end of my marriage on *Loose Women*, with my great pals Andrea, Sherrie and Jane by my side. I faltered a little as I began, knowing what I was going to say, but not quite knowing how I would say it.

'This is going to be really difficult for me,' I said, 'but the *Loose Women* audience over the years have given me so much support, as they have to all of us, and so my family made a decision that we would talk about this today.'

I took a deep breath. 'Tim and I separated some time ago, so I'm not having an affair. We've been living our own lives for some time now.'

I explained how the press furore had taken us by surprise after *Celebrity Big Brother*. 'But there's been nothing in the papers that my family didn't know about,' I said. After thanking everybody for their support, I said, 'Tim and I feel a sense of relief that we don't have to hide this any more. We've actually become better friends since we made the decision, but we wanted to have Christmas with the family without telling anybody.

'I left the house last night to come to London with great hugs from Tim, great hugs from the boys, saying how proud of me they were, and we're all just going to move forward as a family. Tim and I are still going to be co-parents. We love each other very much. I just hope that you'll support us.

'Next weekend, we're co-hosting our big Sunday for Sammy charity do; the following week we're doing something else. The kids love us very much and they wanted me to do this today because if you do it via a newspaper or magazine, they can choose their own headlines and put it in the way that they want. But they're sick of me being annihilated. I'm not having an affair. I'm officially separated. But we do love each other very much and I just want to say thank you.'

It all came out in a fast stream of words, but I think I got my point across, because the audience gave me a big ovation. 'Listen,' said Sherrie. 'You can tell from that' – meaning the audience reaction – 'that everybody loves you. We all love you. You are very brave and we're very honoured.'

There was more applause. 'It's a relief,' I said, because it did feel like a huge load off my mind to have said it, at last. 'I'm going to nick a Dawn French quote that I read this morning. She said that she had far more years in a happy marriage than in an unhappy marriage. And that's how I want to see the twenty-four years that we've been together, and move on while we can still love each other in a different way. I just wish Tim every happiness, and he wishes the same for me. The kids are going to be fine.

'I guess we were scared of saying it, because that makes it official,' I said a little later. 'And obviously the press have forced our hand . . . The kids don't want to see those headlines about me when there's been nothing in the papers that they haven't known about. This is not about anybody else. Our marriage has never been about anybody else. It's just the fact that we are free to move on, should we want to. The kids are great. It's going to be a state of flux. Louis's school have been absolutely fantastic and supportive. I think, to be honest, the kids are quite relieved, because they want us to be happy. And I think that we are going to be happier, and we are still going to spend time together. Since we acknowledged that we are going to talk about this, we're better friends.'

I left the set feeling lighter than I had in a long time. I was glad to have finally said the words that I'd been bottling up for so long. It hadn't been easy, but I had dealt with it. I was coping, I felt. It wasn't until the next day that everything hit me. It may have been a delayed reaction, but it was a terrible shock to wake up to screaming headlines on nearly all the front pages of the tabloids. I read DENISE MARRIAGE SPLIT with a kind of horror. I'd barely had time to get my head around what I'd said on *Loose Women* the day before, and now I was faced with the bare facts of my marriage breakdown, gleefully reported in some of the tabloids. Some were more sensitive than others, but still there was something horribly real about reading about the break-up in the papers.

Suddenly, all the stress and anxiety of the previous weeks came crashing down on me. I was glad to be leaving the marriage after twenty-four years, but it scared me to be alone. It also made me sad to think that the deep love Tim and I felt for each other hadn't been enough to keep us together. I was tired, I was emotional, and I wasn't thinking straight. On my own, in my London hotel room, I broke down and sobbed hysterically.

The worst thing was that I had to keep on working; I had to go on *Loose Women* again that lunchtime. I felt slightly resentful that none of the production people had rung me the night before to see how I was doing. It would have been nice if they'd said, 'Why don't you take a few days off now?' I desperately needed some time to relax and breathe again, but nobody seemed to understand that. I just had to keep on going. I wanted to drink and obliterate everything with alcohol, but I had to fight the urge, because I knew it would make everything ten times worse.

I had seen Lincoln a couple of times since coming out of the house, but I still wasn't sure if I could trust him, and he didn't know if he could trust me, either. We only saw each other for snatched moments, because of the press intrusion, and all our insecurities tended to come out after a drink. We ended up having a couple of blazing rows. He'd storm off and I'd text him saying, 'This is never going to work!' It didn't look like the relationship would withstand the pressure of what was going on.

I was especially mistrustful at the time, because I knew that several people had been trying to sell stories about me, to cash in on the post-*Celebrity Big Brother* press bonanza. They were friends I'd made on nights out, had fun with and taken into my inner circle, despite warnings from others that they weren't to be trusted. Like a mother hen, I was always taking injured birds under my wing. People might say, 'Don't go near him; he's a nasty piece of work. He has a history.' But I always gave people the benefit of the doubt.

One of the people who sold a story about me was Tom Hopkins, someone I'd met at my dear friend Lester's wake in late 2010. It was a totally ridiculous, laughable, unbelievable story about how I turned him from gay to straight and had a sexual relationship with him. Still, I really could have done without it.

Lester's wake was a very emotional occasion for me and all of Lester's friends, including Steven, Pammy and Rose. At the time, we thought that Lester had taken his own life, as he'd made a half-hearted attempt before. I'm not saying that Lester's lifestyle didn't lead to him having a heart attack, but the autopsy established that there were no drugs and very little alcohol in his body when he died. He simply died of a heart attack, and I think it's important that people know that.

The wake was held at the Landor Theatre Pub. I started

chatting to a tall, posh redhead called Tom and we kept going out to the smokers' area together to have a cigarette. 'Who is this Tom guy?' I asked people, as I'd noticed that he was attaching himself very closely to me. Then again, I'm used to that with gay men.

He told me he was a really good friend of Lester's and how devastated he was about Lester's death. He said he'd been with Lester in the last days of his life. That's odd, I thought, as I'd never heard Lester mention him. But then again, I hadn't seen much of Lester in the year leading up to his death, mostly because of the geographical distance between us.

A couple of people told me they didn't trust Tom. There were stories going around that he had made Lester unhappy. Perhaps he'd been the recipient of Lester's generosity – Lester was known for throwing money around in an attempt to make people like him, which he really didn't need to do, because people loved him anyway. 'Were you and Lester lovers?' I asked Tom.

He was absolutely horrified by the suggestion. 'Absolutely not! But I cared deeply for Lester,' he said. I took him at face value and believed him.

He became a chum, and he was very persistent, phoning me a lot. I didn't mind, though, because he was funny and entertaining and we made each other laugh. We saw quite a bit of each other and he became very tactile with me, in a sort of childlike way, a bit like a son with his mother. I forgot all about people's warnings as I got caught up in the intensity of *Dancing on Ice*. I still enjoyed his company. I guess that, until I'm proven wrong, I take people as I find them.

I was staying at the Holiday Inn at Shepperton and he asked if he could come along and watch the show and stay over. 'Yes, that's fine,' I said. I only had a double bed in my room, but I've slept with loads of my gay friends, so I didn't think it was a problem.

It was slowly becoming apparent that Tom felt quite possessive of me. He was always trying to find fault with people I liked and he tried to turn me against some of my friends, which didn't work at all! That night, two of my very good friends, Nick and Paul, came down to see me and we had a hilarious night together. Freddie Flintoff was there and it was all really good fun. Nick ended up singing songs from the shows on Freddie's knee, which was very funny.

Tom was there and I could see that he was really jealous of my relationship with Nick, almost as if he were my boyfriend. He kept giving me possessive looks. 'What are you looking at me like that for?' I asked.

'It's just that I've come all the way down here and I've hardly had your attention for more than a second. You only have time for your other friends.'

'Hello, Tom! I've known these people for fifteen years. I've known you for five seconds.'

He flounced off, which I thought was hysterical, but Nick thought was slightly troubling. 'That's scary behaviour,' he said, but I thought he was overreacting.

We went back to the hotel and Hayley Tamaddon and Matt Evers came up to my room. We were all lying on the bed and I could see that Tom was going to spontaneously combust with anger that they were there. When they left, he went into a big rant about how he wished he was straight, which I found really funny at first. But when I realized he was being serious, I said that most of my gay friends loved being gay and the whole gay scene, the lifestyle and the sex.

I remembered having a friend many years ago who absolutely hated the fact that he was gay. He wanted to be heterosexual and fall in love with a woman and have 2.4 children, so he never let himself form a gay relationship. Every six months he would go out and have some seedy sexual encounter, come home, hate himself for it and not do it again for six months. It was very sad. I told Tom about him and said, 'Please don't be like that. You must embrace the fact that you're gay because it's not something you can work on and change.'

'I know, but I have feelings for you,' he said.

'I have feelings for you, too, but they're not sexual feelings,' I said. 'They're friendship feelings.'

The next day, Tom texted, 'I am completely in love with you.'

'You're *gay!*' I replied.

'I don't care. The soul has no gender,' he wrote back.

I realize now that he was lonely and looking for love, perhaps in the wrong places, but at the time I decided to make light of it and stay friends. If I didn't ring him back, he'd text jokily, 'Excuse me, wife! You haven't got back to me.'

In the end, I went along with the joke. It wasn't hurting me, after all, 'I'm your fiancée, not your wife,' I'd text, but I also used to say to him, 'Oh, stop being so ridiculous, Tom – you're gay.' I got the impression that he was starting to see me as his very own Judy Garland or Doris Day.

There was a point, though, when I started to feel stalked. He was becoming very possessive and my friends were getting cross about it. I'd wake up to eleven missed calls and twelve texts from him, frantic that he couldn't get in touch with me. He'd ring me at all times of the night and he'd phone Pammy if he couldn't get hold of me. Right, I'm going to have to start severing this connection, I thought. However, I didn't want to hurt him, because I knew how vulnerable he was.

Things came to a head at my dear friend Steven Smith's book launch for his memoir, *It Shouldn't Happen to a Hairdresser: Celebrity Tales From My Crimping Days*. Rose, Markaiu and I had made a pact that we would leave at 9 p.m., but as we were leaving, Tom shot across the bar like Clark Kent in *Superman* and said, 'Where are you going?'

'Enjoy the rest of the night,' I said warmly. 'I've got to be up very early for *Loose Women* and Rose is staying in my room tonight. We're all going out to dinner now.'

'With Micarwho?' he said. He always made a point of pronouncing Markaiu's name incorrectly.

'Yes, with Micarwho, because I haven't seen him for a long time.'

'Well, I'm coming.'

'No, you're not coming. You are absolutely not coming, Tom. You're not invited. I'm not being cruel, but I'm going out with Markaiu and Rose and that's it.' Soon after that, I stopped returning his calls. In May 2011, Steven, Pammy and I received a round-robin message from him saying something like 'I think it's time that we drew a line under our friendship. It's clear that you don't want me in your life any more. It's making me ill, so I've decided to sever this friendship. I wish you all nothing but good luck.'

We breathed a sigh of relief, and that was the last I heard from Tom until I came out of the Big Brother house and found out he'd been trying to sell a story about me. My manager couldn't contact me, so he didn't know if Tom's allegations were true or not, but of course I didn't turn him straight! Anybody who knows me knows that it's just too ridiculous for words that I would have a sexual affair with a tall, ginger gay man!

Along with all the nasty newspaper articles, there was an incredible amount of negative stuff being written about me online. I was bombarded with malicious messages on Twitter and called every terrible name under the sun. Some nasty piece of work even wrote a series of horrendous posts calling on me to commit suicide. Although I don't usually get bothered by the unpleasant things people say about me on the Internet, this struck me as beyond the pale and I decided

I would like to take a stand against cyber bullying. I told the people at work and they reported it to the police. At fifty-three, although it affected me, I could deal with it. However, it sent shivers through me to think that it might also be happening to a child of mine, or somebody young and vulnerable whom I cared about. I decided that at some point I would like to do something to fight against cyber bullying.

On the upside, I had a tremendous amount of support from the public. The people who liked me still like me, while the people who don't never will. I always remind myself that they don't know me, though. They don't know anything about me, or about all the charities I work for. There wasn't one charity that wanted to bring an end to our association – that would have horrified me.

All the while I was constantly trailed by the paps. One day when Louis and I were in the park with the dog, we were pointlessly stalked by a photographer. We were oblivious to him, but a lovely couple came up and said, 'Just to let you know, there's a photographer over there.'

'Thank you,' I said gratefully.

When the photographer came closer, I said to him, 'You're not going to make any money out of this, you know. Unless you can capture me falling out of a nightclub or showing off my bra, you aren't going to make a penny. The papers aren't interested in me happily walking a dog in the park with my son. It's not a story to them.'

At this point, Louis put his hands up to shield his head, as if I were about to hit him, the little horror!

Despite all of this, I was determined to fulfil certain engagements that I had committed to many months before. One of these was a performance at the City Hall in Newcastle for Tim's charity Sunday for Sammy, a showcase of north-east talent to mark the life of Ronnie (Sammy) Johnston, a Tyneside actor and a great friend of Tim's who died before his time. It took place on the Sunday after I had talked about our marriage break-up on *Loose Women* and it was to be our first public outing since the announcement. I desperately wanted to take part, but never has learning lines been so difficult for me! I had all this awful stuff going on with the press and I had to learn lines for three comedy sketches. Somehow I managed it, but everything seemed so unreal that at times I felt as if I was living somebody else's life. However, it was worth it when Tim and I walked out on stage together, and 2,000 people rose to their feet to give us a standing ovation. It was a completely overwhelming moment.

For the first time, Matthew took part in Sunday for Sammy. We were all watching in the green room as he walked out with his band and said, 'Hi, I'm Denise and Tim's son.' He'd been dreading it, because he was worried that people would cringe with embarrassment. But they didn't, because Tim and I had showed the world that we were still a unit. It was a tough gig for us and we were so grateful for the acceptance the audience gave us. We did a funny '*Auf Wiedersehen, Pet* do Camelot' sketch that went down very well.

At the end of the show, everyone came on stage to sing Lindisfarne's 'Run for Home' with Lindisfarne, Joe McElderry and all the Geordie mafia, including Angie Lonsdale and Charlie Hardwick. Tim and I went off stage hand-in-hand. It felt as if we were saying, 'We love each other; we've just moved on.'

Unfortunately, because the press forced our hand, we didn't have the opportunity to tell all our friends and family about the separation before I announced it on television. It was difficult for Tim's aunties and other relatives, because the first they heard about it was when they saw me talk about it on *Loose Women*. However, they were very accepting and I realized that the people who love us just want us to be happy. Tim's auntie Margaret and auntie Lillian have never judged me or shown any disapproval when there's been negative press about me in the past. They have always been concerned about me and asked, 'Are you OK?' I think they knew Tim too well to buy into the image of him as 'long-suffering Tim'. They've known him since he was born and have seen him in other relationships, so they knew he wouldn't stay with me if I was the person portrayed in the press. I also worried about how Tim's two dearest friends in the world, Mary and Norman Duffy, would react, because they love us both so much and they're so important to me. They've been wonderful, dear friends through everything and I can't thank them enough.

The weekend after Sunday for Sammy, the Theatre Royal in Newcastle was celebrating its 175th anniversary, and Tim and I had been asked to co-host the celebrations months earlier. When I told Dad that we were going to announce that our marriage was over at some point, Dad, bless him, said, 'Don't you think you ought to wait until the Theatre Royal night is over?'

'Why?' I asked.

'Well, otherwise all those people in the Theatre Royal will feel uncomfortable.'

'Dad, I'm not waiting to announce my marriage is over just to spare the awkwardness of five hundred people in the Theatre Royal!' I said. 'This is about Tim, me, Matthew and Louis!'

Afterwards, it struck me that the old me would have waited, because I, too, would have been bothered about what 500 strangers were going to think. For some time, I had been living my life according to what other people thought but, partly as a result of what happened to me in the Big Brother house, I decided it was time to stop being a people pleaser.

By now I was absolutely exhausted. My life hadn't stopped for a minute since I'd left the Big Brother house, so I was knackered and starting to worry about my depression coming back and bringing my life to a standstill. In the early days of my illness, I would have depression coupled with anxiety. So I had raging panic attacks for no reason and the panic attacks always turned into depression. However, I would also suffer from depression without anxiety, which is how my illness has manifested itself in more recent years, since the anxiety stopped around nine years ago. I've suffered from nervousness, but not full-on anxiety. Unfortunately, my experience in the Big Brother house seemed to trigger something and I started waking up with incredible anxiety in the days and weeks that followed my departure from the house.

What is the difference between depression and anxiety? Well, depression is exactly what it says on the tin: it depresses your whole system so that you have an inability to feel anything. Everything is black. As I've often said, it would be the same to you if someone came to the door and said you'd won four million on the Lottery, or someone came to the door and said your whole family had been wiped out in an airplane disaster. You'd feel nothing either way. Anxiety is where the slightest negative thought makes your heart race. When I'm anxious, I'm frightened of my own shadow. It's as if you're driving along in a car and a lorry pulls out; you think you're going to have a head-on collision and your heart races, your palms sweat. Normally, you'd pull over into a layby and start to feel better once the shock passed. With anxiety, that feeling you're going to crash never goes.

My head was so full I wasn't eating anything, which is always a sign. My appetite disappeared completely, I wasn't looking after myself at all, and I couldn't drink water or eat fruit or vegetables. Everything made me gag. I was also drinking too much alcohol. It was awful, and through it all I still had to go to work.

I had moments when I thought, What would happen if I just went to the airport? I honestly considered leaving a note for my family telling them that I was fine and not in danger, before going to the airport and getting on a plane. The world would continue without me! I thought.

In the early days of my depression, I used to find solace in the thought of suicide. I didn't ever really consider committing suicide, but many people with clinical depression find comfort in thinking of it as an option, so although my sense of loyalty is such that I wouldn't actually do it, the thought was an escape valve. Equally, when I've felt anxious on *Loose Women* in the past, I've thought, If I pulled my lead out now and ran off, it might be front-page news, but nobody would die. I need to feel that I can do it and it wouldn't be the end of the world.

If I hadn't taken a few days off and gone to Tenerife, I think I would have cracked. 'I need a week off, because if I don't have a week off, I'm going to go under,' I told my bosses at *Loose Women*. 'I need to get out of this country; I need to be with Louis and away from everything.'

Every day I felt anxious about what was going to be in the papers the following morning. The press were outside my door all the time and constantly followed me. The kids were being affected by it and I was also worried about them. I was worried about my illness coming back. I had charity commitments and *Loose Women* taking up a lot of my time. It felt as if I wasn't being given any breathing space at all;

then I was going home and trying to be Mum. Several times, I thought I was going under.

Thankfully, four days in Tenerife, even with two days of terrible weather, made me feel a hundred times better. It felt like a month's holiday. I didn't discuss work or business with anyone. It didn't matter that people were saying, 'We've lived here for ninety-seven years and never seen rain like this!' I had a brilliant time with Pammy, Louis and his little pal Thomas, whom we called Caspar, because he's as white as a ghost and never changed colour at all.

It was really interesting for me, because I didn't know how Louis would react when Tim and I told him we were separating. He was absolutely fantastic, though. I felt he'd been putting me down a bit in recent months. I think he was angry with me, because he was aware of the tension at home and he knew that Tim and I were arguing, even if we tried not to do it in front of him. Children have a sixth sense for that kind of thing.

There was never anything in the papers about what 'long-suffering' Daddy got up to. Meanwhile, there was loads about Mum's 'drunken antics' and being seen with other young (usually gay) men. Mum was on the front of magazines under headlines like SEVEN MEN IN SEVEN NIGHTS! (all gay), but there were no headlines or scandals about Daddy.

Louis then found out that Daddy was seeing someone and perhaps he thought, Good! Not, Good, Daddy's seeing somebody, but, Good, it's not just Mummy.

It wasn't a case of 'Whoop-de-doo, they're separating', but I think both Louis and Matthew were relieved to see Tim and me getting on again. There was definitely a shift with Louis when he realized that Mummy wasn't the bad guy, and he was horrified at the way I was treated in the Big Brother house. He enjoyed talking to me about 'the bitch twins'.

'Mummy, you know what they said about you behind your back?' he said. 'I really wanted to meet them, because they were the Playboy girls, but they're absolutely horrible – and they've had bum implants!'

We laughed when, two weeks after I left the house, I received a text saying, 'Hi, Mom, it's your twin daughters. We miss you!'

As I've said, I came back from Tenerife feeling refreshed and much stronger. It was fun to be back on *Loose Women*. Our debates can spring some real surprises, like a sudden confession or recollection from one of the girls that none of us was expecting. There's always a great rapport with the audience as well; it wouldn't be half the show it is without the live audience, and I really enjoy meeting some of them after the show. However, I had a real shock when I met one audience member just after my holiday, and it wasn't a nice shock, either, as I was totally unprepared for what she had to say.

In the course of that day's show, the panellists discussed whether it was OK for modern women to multi-date while looking for a partner. When it was my turn to speak, I said, 'I'm sick of "Modern Woman" and "multi-dating". Doesn't that just mean not being exclusive to one person if you're single; in other words, going out with several people?'

I've never really been single long enough to have a dating strategy, but we certainly never called it multi-dating in my day! We just went out with people. My advice to the 'Modern Woman' was that if you say you're dating exclusively, then maybe you shouldn't 'multi-date', but if you don't say you're exclusive, then surely you can see whoever you want.

We cut to a break and a woman in the audience said, 'Denise, I think that you and I were dating someone at the same time.'

A hushed silence swept over the audience. 'Really!' I said. 'Who?'

'David Easter,' she said.

I was stunned. 'That's my ex-husband!'

'I know,' she said.

I caught my breath. 'Did you go out with him while we were married?'

'No,' she said.

'Can I see you after the show?' I asked, feeling intrigued, but also a little flustered.

When the show finished, I met up with her and her friend. Sherrie Hewson and two pals from the *Loose Women* team came along, too.

'When did you go out with David?' I asked her.

'Between 1981 and 1982,' she told me. 'When did you start going out with him?'

'In 1979,' I said softly, barely able to keep the amazement out of my voice. 'Go on.'

She said she had met him at Chesterfield Theatre, where I had suspected him of another infidelity. He had pursued her relentlessly until she'd succumbed. 'We'd go to his flat in Willesden Green,' she said.

'*Our* flat in Willesden Green?' I burst out.

'Well, yes,' she said. 'I realize that now, obviously! I remember seeing some heated rollers one day and asking him about them, but he made a very plausible excuse for why they were there.'

I harrumphed. This was familiar territory and I wasn't particularly surprised to hear what she was saying. Meanwhile, Sherrie Hewson's mouth had dropped open.

'I used to go to his flat in Chesterfield as well,' the woman went on. 'He met my family. He said he wanted me to move in with him in London. Oh my God, this is so awful!'

'Listen, please, this is not awful,' I said. 'I knew this was going on.' And yet it did feel strange to be sitting down with someone who had been going out with David at the same time as I was. The years fell away and I remembered how suspicious I had been of him, how believable his excuses were and how tangled up in truth and lies I became. And to think, this was the man I went on to marry! It had all happened such a long time ago, but I couldn't help feeling sorry for the gullible, besotted girl I was then. I was so in love with him.

'I swear on my life, Denise, I didn't know he had a girl-friend,' the woman said, and I believed her. She was talking about the days before David was cast in *Brookside* and became a national heartthrob. I wasn't on the television then, either, so we weren't in the public eye. There would have been no reason for her to think that he was going out with me.

'When did you find all this out?' I asked her.

She explained that I had met her husband at a charity dinner event once and he'd apparently said, 'I think my wife went out with David Easter at some point.'

And I had joked back, 'Oh, it was probably when I was going out with him.'

He went home and repeated what I'd said, and she'd worked out the dates and thought, Oh dear!

'How many times did you see him?' I asked her.

'I went out with him for eight or nine months,' she said.

Oh my God! I thought she was going to say, 'Just a few times.' But it seemed they were in quite a serious relation-ship. He called her when he got the part in *Brookside*! She left him after he showed his temper a couple of times, though, sensible girl.

'I realize now that you drew the short straw,' she said.

A shiver went down my spine and I realized that she must have read my account of my relationship with David in *Pulling Myself Together*.

'Thank you for coming to tell me this,' I said. 'He always made me think I was going mad when I accused him of seeing other women. It's comforting to know that it wasn't just my paranoia.'

We then said goodbye and went our separate ways. As I jumped in a taxi to go back to my hotel, I couldn't help smiling. Just another boring day at the office, I thought, furiously burning an effigy of my ex-husband in my mind.

That night, Tim phoned to ask me where the car keys were. 'Where I left them!' I said.

'They're not there,' he complained.

'Well, you've put them somewhere else, then,' I said.

A little later, Lincoln phoned and we had a long, long chat. He had established that the story about us in the *Sunday Mirror* had been sold by one of his ex-girlfriends. (That's employing the word 'girlfriend' very loosely!). She knew about us because the information was out there among our friends, and one of Lincoln's friends had sent her the photo of us on a picture text, never suspecting that she would do anything with it.

I was relieved to hear this. I'd never believed that Lincoln would sell a story on me, but it was good to know, once and for all, that he hadn't. I wanted to see him. I'd really missed him.

'Would you like to go out for a late dinner?' he asked.

'Yes, please,' I replied.

13

It's Really Nice to Be in Love

I woke up in a cold sweat, with clammy hands and a familiar heaviness weighing me down. Oh no, I thought. Not now. Please not now.

It was early March 2012 and I was in London for the rehearsals of *Steel Magnolias*, the play I had committed to six months earlier. I never normally book myself that far ahead and I turn down theatre tours as a matter of course, because touring involves being away from home. I hadn't done theatre for eight years and I hadn't done a tour for over twenty years, since before Matthew was born.

However, I'd seen the letter that had been sent to my agent. 'We know Denise doesn't do tours, but please just ask her to read the play,' it said.

First, I watched *Steel Magnolias*, the 1989 film starring Shirley MacLaine, Sally Field, Julia Roberts and Dolly Parton. I love the film, I thought. Please don't let me love the play.

Then I read the play and loved it. I really wanted to do it. I looked at the proposed schedule. The whole thing would only take up twelve weeks in total, from the beginning of rehearsals to the last night, so, after talking to Tim and the boys about it, I decided it was a doable length of time. After committing to do it, I subsequently missed out on a TV series, but that's life. I'm thrilled I did the play, on so many levels, even though it was such a struggle to begin with that I actually regretted agreeing to it.

My home for the next three weeks was a rented flat near the rehearsal studios at Bankside in Borough. But I didn't want to be there; I wanted to be at home with the children. Although it was exciting to have the opportunity to act in a brilliant play with an amazing cast, I was desperately worried about my kids. They had been through a lot when I was in the Big Brother house, followed by my distress over the press and media attacks, and then splitting up with Daddy. The last thing I wanted was to be away from them for the next twelve weeks. Still, there was nothing I could do.

When I agreed to do the play, I couldn't have envisaged the turmoil ahead of me. Even if I'd known I was going to do *Celebrity Big Brother*, I didn't have a clue how much anguish it would cause me and my family, and it didn't occur to me that the show would cut into my preparation time for the play. Now I was going into rehearsals worried that I wouldn't be ready for the opening night on 2 April 2012 at the Theatre Royal in Bath. What's more, my work commitments made it difficult for me to focus on this new project, just as I hadn't been able to concentrate fully on learning to skate for *Dancing on Ice* the year before. I was taking time out from rehearsals to do *Loose Women*, I had a packed schedule of interviews to publicize the upcoming tour, and I wanted to spend as much time as possible being a mum.

If I was going to do this play, I wanted to throw myself into rehearsals, but so much was getting in the way. And to compound everything else, my depression and that horrible heart-stopping anxiety was still there. Can I do this? I thought, suddenly feeling insecure about my ability to hold my own alongside actresses like Isla Blair and Cheryl Campbell. And can I do it with my head where it is?

I was worried that the other actresses in the play would have been preparing for rehearsals while I was locked away in the Big Brother house, while I hadn't even had time to get my head around it. The cast was stellar: as well as Cheryl Campbell and Isla Blair, Cherie Lunghi, Kacey Ainsworth and Sadie Pickering had signed up to the production. Since I hadn't worked in the theatre for eight years, it was intimidating. It was a really important job to me, but it was being overshadowed by everything else.

I felt very nervous on my first day, but that was mainly the normal nerves that everyone has at the start of a new project. We were rehearsing at the Jerwood Space in Bankside, a lovely, light, airy studio complex, and I was filled with a sense of excitement the moment I walked in there.

I was thrilled to be rehearsing this brilliant play with these amazing actresses and working with the Olivier Award-winning director David Gilmore. On the other hand, I was also concerned about what these grown-up actresses would think of a woman who kept appearing on the front page with her tits out! I was worried they'd think, Oh God! Can't you get someone else?

Within a few minutes, Isla Blair put my mind at rest. 'I thought you were amazing the way you dealt with everything,' she said about my *Celebrity Big Brother* experience, making me feel better instantly. Her husband, Julian Glover, is also an actor, as is her son, Jamie Glover. I worked with Jamie in *Waterloo Road*.

A little later, Cherie Lunghi came up and said, 'My stepson, Rowan, asked me to say thank you very much for looking after him on one of his first jobs. He said you took him under your wing and were very kind to him.'

I hadn't made the connection at the time, but she reminded me that I had worked with Rowan Joffé who was the first assistant director on a BBC1 afternoon play called *Turkish Delight*. I loved appearing in it, even though it was all done and dusted in six days, from rehearsal to filming. I played a woman whose marriage is going downhill until she takes up belly dancing and finds herself again. Needless to say, her marriage is back on track by the closing scenes!

We filmed it in Birmingham and I knew we were all doing it for sixpence, but I hadn't expected it to be quite such a tiny sixpence!

'So, is that per night?' I'd asked when the BBC mentioned money, thinking this was what they were offering for my overnight expenses.

'No, that's your total fee,' they'd told me.

Who said TV pays?

Everybody seemed very supportive of each other as we ran through the play on the first day. It was great to be back among actors again and we got on from the start. There wasn't a hint of the diva about any of them and they all had a great sense of humour.

One of the reasons I was so attracted to the role of Truvy, the owner of a beauty salon, was that I'd have lots of funny lines. 'If I don't get the laughs, I'll get my tits out,' I told everyone.

As I was getting a coffee during a break, Trevor Nunn said, 'Oh, hello!'

I love being back in the land of the luvvies, I thought. I like it when really grown-up people like Sir Trevor recognize me!

On the night of the second day of rehearsing, I went to bed feeling right as rain. But, to my horror, when I woke up the next morning, the black cloud of depression had descended. I felt sick to my stomach and I couldn't eat or drink. How the hell am I going to get through the day? I thought with a deep sense of dread.

Lincoln had stayed the night, and when he got up to make some tea in the morning, he instantly noticed something was wrong. 'Are you OK?' he asked. I'd told him about my depression, but I hadn't gone into detail and he'd never experienced clinical depression first-hand before. Of course, you can't see it. The only sign of it was that I was quieter than usual.

'You're not well, are you?' he said.

Wow, I thought. That's incredibly perceptive, because he doesn't know how my illness affects me. Tim would have known, because he'd lived with it for twenty-odd years; my mum would have known, because she could always tell when I was poorly; but I didn't expect Lincoln to spot it. He was very concerned about me all day and I was grateful that I didn't have to put on a pretence in front of him.

Since I have no more control over my condition than I do over getting a physical illness, I made a decision a long time ago that I would be open about it. It was no good pretending to have a stomach bug. It was much better for everyone if I said, 'I'm really sorry, guys; I'm having a bad day with my depression.'

However, I hated the thought of the cast and the director being concerned about whether I would be well enough to do the tour. They might worry that they're working along-side Mad Minnie, who's liable to crack up at any point and be unable to continue, I thought. They needed the confidence of knowing that we could all rely on one another.

I could have shared how I was feeling with Sadie Pickering and Isla Blair, because, coincidentally, I had described my illness to them just the day before, when we were talking about mental health issues among people's relatives, but I decided to stay quiet and try not to give anything away. I was determined to get through the blackness and come out the other side, as I didn't want to let down the cast, crew or myself.

It was the worst day I'd had since I'd taken Louis down to London to see *The X Factor* in late autumn 2011, though thankfully that attack or lasted twenty-four hours. After that, I'd started thinking that my depression was becoming more transient, coming and going much more quickly. This time, however, my anxiety made me worry that it would last. Maybe this time it would be so bad I wouldn't be able to act.

I found it very difficult to go to work each day. As usual, the nausea became so bad that I threw up before leaving the flat each morning. All the familiar worries assailed me. I don't want to go to the rehearsal! I thought, in a total panic. I can't do the play. How can I keep up with all these brilliant actresses, feeling like this? I bet it lasts a long time. I won't be able to go on stage if it lasts. I'm going to have to pull out.

Depression takes away my ability to control my voice, which tends to develop a thickness of tone when I'm feeling poorly, so it was unfortunate that the voice coach was at the rehearsal on this particular day, listening carefully to our accents and the way we delivered our lines. I wondered what she was thinking. I guessed it would be something like Oh no, she's terrible! Who employed her?

Perhaps Isla Blair sensed that I was feeling bad, because

she confided in me that day. 'Oh God,' she said. 'I went home feeling very anxious after the rehearsal yesterday and Julian had to talk me round.'

Oh dear, I thought, she knows! But it was also a comfort to know that some of the other members of the cast were feeling the pressure, too.

I struggled through the rehearsal and, to my utter relief, I began to feel better by the next day. In the darkest times of my illness, the stress of working on a new play would have compounded how I was feeling, but this time I recovered quickly, despite all the negative thoughts and projections. I felt almost normal the day after that, except for feeling anxious, which was more a case of being insecure about acting on stage again after a break of eight years. It was a knock-on effect of my illness, really. Feeling poorly saps me of everything, and as a result I can't fire on all cylinders, so I felt I'd taken two steps forward and one step back with my accent. I bet the director's wishing he had never cast me in this role, I kept thinking, even though I now know he didn't think that at all. Every time he gave me a correction, I'd assume, He thinks I'm terrible!

We all have good days and bad days, but I could do without having a condition that compounds the normal nerves and insecurities you experience as an actress. Life is stressful enough! Added to all of this, every Tuesday I'd wake up to all kinds of dramatic headlines about me on the front of the weekly magazines. Thankfully, working in a serious theatre role meant that no one in the company was aware of the headlines. They weren't remotely interested in my tabloid world; they knew me as an actress, and a good one, too, although until I found my feet, I didn't think I was living up to that.

Despite the anxiety, I refused to give up. I had missed doing live theatre and I really wanted to prove to myself that I could still do it. Also, the script really appealed to me because it's about women supporting each other, which is a theme close to my heart at any time – and, of course, it's what *Loose Women* is all about. The idea of friends being there for each other and supporting one another through a crisis was especially resonant during my separation from Tim. It was then, more than ever, that I realized how lucky I am to have a group of caring, sympathetic girlfriends to turn to at any time.

Another huge advantage was that it was an ensemble play. After eight years away, I didn't want to go back to the theatre and play a whacking great lead in a production where all the pressure was on me to carry it and sell it, so it had seemed the perfect way to ease myself back in. Obviously, I'd talked it over with Tim, who agreed that it was a great opportunity. We worked out that Louis would be off school for three weeks of the run, over Easter and on a school trip, which meant I could see him much more than if he was at school. Tim very kindly offered to take a break from work to stay at home with Louis for the duration of the tour, which I really appreciated. We'd had these kinds of dilemmas throughout our married life, because someone always had to stay at home if the other one was away working.

When I started rehearsals, Tim had to turn down two jobs so that I could be in London for three weeks. I would have done the same for him if the situation was reversed, of course, but I still couldn't help feeling a little bit guilty. It's important to us that one of us is with Louis, but if Tim was a selfish person in that way, he would have said, 'You're going off on tour. Well, I've been offered two jobs and I want to do them!' He did agree to a TV series in the middle of it all, so there was going to be a bit of juggling along the way, but Tim has to work as well – we're a two-income family and we remain that way.

Lincoln was an incredible support to me while doing rehearsals, and it was during those three weeks that I began to think we definitely had a future together. He would come home and cook for me most evenings, and then go off into a room to work while I went through the play and learned my lines. I really appreciated his care and concern, especially as some of my days were really frantic, what with appearing on *Loose Women* and doing promotional work for the play on *This Morning* and *Alan Titchmarsh*, as well as doing various magazine shoots and, on one occasion, twenty-five back-to-back radio interviews in an afternoon.

People tend to book musicals even if they're not theatre-goers, apparently, whereas with plays you have to reach out to television and radio audiences to sell tickets. Because Kacey Ainsworth and I were the most current TV faces at

the time, it made sense for us to do much of the promo-
tion, and I was happy to help out, but I found it difficult to
keep dipping in and out of rehearsals, especially as a lot of
the scenes involved all or most of us. The others often
couldn't rehearse without me, so they would learn their
lines and hone their accents while I was away. In my anxious
state, I felt they had more time to prepare, leaving me
woefully unprepared, and I found myself longing to focus
on the play and nothing else.

I love doing *Loose Women*, but I kept thinking, I should
be at rehearsals! And it wasn't always easy to go from being
Denise Welch, the personality, to Denise Welch, serious
actress, within half an hour. Followed by Denise Welch,
mum in the evenings and at weekends. People ask me how
I switch around all the time. I guess I just think, This is
what I have to do.

At the time, I comforted myself with the thought that
I could always go to Heathrow and get on a plane. I could
run off like Stephen Fry did and the world wouldn't end, I
thought. My understudy would come on and take over, and
the headlines would say, DENISE RUNS OFF STAGE AND HAS
A NERVOUS BREAKDOWN. End of.

Tim was also very supportive. He knew I was feeling
wobbly, so he rang me to say, 'How are you? Thinking about
you. If you need to call me, I'm here.' I thought that was
really sweet, because it confirmed that we will always be
there for each other in that way. Our love didn't end when
we separated; it just took a new trajectory.

Meanwhile, I was growing closer to Lincoln by the day. He was always making me laugh. He'd send me a text and I'd laugh as if it was a text from Pammy. I'd never experienced that before. Tim is very funny, but Lincoln's humour is different. He makes me laugh in a similar way to my gay friends. Added to which, I fancied him more every day, and he had a way of looking after me that I loved.

Whereas I'm Miss Primark, almost everything Lincoln wears is handmade. 'Not that top with those trousers!' he'd say, appalled by my lack of style and coordination. It made me laugh, because for so long I was married to a man who was happy for me to put out a T-shirt and jeans for him without even noticing the cut or colour of them.

'Are there not enough shops in this country that you have to have things handmade?' I teased. He has the most amazing array of clothes. You'll never see him without a gorgeous jacket, a matching hanky in the pocket and handmade shoes. He says that it's an important part of his job to look good, and I can see that it is, but there's more to it than that. He just loves to be stylish.

The great thing is that I can tease him about it. If he had any of the vanity of my first husband, David Easter, I don't think I would have stuck around, but Lincoln isn't vain. 'Is this gay enough for you?' he'll say, doing a twirl in his latest pink jacket. He has a flamboyant attitude to clothes that I really like. It's important to him how he looks, but he has a sense of humour about it.

At the time, Lincoln often used to see a particular bloke

who had an office in the same building as his. There's a restaurant downstairs and this man used to have breakfast with his wife in the morning. One day, Lincoln walked past wearing a new pink jacket and they said good morning to each other. Lincoln walked off, but then changed his mind and decided to have a coffee in the restaurant instead of going straight upstairs. He sat down on a bench behind a partition, near the man's table.

The man had obviously heard Lincoln walk off, but not walk back again. 'That guy,' Lincoln heard him saying, 'he must wear a different jacket every day.'

'Yes, I've noticed that, too,' said his wife.

They were about to say something else, but Lincoln stuck his head round the partition and said with a wry smile, 'This is actually a new jacket!' They both cracked up. I love this story and started to take a new 'gay' photo of Lincoln in a different jacket every day after that.

One night, we were lying in bed – Lincoln was reading, and I was learning my script – and he said how much he loved me. 'I've never felt like this before,' he said. It sounds corny and it's what everybody says, but he said it in a way that told me he meant it.

'I'm not going to jeopardize this by going on about the age thing,' I said before going on quite a bit about the age difference between us. The papers have made much of the fact that Lincoln is quite a bit younger than me. He's constantly described at 'Lincoln Townley, Denise Welch's toyboy lover', despite being thirty-nine, which isn't the age you'd usually associate with a toyboy. Still, sometimes I wondered if it bothered him being with someone older. There are lots of examples of women who are happy with younger men, from my friend Carol McGiffin to Joan Collins, but I still felt I needed to get it out in the open.

Lincoln's face grew serious. 'You have no idea,' he said. 'You are the perfect age for me! I think I've got you at just the right age. Firstly, I don't think about it, and secondly, the dilemma of whether or not to have children together doesn't even enter the equation.'

He went on to talk about how much I am loved and how aware he is of it. He gave me this whole speech about how I do so much for so many people and how the atmosphere of a room transforms when I enter it and all kinds of other stuff. I listened in awe. 'I see it all as it happens,' he said. 'I just know how much I love you.'

Wow! I thought, realizing that I felt the same way.

I did tell him that I was a bit pissed off about falling in love so soon after my separation from Tim, because I was quite looking forward to being single for the first time since I was fourteen! OK, I have managed to notch up quite a few people in that time, but only 'illegally'!

Interestingly, I've found I have a different attitude to fidelity in this relationship. With every other relationship I've had, it's been possible to separate love from sex. If I had a one-night stand, my partner wouldn't have known about it and it wouldn't have affected the relationship. But now I couldn't bear the thought of having a one-night stand with anyone. It's not something that remotely appeals.

Around the middle of March, the *Sunday People* ran an exclusive revealing that Tim had a girlfriend. What I think happened is that I was overheard at a party saying to some friends that Tim had someone new. A *Sunday People* journalist was hovering nearby and came over to 'introduce' herself. 'Hi, Denise. I'm Halina and we met at *Wicked*,' she said.

I couldn't remember meeting her, but assumed I'd just forgotten. She was friendly and I was friendly back, unaware that she was a journalist. I'm an open person and I forget that the people I'm talking to might not have my best interests at heart. I ought to be more careful, but it's not in my nature to be very private. That's probably why Tim calls me 'Gob o' the Tyne'!

When Halina asked me about Tim having a girlfriend, I probably said, 'Yes, it's great!' without thinking and she had her article. It wasn't a horrible piece and, to be honest, there was a part of me that was quite glad it was printed, to get things out in the open, but I prefer to say things in my own words, which is why I decided to write this book. Also, if I was going to talk to the *People*, I would make sure I was paid for my 'exclusive'!

Three days later, there were pap photos in the paper of Tim and Jo at the pub. It was the first time I'd seen Jo. Tim had seen pictures of Lincoln, but although I knew about Jo, I didn't know what she looked like. I didn't feel jealous or upset; it was just odd. Whoa! There they are, I thought.

'Does it make you feel strange to see that?' asked Sadie at work.

'Yes, it does,' I said. 'It doesn't make me think, Oh my God, what have I done? It's just that it's my husband and his new girlfriend and I've never seen her before.'

Tim was upset that Jo was described as a cleaner in the article and subsequent press. I understand that it might have been difficult for her, because the whole thing was totally outside her experience. On the other hand, I've been called far worse things than a cleaner and it didn't worry him as much! OK, Jo isn't a cleaner; she runs a café and works on a voluntary basis for some older people, which includes doing a bit of cleaning, and that's fantastic and very admirable. But, of course, the press had to present it in an almost derogatory way, because that's the way the tabloid press works. I sympathized, but I said to Tim, 'Unfortunately, she's going out with a famous actor now. If she can't stand the heat, she has to stay out of the kitchen. It comes with the territory.'

About a week later, someone came up to me at a party and said, 'Hello, I met you at Dawn Ward's party. How are you?'

'Great!' I said. She asked me how I felt about Lincoln 'I love the bones of him!' I said happily.

Whoops, another journalist on the prowl! The next day, I was being quoted all over the online newspapers. I didn't mind all that much, although I hadn't planned for the comment to go public, because it was still very early in our relationship and I didn't want to set myself up for a fall. On the other hand, I was in love when I said it, and it's really nice to be in love, and I'm not very good at saying, 'I'm sorry, I can't talk about that.' In future, I'll just have to stay in if I've got something I want to keep to myself.

Lincoln saw the funny side of the coverage, though. The papers were trying to make out that we were one big happy family, because I'd said how delighted I was for Tim that he had a girlfriend. So Lincoln sent me a very funny text that said, 'Stop press! Jo and Tim adopt Lincoln and he moves in with them and Jo's son. "I've always wanted a younger brother," Lincoln laughs, wearing his "signature peaked cap". Next: Denise's dad teaches Lincoln how to do drag on a Friday night.'

However much Lincoln took it in his stride, it takes time to get used to being with somebody who's in the public eye. He finds it lovely in many respects, but difficult in others. I remember one evening when we were in Leicester Square in London and I asked him to flag down a taxi, because I needed to get to the station to catch my train. 'I have to go,' I told him, looking at my watch and panicking, so he darted out into the street to look for a cab.

Suddenly, I was surrounded by a gang of Irish St Patrick's Day revellers, all shouting my name. They were drunk, but they were lovely, so it was a dilemma: I wanted to be nice to them and have a bit of a laugh, but I had a train to catch. It didn't take long to make my mind up, though, and I launched myself into having fun.

Just then, a taxi stopped for Lincoln and he spun round to wave me into it, but by then I'd turned into a leprechaun and was doing an Irish jig in the middle of a group of men in green hats.

'Oye, hoydy toydy! My granny was Irish, to be sure, hoydle, oydle, oye!' I told them. 'Top of the mornin' to ye now!' I started singing, 'How Are Things in Glocca Morra?' from *Finian's Rainbow*. I was having a whale of a time.

Lincoln tried to reach me to let me know the taxi was waiting, but my new friends kept pushing him out of the way. I remember being overlooked in the same way when I was first with Tim and he was famous and I wasn't. It's frustrating, not because you feel resentful about being ignored, but because all these strangers keep getting in the way and you can't get anything done.

Lincoln didn't know what to do. I'd asked him to flag down a taxi, which he'd done, but then he turned round to see me having a party in the street, totally oblivious to him and the taxi, which was revving up to go. 'Get in the taxi,' he shouted, 'otherwise it will go.' No response from me. He jostled through the crowd to get near me. 'Get in the taxi now!' he repeated.

'Don't you tell me what to do!' I retorted, to his consternation.

What's going on? he thought. And who could blame him?

★

Something far more serious than fame was causing us problems, though. Unfortunately, when I drink, I sometimes try to wind up my partner deliberately. It never happens with my friends, just my partner. It's almost as if I'm testing them: How far can I push you?

And when Lincoln has a drink, he bites back. Consequently, we had a big fight one night and I chucked him out of my rented flat. It was very upsetting and I felt devastated the next morning. Before I went to work, Lincoln came over. 'I can't lose you and I won't lose you,' he said. 'I'm going to stop drinking, because it's not worth it if this is what happens when we drink.'

'Well, I'm not ready to stop yet,' I said.

'Fine, but I'm not going to risk another situation like last night,' he said. After that, he showed amazing restraint and had the odd glass of wine, nothing more. I was very impressed he would do that for me. Much as I loved him, I didn't feel I could do the same for him.

As I'm used to getting my own way, I need someone who says, 'No,' and Lincoln is brilliant in that respect; he's very good at setting boundaries. It doesn't always work, but we're getting better at it.

An example of it not working was a night in mid-March when I arranged for a group of friends to meet at the Covent Garden restaurant Joe Allen, a popular haunt of actors and theatre people. I particularly wanted Matt Evers and Lincoln to meet again, because when they'd first met, it was a bit of a crazy night.

Lincoln and I had been living an insular life in the flat until then, while I focused on rehearsals and he worked all hours on his new business. I was itching to go out and be sociable, but I was also aware of the need to be sensible. 'I have a run-through of Act One in the morning,' I told Lincoln. 'I can't be out late, so we're coming home at eleven, all right?'

Lincoln smiled, but I was deadly earnest. 'That's how it is, Lincoln. We can't stay out later than eleven. Under no circumstances! For goodness' sake, don't let me go on anywhere else.'

'That's fine with me,' he said. 'I want to be in the office early tomorrow.'

Matt Evers came; my newly married friend Daran Little came with his husband, Andre, whom I was dying to get to know properly; Sadie Pickering, with whom I was working, was there, along with Zara Dawson, who played my daughter in *Down to Earth* and her boyfriend Lex James, Markaiu and Josh Bedingfield, Daniel Bedingfield's brother. It was a random collection of people and it was fantastic.

Lincoln and I arrived early and I ordered a glass of rosé, which came in a mini carafe. Seeing this, Lincoln told me a story that really made me laugh. A couple of years ago, he took some guys from Porsche out, in an attempt to impress on them how he was going to organize the most amazing corporate party for them. Beautifully turned out in his fly suit and Gucci belt, he ordered a glass of expensive red wine, and the waiter brought him a mini carafe and a glass.

Lincoln put his briefcase on the bar, unknowingly concealing the glass, so he proceeded to drink from the carafe, assuming it was what he was supposed to do. 'Hmm, this is an angry little Beaujolais,' he said, sipping away, wondering why his clients were giving him odd looks. A few minutes later, he took his briefcase off the bar, saw the glass and went bright red!

Everyone arrived and we had a lovely dinner. Some other friends were going to see our Irish pal Rose-Marie in concert, so I told them to meet us at Joe Allen afterwards. Instead, they called after dinner and said, 'Please come to the Rose-Marie after party!' By then, I'd had a few glasses of wine.

Lincoln looked at his watch. It was nearly eleven o'clock. 'Right, we're going,' he said.

'Shall we just go along to the after party for one?' I said.

'No, we're going home,' he said firmly.

I could see the surprise in my friends' eyes. Uh-oh, they were thinking – they didn't know about my earlier insistence on getting home at a reasonable time. Of course, I wasn't thinking quite so sensibly after a few sherries.

'Hey, don't tell me what to do!' I blasted back. 'Come on! Let's go for a drink,' I wheedled.

'No!' he said, knowing how important it was to me to get home. He stood up to leave and I had no choice but to go with him, which caused some raised eyebrows among my friends.

Back at the flat, Lincoln expressed his frustration with the situation. 'I didn't know what to do,' he said helplessly. 'You made me look like a control freak. You said, "Don't let me go anywhere else," but if you want to go to a party, that's fine. It's just that I thought you wanted to come home.'

The next morning, I woke up feeling slightly fuzzy from the wine and thought, Thank God I didn't go to the Rose-Marie after party! Lincoln was right. I would have stayed there for another two hours and not been able to do my job properly the following day.

Perhaps I will give up drinking at some point, I thought. Maybe that's what I need to do to keep my life on course.

However, giving up booze wasn't remotely on my mind when I opened the newspaper a little earlier in the month to see that Michael Madsen had been arrested in California for child cruelty after an alleged fight with his teenage son. When I saw his mugshot in the paper with bail set at $100,000, I drank a bottle of champagne at home on my own and skipped around the kitchen, toasting myself in the air. 'Karma, karma, karma chameleon!' I sang. It was brilliant.

14

I Can Be Happy for Tim

'Oh, and Jo says hi,' Tim said, at the end of a phone conversation about Louis's weekend travel arrangements.

'Hi, Jo,' I said. 'Hope to meet you sometime.'

I put the phone down, wondering if I really meant that. In theory I wanted to meet Jo, but in practice I was slightly reluctant, although I wasn't sure why. It had to happen at some point, but I didn't know when or how.

Towards the end of my rehearsal period in London, I went home for the weekend. On the Sunday, Louis and I had to nip up to Marks & Spencer to get a few bits and bobs. When we got to the checkout, my credit card was refused because some money hadn't been transferred. I phoned Dad, but there was nothing he could do about it on a Sunday. 'Can I leave my stuff here while I go and get another card?' I asked the assistants, and they kindly said I could.

On the drive home, I saw Tim's car outside the local

pub. I knew he'd been doing a charity event earlier. 'Would you run in and tell Daddy to come out?' I asked Louis. 'I want to borrow his card.'

The sun came out while Louis was gone. There were newspapers on the tables outside the pub and I thought, When Tim comes out, I'm going to suggest we have a beer and sit in the sunshine for half an hour.

Louis came running out of the pub. 'Jo's inside,' he said. 'I'm going to tell her to come out and meet you.'

'No, don't!' I said. 'I'm not in the right frame of mind to meet Jo. I'd like to prepare myself first.'

Lo and behold out comes Tim, asking if I want a drink.

'Apparently, Jo's here?' I said.

'Yes, she's here with a couple of friends,' he replied, and at that moment, Jo came out of the pub.

So that's how I met her. It just happened, really.

'Hello, at last,' she said.

'Yes, it's lovely to meet you,' I said. Before I knew it, Tim, Jo, Louis and I were sitting in the sunshine having a drink and chatting as if we'd known each other for ages.

I'm at the pub, talking to my husband's girlfriend! I kept thinking. This ought to feel really weird, but it doesn't. That's when I realized that the root of relationship jealousy is sexual, and as there was no sexual jealousy and Jo seemed to be a very nice person, I could only be happy for Tim. If I'd moved out of home and she had suddenly moved into my house, I would probably have felt territorial, but when Tim said, 'Jo and I are taking Louis and his friend to

Blackpool for the weekend,' I thought 'Fabulous! I'm away on tour and Louis is having a brilliant time.

It's not like Jo is going to try and be Louis's mother. I am completely secure about my children's affection for me. She has her own son, and she doesn't want another one. She can be their friend – and that's all Lincoln wants to be to my boys.

I didn't decide to introduce Lincoln to my children; they decided to meet him. It was very much their decision. I was never going to say, 'Come and meet "Uncle Lincoln",' while there was a risk that Uncle Lincoln would be gone in a fortnight and Uncle Bert would have taken over. That was never going to be the case.

Obviously, Matthew knew about Lincoln, but when Louis became aware of him, he kept deleting his number from my phone. I had to file Lincoln under various pseudonyms, because Louis kept deleting them. 'Is that *Lincoln* on the phone?' he'd say whenever he sensed I was speaking to him.

One day, Matthew said, 'I'm coming down to London. Is Lincoln going to be around?'

'He can be or he won't be, whichever you want,' I said.

'I'd like to meet him,' he said. It was his choice. Matthew's a cool kid: he was twenty-two, Lincoln was thirty-nine, and they had music in common that I'd never even heard of! When Lincoln said he used to run Stringfellows, Matthew's eyes lit up and he casually, but hopefully, mentioned that it was his birthday soon and he would probably be coming to London with some friends!

When he went back to Cheshire, he naturally told Louis about meeting Lincoln. The next thing I knew, Louis wanted to meet Lincoln, too, so we arranged for him to come to London and spend the weekend with us in my rented flat.

It was Louis's first ever trip to London on his own. Daddy put him on the train in Cheshire and had a word with one of the guards, and Lincoln and I met him at Euston station. Unfortunately, there was some kind of signal problem and the train was an hour late, so I was a nervous wreck as I waited at the station. Then the trains started arriving at different platforms to the numbers listed on the boards. It was awful. At one point, there was an announcement saying, 'Would Mrs Papoudopolis please come to the information desk?' and I was in such a state that I thought it said, 'Would Denise Welch please come to the information desk?' Of course, Louis was cool as a cucumber when he finally stepped off the train, acting as though he always travelled solo!

Now it was time to introduce him to Lincoln. It was a tricky situation. Lincoln was very friendly, but I could see that he was being careful not to be over-chummy. Fortunately, he has a son, so he knew how to play it, but that sort of introduction is never easy.

They were thrown in at the deep end the next morning, because the *Steel Magnolias* director had decided to hold an extra rehearsal, which meant I wasn't going to be around.

'What do you think of the Natural History Museum?' Lincoln asked Louis.

'I'd love to go there,' Louis replied, and off they went.

As I was coming to the end of the rehearsal, I texted Lincoln. 'Mind, don't let him take the mickey out of you!'

'Too late,' he replied. 'We're at Hamleys. I've just bought him a remote-control Porsche.'

That kid's not daft, I thought.

It turned out to be a good weekend. Lincoln and I were affectionate with each other, but we were careful not to be kissy-cuddly and we didn't sleep together. Louis shared my room while Lincoln took the spare bedroom, and Lincoln was very keen that we did things that way. Things have moved on now, but that's how it was for quite a long time.

The next time Louis came for the weekend, he gave me a much tougher ride. He came with his friend Solomon and Solomon's mum, Keeley, who's become one of my really good friends over the last few years. Louis and Solomon have a bit of a naughty dynamic and they tend to wind Keeley and me up when they're together. Unfortunately, I'd had another anxious day at work and was not only worried that my anxiety was going to get in the way of my performance but that it would ruin my precious weekend with Louis.

I worked on the Saturday morning and Lincoln was at the flat to let everyone in. As soon as I got back, Louis started misbehaving, answering back and putting me down.

'You aren't being very nice to Mummy and it's upsetting

me,' I told him, but he just made a face. 'I'm just feeling a bit anxious,' I explained.

'What are you feeling anxious for? You're only doing a stupid play that you're probably not going to be very good in anyway.'

It was unlike him to say something so harsh and it really upset me, especially as it echoed my own fears.

I spoke to Matthew on the phone about it. 'Mum,' he said, slightly impatiently, 'you have to understand that while Louis and I totally understand and accept that you and Dad have made the right decision to separate, of course Louis is going to kick off a little bit. His life has changed. Although you and Dad have been planning this for some time, no one else knew it was coming. For Louis, it's all happened in a blaze of publicity, in what to him is a very short space of time. It's not that Louis blames you or doesn't agree with it; it's just that change is difficult for people, especially children.'

Of course, he was absolutely right. 'What about you?' I asked. 'How are you feeling?'

'It's weird, because I'm in a house that I love, that I've grown up in, but I feel like I'm here on borrowed time,' he said. 'It's fine, but things have changed and we need time to adapt.'

'I wish I wasn't doing this play,' I said, feeling horribly guilty. 'It's totally the wrong timing.'

'It's just that it's going to be hard for me to move out of this house, as it's where the band developed. There's lots of sentimental stuff going on.'

My guilt made me feel a bit cross. 'Unfortunately, our finances don't allow for sentimentality, Matthew,' I said. 'This is how it has to be.' I tried to change the subject: knowing that he had met Jo for the first time the night before, as Tim had taken her to Matthew's gig, I asked, 'What was Jo like?'

'She was fine,' he replied tersely. By the time the conversation ended, I was feeling upset all over again.

Half an hour later, Matthew sent me a long text. 'Mum, I was really moody earlier, just woken up. Listen, I love you so much. Please don't feel guilty. Mostly I'm fine about everything. It's just that I'm a little bit scared of change. Also, Jo is very nice. I didn't spend much time with her, but for some reason it was much harder meeting Jo than it was meeting Lincoln.'

I thought about this afterwards and wondered if it might have been harder to meet Jo because Tim hadn't been honest with Matthew about Jo, whereas I had been very open with him about Lincoln. There wasn't really time to dwell on anything, though, because Louis, Keeley, Solomon and I were off to see the musical *Matilda* at the theatre. It was the hottest ticket in town and it was fantastic. Everybody in it was brilliant. I didn't look at the programme, but I didn't think I knew anybody in it.

Afterwards, Louis said that he thought the ten-year-old playing Matilda was absolutely amazing. 'Can we go and meet the cast afterwards?' he asked.

'Well, OK,' I said. 'I don't know everybody, Louis, and

I don't know anybody in this production, but we'll go round to the stage door and see.'

As it happened, the actress playing the horrible mother turned out to be Josie Walker, whom I do know. I had a little chat with her and then I said to the stage-door man, 'My son Louis would love to meet Eleanor Worthington-Cox, who's playing Matilda tonight.'

The children's chaperone wasn't sure if it would be all right for us to meet Eleanor, but she relaxed when some of the other kids from the show started coming out and a few of them recognized me. 'That was absolutely brilliant!' I kept saying. Then Eleanor arrived and Louis went gooey-eyed. 'Darling, you were amazing!' I said, and I really meant it. 'Can I get a little picture of you with Louis?'

'I'm really sorry, but it's not allowed,' the chaperone said.

'Never mind, it was nice to meet you,' I replied.

The chaperone darted away and quickly returned. 'Eleanor's mum is outside and she said it's fine,' she said, so Louis and Eleanor had a picture taken together.

The next morning, we were in a shop and Louis said, 'Will you buy me a card?'

'A card for . . . ?' I asked.

'Shhh! Just get me card! A blank card.'

So I bought him a blank card and he wrote on it, 'Dear Eleanor, I'm Denise Welch's son, Louis. I met you and had a photo taken with you after seeing *Matilda*, in which you were amazing. I think you are so beautiful and I would love you to write back to me . . .'

'Mum, will you take it to the stage door?' he asked.

'I can't,' I said, 'but perhaps Lincoln can.'

Later on, we went to the London Bridge Experience, which tells the history of London and London Bridge in vivid detail. The 'experience' comes in two parts, one of them being the London Tombs, a scary visitor attraction situated in a former plague pit!

Louis was really looking forward to going and was full of bravado, saying, 'Scary things, yeah! That's me!' But when we arrived at the door, he refused to go in. We had thirty-five false starts, but didn't get beyond the ticket desk.

Keeley and Solomon tried to reassure him. 'There are two segments, Louis,' they said. 'First, there's the history of London Bridge; you don't have to go through to the scary part unless you want to.'

He wouldn't believe them, though, and said he wouldn't go in unless Lincoln came with him. So I had to ring Lincoln and ask him to cut short his gay shopping trip in the West End, where he was buying more pink jackets.

While we waited for Lincoln, we bought a sandwich and went to eat it in the grounds of Southwark Cathedral. One minute, Louis was by my side; the next, I turned round and he wasn't there. Panic, panic, panic! 'Have you seen my son?' I asked an official breathlessly.

'I think he went into the cathedral,' he said.

I rushed inside and spied Louis kneeling at a pew. He was praying for the soldiers in Afghanistan, which was interesting, because he isn't normally religious. When he'd finished, we walked through the cathedral looking at the amazing sculptures and statues, then Louis went into the private prayer room to pray for his nana. 'I've just decided that I believe in God again,' he said when he came out. 'But I don't want to tell my friends at school because they'll take the mickey out of me.'

'It's brilliant if you believe in God,' I told him. 'Life is tough as you get older, and if you can believe in something and it gets you through, that's amazing.' Shortly afterwards, Lincoln turned up and we finally made it into the London Bridge Experience.

By the end of the weekend, Louis didn't want to leave. It was horrible saying goodbye. Later, Keeley texted me to say, 'All fine. Kids were great on the train and, by the way, Solomon thought Lincoln was gay for the whole weekend!'

That evening, I had four calls from Louis. 'When is Lincoln taking the card? Will she write back? What if she doesn't write back?'

'I don't know Eleanor Worthington-Cox,' I said. 'I'm sure she'll be very flattered that you've written to her, but maybe she won't, I don't know.'

'Well, I've just finished with Samantha,' he said, mentioning the latest of my eleven-year-old son's string of 'girlfriends'.

'You haven't finished with Samantha because of Eleanor?'

'No.'

'Why have you finished with her, then?'

'It just wasn't working out.'

'OK, what did you say?'

'"Samantha, it's Louis. I really want to be your friend, but our relationship really isn't working out."'

'What did she say?'

'"OK, fine." But I could tell she was upset.'

He phoned me several times a day after that. 'Mummy, have you found out exactly which days Eleanor is playing Matilda? I want to know if she's got the card yet.'

'No, I haven't,' I said. In the end, he nagged me so much that I rang the stage door to leave a message for Josie Walker asking her to find out if Eleanor had received the card and to beg her to at least write something to Louis. He was absolutely smitten by this ten-year-old!

'You know, some people are impressed because Mummy is on the television, but I don't think Eleanor Worthington-Cox will write back to you just because your mother is a Loose Woman and is now in *Steel Magnolias*,' I told him. Then I felt bad, so I added, 'If she doesn't write back, the only reason will be that the Royal Shakespeare Company don't allow child cast members to reply to people. It may be their policy.'

A couple of weeks later, Eleanor wrote Louis a sweet card saying, 'Of course I remember you and it was lovely to have met you. Wish me luck in the Olivier Awards.'

It so happened that Louis had just dumped his next girl-friend (the one after Samantha) and was feeling too low to really enjoy the moment. 'The timing couldn't have been worse,' he told me. 'I'd just walked in from her house when I found the card from Eleanor. She said to wish her luck in the Oliver Awards.'

'It's the Olivier Awards, darling,' I said.

'Mum, it's the Oliver Awards!'

Well, she only went on to win the 'Oliver Award' for best actress in a musical! You've got to give it to him, Louis can spot talent!

So Louis had met Lincoln – and liked him. I wondered what he would think of Jo. I soon found out. 'Oh, Mummy, I met Jo today,' he told me on the phone a few days later. 'She's very nice.' Phew!

Around this time, Tim and Lincoln bumped into each other in Soho, though they only acknowledged each other, as far as I know. Tim might disagree with me, but I think it's harder for men. It's a gender thing. They're a little bit like stags! Tim has never said anything negative about Lincoln, and I sense that his only criteria for the person I'm with is that they are good to me and good to our children, which mirrors my criteria for the person he's with.

Certainly, we have no desire to swan off into the sunset as a foursome. I said to Tim that, of course, I'd like him to bring Jo when he came to see me in the play, where he might well bump into Lincoln, but that we wouldn't be going on holiday together or anything. 'Well, not until next year, anyway!'

While all this was going on, it felt very strange that Mum and Dad hadn't met Lincoln yet. In fact, I hadn't spoken much to Mum about him, because her speech was bad and I couldn't understand her very well on the phone. I tended simply to say, 'Love you, love you,' before Dad took the phone again.

Then one night in late March, Dad said, 'Your mum has had a really good few days. She hasn't been using her nebulizer and her speech is better. Would you like to talk to her?'

Lincoln had gone to bed to read and I was going over some lines in the lounge. I got on the phone to Mum and found myself talking about my sister and the fact that we still weren't speaking.

'I think it's really sad that you're not,' Mum said.

For the first time, I gave my side of the story and Mum listened patiently; then we moved on to the subject of Lincoln. Mum said that the only thing that worried her was that it had all happened so quickly. I think it was quite odd for both her and Dad, because circumstances meant that they hadn't met Lincoln. They could see my feelings growing for him, but they didn't know him.

'It does seem like I've jumped out of one relationship into another; it does seem like it's been very quick,' I agreed. 'But, actually, it hasn't. It just seems that way. Oh, Mum, I really, really want you to meet him, and I really, really want you to like him!'

Because of who I am, my parents' opinion and approval are always hugely important to me. If they hadn't liked Tim, for instance, I don't think I would have stayed with him. Perhaps I would, because they couldn't stand my first husband and I stayed with him, but a huge part of the attraction with Tim was that he got on so well with my family and friends.

However, I'd changed after my *Celebrity Big Brother* experience. I'd become more certain of myself, I suppose. So I knew that if for some reason Mum and Dad didn't like Lincoln, it wouldn't change my feelings for him, whereas it might have done before. Of course, I couldn't see why they wouldn't like him, as long as he was being good to me and the kids. They've always been very generous people and never prejudged anybody, and I knew they understood why Tim and I were no longer together. I think everybody close to us understands.

'I'll meet this Lincoln when I come to see the play in Newcastle, won't I?' Mum said.

'Or we'll try to get up for a visit when the play is at Bradford or York,' I said. 'Love you, Mum, love you. Bye!'

I put the phone down thinking how much I loved talking to Mum. I had hardly seen her all year and I missed her.

Mum Will Always Be in My Heart

You're going to mess this up, I thought, as I got into my costume backstage at the Theatre Royal in Bath. You're not good enough. You'll let everyone down. I felt sick with dread.

The opening night of *Steel Magnolias*, on 3 April, was terrifying. It doesn't matter which play you're in, you always think you need more rehearsal time. Unfortunately, when you're on tour, you rarely have enough time to get used to a new theatre space before you go on stage. We'd only had a couple of hours to rehearse in Bath, so we went straight from the rehearsal rooms to the stage, which was difficult.

What made it ten times worse for me was that I was feeling anxious already, on top of the usual first-night nerves. I felt pissed off and sorry for myself. Why do I feel like this? I thought resentfully. Why can't I just be a normal person with normal nerves? I felt envious as I looked around at the other actresses in the company. They were all worried in the usual way, while my anxiety was creating catastrophic scenarios in my mind. In the end, I got through it, but I didn't enjoy it.

It was great that I had good reviews, and it was amazing that the writer, Robert Harling, told me afterwards, 'You *are* Truvy!' Bearing in mind that he'd based Truvy on someone he knew, what more could I have wanted? Added to this, Bath is a beautiful place and Lincoln was with me, bless him. I was falling more deeply in love with him every day.

However, my anxiety cast a shadow over all the good things that were happening. What if this feeling doesn't go away during the whole tour? I started thinking. That's what happens with anxiety: you project and it gets worse.

I reassured myself in the same old way: I could always walk off stage and run away if I needed to. Back in the days when I toured and wasn't well known, that wasn't an option, because we didn't have understudies. Now we had three understudies between the six of us. Although I hoped very much that I wouldn't have to use them, they gave me a security blanket. Just in case, I thought, I have a competent actress who can go on in my place. Yes, the audience will be disappointed, but after three minutes they'll forget their disappointment and become absorbed by the play.

I had overcome the insecurity I'd been experiencing during rehearsals, when my fear and anxiety built up to the point that I decided to take the director aside and tell him how I was feeling. By the time I'd got up the confidence to do it, the character of Truvy had clicked for me and the director was showing visible relief at my improvement. I enjoyed finding Truvy, but it took a while, because she isn't drawn as obviously as some of the other characters. She's not right there on the page when you read the script. You have to dig to find her.

Researching Truvy reminded me of how much I love theatre. For eight years, I concentrated on TV acting, where your whole performance is controlled by the cameras and the editing. Exploring a character is a different process when you're doing television today, because you have very little time to complete filming. It's all about getting it done as quickly and as cheaply as possible. That's just how it is. Often, you're filming out of sync, the scripts are changing all the time, and they're handing you new pages just before you film a scene, so you don't have the chance to invest in the whole journey.

You can find that the storyline you filmed is rather different when you see it on the television. In one scene your brother dies and in the next scene you come skipping into the pub with a bunch of balloons. Hang on, you think. There were eighty-four scenes in between. Why have they been cut?

'You didn't seem very depressed about your brother's death,' your friends and family say.

'Because they cut that bit out!' you cry. Or, 'Because I filmed one scene in June and the other scene in September! I'd forgotten my brother had died!'

My dad, who is my biggest fan and my harshest critic, will say, 'Well, I thought you could have had a bit more of an emotional journey before the balloons!' It's frustrating.

TV is all about the cameras. You might want to be in a certain place in a scene, but if the cameras can't accommodate that, you may have to say your lines in a very awkward position in the corner of the room, because that's the best angle for filming. As you become older and wiser and more confident of your status within the industry, you can say, without being a diva, 'I'll go along with it to a degree and do this, but I'm not doing that.' Live theatre has far fewer restrictions, which is what I love about it.

On the other hand, though, in TV you can go again if you fluff your lines, whereas once you're on stage, it's just you for two hours. But that's also what makes it so blissful. You have no one controlling your performance. The time had come when I really needed to do what I do without someone shouting, 'Cut!'

Unfortunately, two weeks into the tour, my anxiety still hadn't lifted, so there was very little bliss in performing. There came a point when I had to face it full on. 'OK,' I said to my illness, 'I've done this play and had really good reviews. The writer told me, "You *are* Truvy," and he wrote the character based on someone he knew. I've managed all of this with you bearing down on me, you little bastard! So, if I can do it with you, I can be ten times better without you.' That's how I have to talk to it and I always have done.

Off it went. Joy!

Now, my only problem was trying not to look at Cheryl Campbell on stage, because we're terrible corpsers, the pair of us. If I made eye contact with Cheryl, it was game over. I'd start to speak with my 'corpsing voice', which is slightly high-pitched and trembles as I try my best to mask my laughter.

For the first few performances, Cheryl and I were absolutely terrified of corpsing while having to speak with a Louisiana accent. Knowing Cheryl's work as I do, I didn't think she'd be the giggly type, but she's great fun. Everyone in the company is. Once you've been doing a play for some time, the giggles can set in when you're doing a wet and windy afternoon in Skegness. We never actually corpsed, but there were some performances in which I had to play lines to Cheryl's breasts, rather than look at her face!

One thing that did make me laugh was having to look every night at an authentic 1980s magazine with a cover photograph of the model with whom David Easter had an affair while we were married. When I told Kacey Ainsworth, she picked her nose and rubbed a bogey in it.

Lincoln came on tour as much as he could. I always thought I would hate anybody to be out on the road with me, but I loved him being around. I also thought I'd hate to sleep in the same bed as somebody every night, because I like my own space, but I have found I always want Lincoln there with me. Oh my God, I've turned into this pathetic in-love person! I miss him as soon as he's away. It's really nice to feel that way, but it's also quite scary.

What's funny is that at the beginning of 2012, I didn't feel that anything more could go wrong with my life. When I came out of the Big Brother house, the press was horrendous, my marriage was breaking down, I knew that my mum's health was failing, I didn't know if my relationship with Lincoln was going to survive, and my relationship with my manager was starting to deteriorate, because I unfairly half blamed him for putting me on *Big Brother*.

Now, things seemed to be slotting into place. My anxiety had gone, I was loving the play and getting good reviews, and my relationship with Lincoln was going from strength to strength. It was around this time that I decided to give up drinking for the sake of our relationship. I wasn't going to lose Lincoln because of alcohol, so I stopped. Everything came to a head after I organized a celebrity night for *Steel Magnolias* when it moved to the Richmond Theatre. It was the nearest to London we were getting and I wanted to have a bit of a glitz and glamour night when my celebrity friends would come and see the play. As usual, I was on a high when the play finished and there were lots of friends there I hadn't seen for ages. People were thrusting glasses of wine in my hand at the party afterwards and I got far too drunk far too quickly. On the tour, I had been moderating my drinking because, as a professional actress, I cannot be hungover on stage.

I woke up feeling appalled that I'd let myself get so hungover, with two shows to do that day, but much worse was to be told by Lincoln that I'd turned into a monster towards him. I had no recollection of it but he was devastated by the things I'd said to him, all of which were completely untrue. Unlike the Big Brother house, where alcohol gave me the courage to confront people about the things that were upsetting me, this time it had turned me into a person I did not know. I was mortified by the fact that I'd become this person. I had always hated people who turned into monsters when they drank.

Lincoln picked me up that night and I listened to him talking from Richmond to Kensington and didn't say a word. He didn't give me an ultimatum but he did say, 'I love you so much that if you are going to continue drinking and I'm not, you will have to do it when I'm not with you, because I can't live in fear of that person coming into the flat at night.'

That struck a chord with me, because I've experienced that dread of a person coming in, even if it wasn't necessarily because of their drinking. That's when I thought if this relationship ends because it ends, that's life. But I'm not having this relationship end because of alcohol. I haven't drunk since that day. I've eaten a lot of chocolate, though! I feel like my appetite has increased so much that at this rate I'm going to have to be be winched out of the house. Or they're going to have to knock the front wall down to get me out.

To be honest, I think the monster that can come out when I'm drunk is a side to me people have seen over the last two or three years. I have changed medication and the new regime is working for me but my doctor did warn me there could be a reaction between the medication and alcohol. In the past, I was always a happy fall-about drunk, which I can still be in certain circumstances. But now it seems that if anybody very close to me questions me about anything, I can let them have it in a nasty way. I *never* used to do that.

The fact is, if I have to make a choice between my mental health and my drinking, there's no decision to make. I didn't tell anyone I'd stopped drinking because I didn't want people watching me and waiting for me to buckle. But this time I knew I was ready.

I even managed to stick to my resolution in what could have been a potentially awkward situation, when Lincoln and Tim met properly at home in Cheshire in April. As it turned out, it couldn't have been less awkward. Lincoln was trying to mend Tim's phone for him when Jo came over. We all sat in the garden, chatting and laughing, Pammy, Rose, Lincoln, Tim, Jo and me, as if it was all perfectly normal.

We tested the latest non-alcoholic wines together. 'The red wine tastes like someone's been sick in a sock and they've stained it red and put it in a glass!' I said, wincing at the first sip, and Jo offered to pop to an off-licence in South-port the following Tuesday and find me something nicer. While Jo and I discussed non-alcoholic beverages, I looked across the lawn to see Tim and Lincoln swinging Louis between them. You couldn't make it up.

I've often said that Tim and I are not trying to be the poster couple for amicable separation; we've just done the best we can. It's never been forced. We weren't pretending to smile in front of the children. It was just how it worked out. Sometimes it's like a scene from *The League of Gentlemen*, though, such as when Jo's brother, Alwyn, a big amiable guy, came in and tried to talk to Pammy about God; and when Pammy's sister mistook Jo's son for Matthew. She couldn't understand why he stood stock still as she hugged him. 'I haven't seen you since you were knee high to a grasshopper,' she gushed. Poor boy!

On the day of the non-alcoholic wine-tasting, Tim and Jo took the kids out. After making twenty false exits, they finally left: Tim, Jo, Louis and Harrison, Rose's son. Off they drove. We went into the kitchen and Lincoln noticed a phone on charge on the counter top. 'Whose phone is this?' he asked.

'It's Matthew's,' I said. But of course it was Tim's. He'd left it behind – yet again!

Twenty minutes later, the car came back into the drive. As I handed the phone to Jo, I said, 'Welcome to my world. Bye!' And we raised our eyes to heaven together.

Mum's health had deteriorated over the last few years, but we hadn't always connected that to her cancer, which we knew couldn't be cured. She continued to have her three-month checks and they kept saying there were no changes. The cancer hadn't spread or grown so part of me believed she would bounce back and be Joan Collins again, as she'd always done in the past. But I knew they couldn't get rid of the cancer so it was just a matter of time. I wished I could do more to help. I was glad that my sister lived nearby, as she did a lot for Mum.

In early May, *Steel Magnolias* moved to the Grand Opera House in York, an hour and a half's drive from Mum and Dad's. 'It feels really odd that I'm in love with you and you haven't met my parents,' I said to Lincoln.

I hadn't seen Mum since February, because I hadn't been able to get up to the north-east and Mum hadn't been well enough to come and see the play in Bradford with Dad, two weeks earlier. I now know that having difficulty breathing is a condition related to cancer, which, added to her emphysema, was obviously making her more poorly, and I could see that Dad was becoming increasingly stressed about Mum's health. Often, when I phoned home, he would say, 'Hang on a minute, I've just got to go and see to your mum . . .'

'Do you think you'll make it to Turkey?' I asked him. I was so glad that we'd hung on to our house in Hisaronu, because she loved it there so much.

'I'm afraid she isn't well enough,' he said.

Poor Mum! I thought. It upset me to hear that she wouldn't be able to go that year.

She was maintaining a decent quality of life, though. Dad told me that she had recently been to the Metro Centre with Debbie, so she was getting out and about.

'Do you fancy driving up tomorrow?' I asked Lincoln. 'OK,' he said.

I phoned Dad. 'I'll ask Mum if she's well enough,' he said.

My heart flipped. 'Wow! OK.' I waited for him to come back to the phone. It hadn't occurred to me that Mum might be too ill to see me.

'Yes, she said it's fine,' Dad said.

'I'll ring again tomorrow, just to make sure,' I said. 'I don't want to tire her out.'

The next day was one of those days that really get me down. The sky was a black-grey and the rain was constant. It was awful. I don't have full-blown SAD, but there's a trickle of it in my system, and I felt a bit sweaty-palmed. 'I'll ring Dad to say I'm not coming today. I don't feel up to it,' I said to Lincoln.

'But I'm going to London tomorrow,' he said, sounding disappointed. 'You know I really want to meet your parents.'

'OK, let's go, then,' I said, changing my mind in an instant. 'I expect I'll feel better when I'm out.'

When we arrived, at about midday, Dad said, 'Mum's still in bed.'

I went upstairs and opened her bedroom door. Although I was expecting Mum to look ill, I wasn't prepared for the sight of her lying there dying of cancer. She's not going to get better, I thought despairingly. It was the first time I'd sensed that she was dying in the twenty years that she's had cancer on and off. Every other time I had seen her looking ill, I'd thought, Well, she's like this now, but she'll be Joan Collins again next week. And, true to form, she always was. I knew this time was different, though.

Mum and I chatted for a while; then I said I was going to bring Lincoln up.

'Hello, Lincoln. I can't believe you're seeing me like this,' she said brightly. 'Don't try this dying malarkey – it's not much fun!' That was her sense of humour. Ha. Ha.

'Oh, Mother, you morbid bugger!' I said.

Lincoln had brought her some beautiful perfume, in a diamante bottle, as a gift. 'Well, if you haven't used much of that before you pop off, I'll be having it,' I joked.

After a little while, we left Mum to rest. I slipped out of her room and walked straight into what used to be my bedroom, where Dad now sleeps, feeling shocked and devastated. I burst into tears. Lincoln put his arms around me and did his best to comfort me.

When I'd calmed down, I went downstairs and said to Dad, trying not to be dramatic, 'She doesn't look well.'

Dad wasn't in denial, but when you see someone every day, you don't notice it as much. In the weeks that followed, he kept saying, 'She's sleeping a lot!'

'I think she's dying,' I'd say gently.

I'm so glad I went home that day. It was the last time I had a conversation with Mum. I desperately wanted to stay and spend more time with her, but she needed to sleep and I had to get back to the theatre for the evening's performance.

Lincoln drove me down to York through torrential rain and I cried for the whole journey. I was incredibly upset.

I found it tough going on stage that night, because one of the characters in *Steel Magnolias* is dying. Mum was constantly on my mind. I hated to think of my wonderful, beautiful mother suffering, and I was desperately worried about Dad, too. He was exhausted and strung out. I longed to give him more than support on the phone. Not for the first time, I wished I wasn't doing the play. At the same time, I was glad that I was, because it's a wise, moving, humorous play with many lines that resonated with what was happening in my life. I quote lines from it on a daily basis. And I couldn't have wished to be with a more wonderful group of women than the Steel Magnolias, especially as most of them have been through the loss of parent themselves. Their love and support got me through, and that's one of the reasons the play will remain in my heart for ever. It's almost as if I was meant to be playing Truvy at that heartbreaking time in my life.

On Sunday, 20 May, Dad called and said that we needed to go home, because Mum was fading. Lincoln drove Pammy, Louis and me, while Matthew drove up separately.

Matthew and Louis both wanted to spend some time alone with their nana, even though she wasn't hearing anything by then, or so we thought. It was their first experience of losing someone so close.

When the boys came down, Pammy said, 'Can I go up and see her?'

'Yes, go and spend some time with her,' I said.

Pammy tiptoed into her room, sat next to her and said, 'I'm going back today with Matthew and Louis, because I'm looking after Louis.'

Louis had his first school trip that week, which seemed like perfect timing. 'The other reason I have to go today,' Pammy went on, 'is that I've had the Molly Maids in to clean the house and I can't bear the idea of Matthew and his friends making a mess. It's the first time Denise's house has been so clean!'

Just then, much to Pammy's surprise, Mum came round and smiled. The Macmillan nurse said that she had only ever seen that happen in one very young cancer patient. It was wonderful, because Mum was conscious again for an hour, and when my boys went to say goodbye to her, she knew they were there. She knew we were all there. Of course, Pammy now thinks she's an evangelical-type figure who can make people get out of their wheelchairs!

Mum slipped away slowly. 'Please don't hang on. If you want to go, just go,' I told her the next night. When we knew the end was near, I went upstairs with Dad. Mum became uncomfortable and we could see signs of stress, so we called the district nurses, who were just fantastic to Mum. My experience of the NHS has never been any different, including the time when Louis was poorly. The nurses came out and said that they didn't think Mum had long. That meant we were able to phone my sister, so Debbie and Peter and the kids came along, early in the morning, about six o'clock, and we were all around Mum's bed until she died. Tim was really upset he couldn't be there, because he was in Turkey with Jo, but we knew how much he loved her.

Mum passed away that morning, as pain-free as they could make her, in her own bed, with her family, who loved her, around her. An amazing sense of peace came over me that morning. I was hugely relieved that Mum wasn't suffering any more. It had been a struggle for her in the last few days and I couldn't have borne seeing her go on like that for months.

Lincoln was in the house when she died. He didn't intrude on our family at the bedside, but he was there to support me and he was wonderful. Still, it must have been awkward for him. He had only met my dad a fortnight earlier, and he hadn't met my sister and her family at all. He kept asking, 'Would you like me to go?'

'I don't want you to go, but if you want to go, that's fine,' I said. He stayed.

It felt very special that Mum actually died on my birthday. I was reminded of a line in *Steel Magnolias*, when the mother says of her daughter, 'I was there when this beautiful creature drifted into my life and I was there when she drifted out.'

Some people felt awkward about it. 'Oh God, we can't say, "Happy birthday!"' they cried. But I was quick to reassure them. 'It's the most wonderful thing that my mum has died on my birthday,' I said. 'She brought me into this world on 22 May, and I was with her when she left this world on 22 May. She will always be in my heart. Now my birthday will always be a celebration of my birthday and of her life. I think it was meant to happen.'

That morning, I looked through her perfume collection, with which she could have set up her own House of Fraser. Recalling the joke I had made about it, I sprayed some of Lincoln's diamante perfume, first on Mum and then on myself.

Despite the obvious temptation, I didn't have a drink when Mum died, even though I wouldn't have blamed myself if I had. As a surprise, two days later Lincoln took me away to Pooley Bridge in the Lake District, where Mum used to go. One afternoon, we went to Ullswater and, on impulse, popped to Ambleside, where I bumped into Auntie Jackie, Mum's best friend! It was totally unexpected and the most incredible coincidence. Auntie Jackie burst into tears when she saw me.

It was all too much for me. 'I'm struggling, Lincoln,' I said. It was a hot day and everywhere I looked people were enjoying cold pints of beer in the sunshine. 'I feel I need a beer.' So we bought some Becks Blue alcohol-free lager, which wasn't too bad. When we got home, we stocked up on a whole range of non-alcoholic beers and wines. I still think you might as well drink some old pop out of your sock, but I'll keep searching for the placebo effect. I don't know how Carol McGiffin will cope with me being teetotal, though!

I'm very grateful to Andrea McLean for being there for me during Mum's illness. She and I had very little in common when she first joined *Loose Women*, but over the years she's become a really good friend. We don't see each other a lot out of work, simply because she lives in Surrey and I live in Cheshire, but she's somebody I go to for a chat.

I can't thank my friends Pammy and Rose enough for how much they are there for me. Pammy turned into Bridgit Fonda for a while, when she moved into our house to look after Louis while I was on tour and Tim went off to film his new TV series, *The Spa*, a Derren Litten project, by the writer who wrote *Benidorm*. She was living my life and trying to push me out gradually like Bridgit Fonda in *Single White Female*! Seriously, without their support, my life would be very difficult. My friend Lesley Wheetman has a lot of stuff going on in her life and yet she's still been there for me, which I thoroughly appreciate.

I took a week off after Mum died and stayed with Dad, then I went back to the play at the Theatre Royal in Newcastle, because that's what Mum wanted me to do. On the first night, fifty friends and family came along to support me. We were given a standing ovation at the end of the play and it was overwhelming. There were more great reviews in the morning, too. I love the way they call me 'our Denise' in the papers in the north-east. Even though I live in Cheshire, the north-east will always be my home.

Mum wanted a humanist service at the Hemmel, our family home. It was a celebration of her life, a sad day, but also full of laughter. One of Truvy's lines from the play kept coming into my mind: 'Laughter through tears is one of my favourite emotions.'

Mum's sense of humour was ever present, even when it came to choosing her exit music at the crematorium. We had to put in the order of service that she'd requested '(Burn, Baby, Burn!) Disco Inferno' as her coffin went down. We wrote, 'Annie said, "Please feel free to dance!"' She was unique and we all missed her so much.

People asked, 'Is it wrong for me to say that it's been one of the loveliest days I've had in years?' I thought it was the biggest compliment they could give Mum. So many people were there.

I could not have been prouder of Matthew, Louis and Debbie's children, Olivia, William and Alex for the way they held themselves together at the service and back at the house. The humanist who took the service was wonderful; he used the stories we gave him about Mum and spoke as warmly as if he had known her for years. Dad read a wonderful poem he had written about Mum, called, 'I'll Never Forget'. My sister spoke, as did my mother's longest-standing friend, Kath McCoull, who told some wonderful stories that I know Mum would have loved to hear!

Tim sang 'Wonderful Tonight'; Jamie Squire, my godson, sang 'Annie's Song.' Louis read a poem he'd written for Nana. Matthew helped him through the first two verses, because he was struggling, and then he composed himself, bless him, and did the rest. Matthew gave what people have said was one of the best speeches they've heard at a funeral as he spoke about his nana and his connection to her. Olivia talked on behalf of Debbie's kids, and we laughed because she looked so beautiful and sounded so posh! I looked at them all and thought, I couldn't be more proud of these people at this time.

It meant a lot to me that Mum lived to see me make some very positive changes in my life. I think she hung on to see those happen. Of course, some things were happening faster than others. There was a lot I wanted to do differently and I accepted that it wouldn't be possible to do it all at once.

One thing is certain: I can't work at this pace for ever, because it's exhausting. I want to be able to take my foot off the pedal. Sadly, in this industry, people think you're dead or retired if they don't see you on television, so I've started to diversify into business a little bit. My friend Gaynor Morgan and I have begun a business that will run alongside my other work and hopefully be a success.

Before she moved to Portugal five years ago, Gaynor had been an events organizer for a long time. We both wanted to start a business and were thinking of opening a kind of photography studio/shoot location until we had a conversation with our dear friend, my favourite celebrity photographer Nicky Johnston. He flagged up a gap in the market for a location service in the north of England. Sometimes photographers and location people need to find somewhere to do a shoot with very little notice, so we've formed Welch Morgan Locations, which has over a hundred and fifty locations, ranging from stately homes to hairdressers, from greasy spoon cafes to wonderful old Jacobean buildings. It just takes one call to Gaynor, who will source the location and everything they need – and then they can just turn up. I'll be using my name and connections to draw people to us and Gaynor will be running the show. Who knows, it might make enough money for me to slow down a little. I'd definitely like to do more theatre, which doesn't always pay very well.

Although I complain that my life is chaotic, whenever it calms down I seem to recreate the chaos again. It's something I do subconsciously and I need to work out why. It might help to start seeing a counsellor. I won't talk about my depression; the sessions will be about me. I want to understand myself and why I do the things I do. For instance, I hate it when my phone rings all the time and I have to wade through my messages, but I get worried when I don't have a thousand messages on my phone each day!

One of my repeating patterns is that I will book myself up with work and say that I don't want to think about another job beyond, say, Christmas, but if nobody comes along and offers me a job for January, I panic. There must be a tour of *Drop Your Knickers and Cry Murder* I can do! I think, in desperation. It's human nature to want to be wanted, especially in my industry, but it means I'm my own worst enemy, because I become exhausted by overwork. Thankfully, it's something I'm beginning to address.

As I've said, I'm trying to take the dead wood out of my phone book and stick with the people I know and love. On the other hand, I love meeting new people and experiencing new energy and new experiences. I just need to learn not to go headlong into things, but it's difficult, because going headlong can be fun.

'Why are we going out with all these people when all you want to do is be at home?' Lincoln has teased a couple of times.

'Because I want to see them,' I say, 'but I also want to cosy up on the sofa!' I want to spend time at home and be with Lincoln, but I can't totally suppress the sociable side of myself. It's all about finding balance, and balance has never been my thing. Still, I'm trying.

I'm not a spiritual person, although I'm not quite sure what the definition of spirituality is. I just know that I'm not religious. I don't believe in God, as in the Bible, but I do believe that there's a power in the universe. So many things have happened that have made me feel there's something there – and whatever it is has had a profound effect on me this year. It appears to be working for me, right now. My children are amazing; I'm in love with a wonderful man; Mum isn't suffering any more; Dad's getting through; I've made up with my sister; Tim's happy; I've rediscovered the joys of live theatre; and I've started making some positive changes in my life.

My sister and I are very different in many ways, but we have been incredibly close over the years and I was saddened that out relationship seemed to have gone downhill a bit. However, the combination of our love for Mum and Deborah's joy at me giving up drinking, because she always worried about it, has brought us together. We're now friends again and I'm so much happier that our relationship is back to normal. I can also tell that it's nice for our children, because they all love the bones of both of us. Although they didn't interfere, they're much happier with the way things are now.

Tim's and my separation went very smoothly, although it was tough making the decision to sell the house, because you can't help but be attached to a property you've lived in for a long time. A home isn't just bricks and mortar. On the other hand, we both accepted that it was time to move on. Tim soon found a great house to rent a couple of miles away, but I could do very little at the time, because I was on tour and Mum had just died. As it turns out, we still haven't sold the house, and a part of me is hoping that I'll win the lottery and be able to keep it. But maybe that's because I haven't had a chance to look for anywhere else yet.

A few weeks after Mum died, Lincoln booked a weekend for us in Nice. He organized everything, which was lovely, because I've always been the one everyone turns to and asks, 'Where are the passports?', 'Where are we staying?' So it was great to have someone say, 'We're going to Nice and I've sorted everything out.'

Off we went and we had a lovely two days in a beautiful

hotel. But on the third day, Lincoln seemed very twitchy. A couple of times he asked me a question that didn't seem to relate to anything. While we were at the beach, I happened to point out a gorgeous necklace I saw someone wearing. He immediately asked, 'Who's your favourite jeweller, then?'

'I don't know,' I said, thinking it was a bit of an odd question. 'The only one I've really heard of is Tiffany. I'm more of a costume jewellery person.'

Back at the hotel, he said he had to nip off and sort a couple of things out. I was still in my bathing costume when he came back. Earlier in the day, we'd talked about having a couple of non-alcoholic beers down by the coast, but now he said, 'Let's go for an early dinner instead.'

He was still twitchy. 'Are you all right?' I kept asking him. 'Are you hiding something from me?'

'I'm fine,' he assured me. 'I just really want to go for dinner now. I'm starving.'

'OK, then,' I said, even though I wasn't feeling hungry. I had a shower and got ready.

We left our room and went down to the hotel reception, at which point Lincoln said, 'I've booked us a table in the restaurant here.'

Until then, we had always gone to the coast to eat, so we hadn't explored the hotel restaurant. 'Oh,' I said, 'isn't it indoors?'

'Yes, but we've got a lovely table.'

The restaurant was completely empty. We were shown

to a table in the corner. It was a lovely spot, but the table next to it was really close and I was worried that someone would come in and sit there. 'I'm not sure about this table,' I said, because I hate it when people are sitting close enough to be able to listen in to your conversation.

'It's fine! It's fine,' he said.

'You have the restaurant to yourselves,' the waiter said.

Lincoln looked at me and smiled. Oh my God, he's booked the whole restaurant. That's so romantic! I thought.

Lincoln reached into his pocket and started pulling something out. What's going on? I thought. I noticed he was shaking. As a ring box finally emerged, I felt myself go into a cold sweat. It wasn't a feeling of horror; it was because I knew that something momentous was about to happen.

Finally, he opened the box. Inside it was a Tiffany Time ring, which he was giving me to represent a new time in our lives. 'Will you marry me?' he said.

I burst into tears. Then he burst into tears!

It was such a shock. All the while, I was thinking, I can't believe I'm being proposed to and I'm saying yes, when a year ago, if somebody had said to me, 'Will you marry again?' I would have laughed in their face. I would have said, 'Not in a million years! I've got my children, I've already been married twice. Why would I get married again?'

And yet there was nothing I wanted to do more than say yes to Lincoln and marry him. He is so good for me.

A few weeks later, I chose a solitaire ring from Harrington and Hallworth. So I now have two favourite jewellers!

Of course, Lincoln's proposal spurred me on to get divorced and it's been the most painless divorce that anybody could have. We all went on to spend Christmas together at the Hemmel, our house in the north-east: Tim and Jo, Lincoln and I, my sister and her husband and all the children, apart from Lincoln's son Lewis, who spent Christmas with his mum. Other people find it more difficult to understand than we do, but I keep saying to them, 'Tim and I never split up because we hated each other. I couldn't be happier to see him with Jo.'

I feel very lucky, though. I have friends all around me who are going through awful, acrimonious divorces. In our case, most of our friends saw it coming and were thinking for a long time, 'Just get on with it!' Nobody's had to take sides because we're all pals.

Louis and Lincoln have gone on to form an amazing bond. Almost as soon as they met, Lincoln said to Louis, 'There's no way I'm ever going to try to be your dad. I have a son of my own. You've got a fabulous dad. All I want to do is be someone that you can rely on.' They've become really good pals. I'm also thrilled to say that Matthew's band is doing really well and they're off on tour for most of this year.

At the time of writing, it has been nine months since I gave up drinking and it's the best thing I've ever done. Everything about my life is better since I stopped. However,

I've found that it's much harder not eating than not drinking. In the past, I'd often have a glass of wine to replace a starter or a dessert, but I now think of food from the moment I get up in the morning! Still, I refuse to be a fat bride, so I'll have to rein myself in somehow.

Lincoln and I are getting married in Portugal in July 2013, at my friend Gaynor Morgan's villa. I'm determined to have a laid back, summery wedding, because I've had two weddings in this country where I've panicked about the weather and had the reception in a stately home and everything, and I don't want that again. I did intend to keep down the numbers but they're creeping up, of course. Julie and Lincoln are planning it. They don't really want me involved, which is great, because I'll just turn up and it will all be done! It's a bit like that programme, *Don't Tell The Bride*.

I said last year that 2013 would be my year of reminding people that I'm a good actress and I've been offered the perfect vehicle, a play called called *Smack Family Robinson*. Richard Wilson asked me to do it; he's directing and I'm starring opposite Keith Allen. It's a comedy about drug dealers living in middle-class Kingston, written by Richard Bean, who wrote the West End hit *One Man, Two Guvnors*. It was originally set in Whitley Bay, but he's changed the setting to Kingston, so I won't get to play it in my home town accent after all. Still, I'm very excited about working with such a great team of people.

When I look back on the last year, I sometimes find it

hard to believe that I managed to get through all the ups and downs. So much bad stuff happened, but somehow, bar Mum dying, it led to all this good stuff. It's fantastic to be excited about what's still to come. Everything is very different now, which can be a bit scary, because we all fear the unknown, but it's also exhilarating. I feel renewed, as if I'm making a fresh beginning in life. There's so much to look forward to, and I'll do my best to make things work out. At last, I'm starting over.

Acknowledgements

I would like to thank the following special people:

My two boys Matthew and Louis: my pride,
my joy, my stress!

My dad Vin, for being with me
every step of the way. Love you, Dad.

Tim, for being my friend.

Jo, for making him happy.

Rose, Steven and Pammy, my oldest friends.
In fact, probably a bit old for me now . . . !

Lester Middlehurst, Lindsay Granger and
Olwyn Cumberland – I hope you're not leading
my mum astray! Miss you all.

My godchildren: Olivia, William and Alex Dedes;
Harrrison Hirst, Poppy Haddigan, Harry Acton,
Jessica Morgan-Hoole and Owen McKie. Love you all,
even though I'm rubbish at remembering your birthdays.

My 'adopted' godchildren: Tilly and Willis Sharrock;
Taylor Ward and Nikki Adams, Bella and Pixie Lomas.

And finally Lincoln, for giving me the chance to fall in
love again. You've made an old bird very, very happy!

Picture Acknowledgements

All photographs courtesy of Denise Welch, apart from:

Pages 2, 9 (all images), 10 (top image) © Rex Features

Every effort has been made to contact copyright holders
of material reproduced in this book. If any have been
inadvertently overlooked, the publishers will be pleased
to make restitution at the earliest opportunity.